SAMUEL BECK

DIALOGUE
1

Edited by

Michael J. Meyer

Samuel Beckett's *Endgame*

Edited by
Mark S. Byron

Amsterdam - New York, NY 2007

Cover Design: Pier Post

Cover photo: António, *Statue dialogue*

The paper on which this book is printed meets the requirements of "ISO 9706:1994, Information and documentation - Paper for documents - Requirements for permanence".

ISBN-13: 978-90-420-2288-1
©Editions Rodopi B.V., Amsterdam - New York, NY 2007
Printed in the Netherlands

Samuel Beckett's *Endgame*

Contents

General Editor's Preface

The original concept for Rodopi's new series entitled Dialogue grew out two very personal experiences of the general editor. In 1985, having just finished my dissertation on John Steinbeck and attained my doctoral degree, I was surprised to receive an invitation from Steinbeck biographer, Jackson J. Benson, to submit an essay for a book he was working on. I was unpublished at the time and was unsure and hesitant about my writing talent, but I realized that I had nothing to lose. It was truly the "opportunity of a lifetime." I revised and shortened a chapter of my dissertation on Steinbeck's *The Pearl* and sent it off to California. Two months later, I was pleasantly surprised to find out that my essay had been accepted and would appear in Duke University Press's *The Short Novels of John Steinbeck* (1990).

Surprisingly, my good fortune continued when several months after the book appeared, Tetsumaro Hayashi, a renowned Steinbeck scholar, asked me to serve as one of the three assistant editors of *The Steinbeck Quarterly,* then being published at Ball State University. Quite naïve at the time about publishing, I did not realize how fortunate I had been to have such opportunities present themselves without any struggle on my part to attain them. After finding my writing voice and editing several volumes on my own, I discovered in 2002 that despite my positive experiences, there was a real prejudice against newer "emerging" scholars when it came to inclusion in collections or acceptance in journals.

As the designated editor of a Steinbeck centenary collection, I found myself roundly questioned about the essays I had chosen for inclusion in the book. Specifically, I was asked why I had not selected several prestigious names whose recognition power would have spurred the book's success on the market. My choices of lesser known but quality essays seemed unacceptable. New voices were unwelcome;

it was the tried and true that were greeted with open arms. Yet these scholars had no need for further publications and often offered few original insights into the Steinbeck canon. Sadly, the originality of the lesser-known essayists met with hostility; the doors were closed, perhaps even locked tight, against their innovative approaches and readings that took issue with scholars whose authority and expertise had long been unquestioned.

Angered, I withdrew as editor of the volume, and began to think of ways to rectify what I considered a serious flaw in academé. My goal was to open discussions between experienced scholars and those who were just beginning their academic careers and had not yet broken through the publication barriers. Dialogue would be fostered rather than discouraged.

Having previously served as an editor for several volumes in Rodopi's Perspective of Modern Literature series under the general editorship of David Bevan, I sent a proposal to Fred Van der Zee advocating a new series that would be entitled Dialogue, one that would examine the controversies within classic canonical texts and would emphasize an interchange between established voices and those whose ideas had never reached the academic community because their names were unknown. Happily, the press was willing to give the concept a try and gave me a wide scope in determining not only the texts to be covered but also in deciding who would edit the individual volumes.

The Endgame volume that appears here is the first attempt at this unique approach to criticism. It features several well-known Beckett critics and several whose reputation is not so widespread but whose keen insights skillfully inform the text. It will soon be followed by volumes on Richard Wright's *Native Son* and Arthur Miller's *Death of a Salesman*. It is my hope that as each title appears, the Dialogue series will foster not only renewed interest in each of the chosen works but that each will bring forth new ideas as well as fresh interpretations from heretofore silenced voices. In this atmosphere, a healthy interchange of criticism can develop, one that will allow even dissent and opposite viewpoints to be expressed without fear that such stances may be seen as negative or counter-productive.

My thanks to Rodopi and its editorial board for its support of this "radical" concept. May you, the reader, discover much to value in these new approaches to issues that have fascinated readers for decades and to books that have long stimulated our imaginations and our critical discourse

Michael J. Meyer
2007

Introduction: *Endgame*—Very Nearly, But Not Quite

Mark S. Byron

BECKETT'S centenary year saw a multitude of celebrations honoring this singular author. 2006 saw major Beckett festivals in Paris, Reading, and Dublin; there were academic conferences in these cities as well as in cities in Denmark, Japan, the United States, and elsewhere; moreover, already existent literary festivals, from Buenos Aires to Sydney, gave pride of place to performances, roundtables, and discussions of Beckett's work; and finally, countless theaters around the world continued to stage his plays, as ever and as always.

This volume of essays on *Endgame*, Beckett's most famous play next to *Waiting for Godot*, comes into being soon after this time of celebration. If the timing of such a publication is propitious, the question remains: why *this* play? As the editor of this collection, I believe there are several compelling reasons for this renewed attention to *Endgame*. It is a deeply complex play and repays intense scrutiny from readers and critics: the range of its thematic concerns—theology, ecology, literary inheritance, companionship (and its twin, abandonment), philosophy, perception, art itself—provide frames of reference within which to position the action; in addition, the possibilities and challenges of staging the play draw attention to the dramatic medium, its limits and its *terra incognita*; and crucially, Beckett's exploration of the ways in which language and gesture assert control or submit to force or ineffability, creates a masterwork of human expressive modes—and their shortcomings.

Precisely because of this variegated texture of themes, modes, and levels of awareness (psychological, rhetorical, dramatic), *Endgame* has inspired a profound critical heritage. From the earliest days of its public existence, the play has received perceptive and subtle reviews and critical commentary. Ruby Cohn and S. E. Gontarski explored *Endgame*'s complex journey of composition years before such matters were at all understood to be central to any critical reading of the play. Other early critical readings of the play—Hugh Kenner's "Life in the Box" foremost among them—established major vectors of interpretation upon which many other critics have elaborated, and from which they have occasionally diverged.

Several dominant interpretations of *Endgame* might include: its walls and windows standing in for a skull and eyes, and its action a dramatization of a rational mind, an unconscious, and its emotions and memories; an enactment of the inability to bring an intolerable situation to an end, even as it draws towards a close; a meditation on inheritance, progeny, orphanhood, parental surrogacy; and a performance of the slapstick couple and their routines both physical and rhetorical. These and other influential trajectories of criticism might be thought to map out the interpretive field. Yet scholars and theater practitioners continue to produce exciting, groundbreaking work on this play with its limitless potential to stimulate creative and critical thinking. This volume brings together some extraordinary essays on *Endgame* that illustrate the play's multifaceted nature. Younger scholars explore previously overlooked themes and the legal, artistic and aesthetic implications of staging the play; senior scholars push into new territory, building upon vast expertise to create new ways of thinking about *Endgame* and its larger role in theater and literature and society.

This volume, initiating Rodopi's Dialogues series, collects twelve fine, astute studies of *Endgame*. Its distinction is the way in which the essays converse with each other: essays by junior scholars and more established scholars set up numerous networks of communication and conduct complementary, as well as contradictory, analyses of the play. These dialogues are not positioned strictly as paired, structured responses, yet affinities between particular essays will be immediately clear to the reader. It is my pleasure to invite the reader to think about and form still other links, responses, and correspondences between the essays, ways that open novel ways of perceiving Beckett's dramatic gem. From this mode of critical reading new ideas will spring, allowing the reader to engage the essays in a more nuanced and complex iteration of dialogues. Beckett's inexhaustible text is given renewed attention in this volume of essays, but this is only the starting point: readers and audience members are utterly central to the production of new critical energy and new ways of perceiving Beckett's dramatic art. His aesthetic of indigent inexhaustibility comes from a deep interrogation of what it is to produce art, and what art might actually be. We too need to rethink this with every reading or viewing, and with every critical engagement we read. Such a fundamental rethinking of art is the central concern of Beckett's aesthetic. As Hamm repeats to Clov:

"Use your head, can't you? You're on earth. There's no cure for that!"

Mark S. Byron, The University of Sydney

'Hard-to-hear Music in *Endgame*'

Thomas Mansell

1. *Endgame* and Music

In a note in *Damned to Fame*, James Knowlson remarked on one of the most glaring omissions in the well-furrowed field of Beckett criticism: "Only now, after so much has been written about Beckett, has a book on the significance of music in his work been prepared by Mary Bryden" (Knowlson 740 n. 132). Bryden's volume, *Samuel Beckett and Music*, appeared in 1998, closely followed by *Samuel Beckett and the Arts*, edited by Lois Oppenheim (1999). Unsurprisingly, neither in these volumes nor in subsequent essays in the growing field of Beckett-and-music studies has *Endgame*[1] figured large. Indeed, regardless of venerable tropes linking music and suffering (the dying swan, the nightingale), one can think of few things further removed from the unremittingly bleak and brutal world of *Endgame* than music. Beckett himself admitted to Alan Schneider, in a letter of 21 June 1956, that it was "more inhuman than *Godot*" (Harmon 11); he might have added, inhumane. Nevertheless, at least one recent critic has made the case for considering *Endgame* in the light of classical music.

In "Beckett et la Forme Sonate," Emmanuel Jacquart argues that Beckett quite deliberately structured *Endgame* on the model of classical sonata form. Jacquart finds parallels to the key elements of a sonata movement—exposition, development, recapitulation, and coda—further noting that *Endgame* is built, just like a paradigmatic sonata, around two strongly contrasting themes which become motifs throughout the play. Despite being predisposed to the notion of music's operation in Beckett's work, I find Jacquart's argument ultimately unconvincing. Before attempting to persuade us of the significance of sonata-form to *Endgame*, Jacquart establishes the relevance of music to Beckett's work as a whole, marshalling such evidence as primary texts, key interviews, and remarks by major collaborators; but presumably this material cannot continue to be wheeled out for every previously unacknowledged "musical" work by Beckett. For a play to have any unity at all one would expect to find its initial motifs recurring throughout (or, to put it another way, for its principal themes to be featured prominently early in the piece). One wonders whether repetition and development could not be subsumed within the standard theatrical terminology of "subplot," and whether *Endgame*'s attribute of two strongly contrasting themes is sufficiently distinct from the kind of dramatic tension upon which any successful play depends to warrant Jacquart's claims for a specifically musical model. In any case, no less a musician than Theodor Adorno aligned the same characteristic with another musical form entirely, namely a double fugue.[2]

Despite Beckett's own avowed fondness for *Endgame*—he told Tom Bishop "I suppose the one I dislike the least is *Endgame*" and admitted to Michael Haerdter that he had chosen *Endgame* for his directorial debut because "[i]t's the favorite of my plays" (McMillan and Fehsenfeld 163 and 230)—it continues to polarize audiences and critics. Some find it excessively formal and abstract: for example, Xerxes Mehta has described *Endgame* as "dramatically inert—cold, hectoring" (17), satisfying an aesthetic in which "Beckett confused formalism with form" (16), and evincing "a contempt for theatre" (18). Others are struck rather by its raw emotional impact. Kenneth Tynan's review of 7 April 1957 in the *Observer* is a case in point:

> I suddenly realised that Beckett wanted his private fantasy to be accepted as objective truth. And that nothing less would satisfy him. For a short time I am prepared to listen in any theatre to any message, however antipathetic. But when it is not only disagreeable but forced down my throat, I demur. (Graver and Federman 166)

Though these characteristics are not exactly mutually exclusive, it is rare indeed for one play to provoke such strong contradictory reactions, and, once found, for each of these traits to be cited in terms of both praise and approbation. Such paradoxical dichotomies are reminiscent of nothing so much as Beckett's own ambivalent reaction to music, figured diversely as the ultimate spiritual art and as the art closest to the senses, the emotions, and the body.

Beckett's remarks about *Endgame* reveal a parallel ambivalence: while writing the play, Beckett described it in terms of torture and intense physical pain (on 17 February 1955 he wrote to Pamela Mitchell that he hoped to "kick them [his characters] into better groans and howls" [Knowlson 406]); whereas in rehearsal, Beckett sought to sublimate any suggestion of pain, using the terminology of music to lift *Endgame* to an otherworldly disinterested realm of pure play (McMillan and Fehsenfeld 222-23). Clearly *Endgame* is an unusually powerful and contradictory work. I believe that it does tell us something about Beckett and music; but not if we pretend that music operates solely as an ideal of formal purity, nor if we consider all trace of music to be obliterated by the general atmosphere of pain. We must directly confront the recalcitrance of *Endgame*—as it confronts us with the disturbing thought that the worlds of music and pain might be not distinct but related.

Let me be blunt: there is no music in *Endgame*. At one point Clov is on the brink of song, but only (he cryptically claims) in order to bring the whole sorry business to an end (*CDW* 127).[3] Clov's humming, however, is immediately cut short by Hamm; later Beckett himself would enact a similar injunction, excising the entire exchange when directing the play in Berlin in 1967 (*ThN2* 37). The thoroughness with which music is eradicated from *Endgame* might itself prompt comment; but while there is no music *per se*, sound was most definitely on Beckett's mind, as Bud Thorpe, who played Clov in London in 1980, recalled.

> He said to us, "Now I am going to fill my silences with sounds." And added "For every silence there will be sounds, be they the shuffling of feet, steps, dropping of things, and so on." (Knowlson 628)

Though no words are spoken during the unveiling, the opening of the play is far from silent. Donald McWhinnie recalls that Beckett was most concerned that the play open with the sequence of sounds: "the first curtain, the second curtain, the first dustbin, the second dustbin" (McMillan and Fehsenfeld 176-77). Clov's limp gives the sound of his shuffling feet a distinctive character; Beckett christened it "this whispering tread on the earth" (McMillan and Fehsenfeld 236). So fine is Beckett's attunement to sound that I think we must reassess Rosemary Pountney's verdict that "it is not until after his initial experience with radio that Beckett really begins to experiment with the possibilities of sound onstage" (176); the attention to sound is written into the text itself. This essay will attend to three of *Endgame*'s sounds in particular: those of the sea, the alarm-clock, and Hamm's "headheart." First, though, we need a theory of sounds that takes us beyond the binaries of "noise" and "music."

2. Hard and Soft Sounds

In the chapter titled "*Boîtes*" in his book *Les cinq sens*, Michel Serres frames his discussion of hearing in terms of "*dur ou doux*" (118), "hard or soft."[4]

> *Doux se range dans les énergies petites, celles des signes; le donné dur quelquefois se classe dans les grandes qui giflent, renversent, déchiquettent le corps* [...] (120) [The soft finds itself in small energies, those of signs; hard phenomena are sometimes a matter of large energies which slap us, turn us upside-down, tear us to pieces [...]]

It is the mysterious work of the senses to translate the "hard" input of energy and physical (perhaps painful) stimulus into the "soft," meaningful, pleasurable realm of information.[5] Though Serres's notion of "hard and soft" enables us to progress beyond certain simplistic dualisms, it too is something of an artificial convenience; as Serres acknowledges, most of our inputs are mixtures of both hard and soft.[6] The principle thrust of philosophy and the arts is a movement towards the soft, "*un adoucissement*" (122). The effort required to translate hard into soft becomes too much for Malone in *Malone Dies*:

> the noises of the world, so various in themselves and which I used to be so clever at distinguishing from one another, had been dinning at me for so long, always the same old noises, as gradually to have merged into a single noise, so that all I heard was one vast continuous buzzing. The volume of sound perceived remained no doubt the same, I had simply lost the faculty of decomposing it. The noises of nature, of mankind and even my own, were all jumbled together in one and the same unbridled gibberish. (Trilogy 207)

However, Malone does not appear to consider this any great loss, to the point where he hesitates whether to call his state a misfortune or a blessing. One might have expected the ability to make sense of the mass of information, to make meaningful music from the material of noise, to be called "composing" rather than "decomposing." Malone's choice of verb indicates both an awareness of the lack of qualitative difference between noise and music and an alternative attitude to the traditional evaluation of each—an attitude equally tangible in Serres.[7] It seems that Serres too would have us swim against the tide of "*adoucissement*":

> *L'éloquence commence par le concassage des cailloux dans les dents face à l'océan chaotique et sur le sable rugueux et s'accomplit dans le sublime.* (121-22) [Eloquence begins with the crushing of pebbles in the teeth of a chaotic ocean and on the rough sand, and is completed in the sublime.]

The sea and the alarm are examples of hard and soft sounds in *Endgame*. I expect few people would have difficulty characterizing these two sounds as either hard or soft in the everyday sense of the words, even though this binary division is entirely metaphorical and arbitrary. Although the two sounds share a certain relentless repetitiveness, most would attribute to the sea a pleasing softness, whereas the alarm resounds with an unpleasant hardness. One would be hard pressed to imagine sounds that are neither clearly hard nor soft, or which suddenly change from one to the other. However, this is precisely what occurs with the sea and the alarm in Beckett.

The sound of the sea features prominently in several of Beckett's works in the periods immediately before and after *Endgame*, by turns soothing and distressing, familiar and strange. For example, the narrator of "The End" (1946) sets the tone, declaring "I couldn't bear the sea, its splashing and heaving, its tides and general convulsiveness. The wind at least sometimes stops" (Beckett 1995, 89). In the unfinished, unpublished work known as "On le tortura bien" ("He was thoroughly tortured") (1952), the three characters live beside the sea (Cohn 2001, 204-205). In Beckett's radio play *Embers* (1959), Henry summons other voices in an unsuccessful attempt to quell the insistence of the sea's sibilant sounds (*CDW* 251-264; Cohn 2001, 245). In the course of the Trilogy, the sea becomes a character in and of itself. Malone endows the sea with its own "voice" when telling the tale of Lemuel and Macmann:

> And often the two of them remained there for some time, in the bush, before going in, huddled together, for the lair was small, saying nothing, perhaps listening to the noises of the night, the owls, the wind in the leaves, the sea when it was high enough to make its voice heard, and then the other night sounds that you cannot tell the meaning of. (Trilogy 276-77)

The Unnamable cannot even distinguish between his own voice and
that of the sea; but then seeks to rid himself of that particular image:

> I listened. One might as well speak and be done with it. What liberty! I
> strained my ear towards what must have been my voice still, so weak, so
> far, that it was like the sea, a far calm sea dying – no, none of that, no beach,
> no shore, the sea is enough, I've had enough of shingle, enough of sand,
> enough of earth, enough of sea too. (Trilogy 311)

Molloy had also experienced a similar identification with the sea, in a
passage that has particular relevance in relation to *Endgame*.

> Much of my life has ebbed away before this shivering expanse, to the sound
> of the waves in storm and calm, and the claws of the surf. Before, no, more
> than before, one with, spread on the sand, or in a cave. (Trilogy 68)

To describe the sea as a "shivering expanse" immediately makes it
akin to a sentient animal, and the deictic "this" virtually assigns it an
individual soul; the merging of subject and object is beautifully
anticipated by "my life has ebbed away"; and there is something
distinctively Beckettian about Molloy's attentive sensitivity to the
sound of the waves in *calm*. Especially striking, though, is the phrase
"the claws of the surf." One is incidentally reminded of Beckett's
remark to Alan Schneider that *Endgame* depends for its effectiveness
on "the power of the text to claw" (Harmon 11); but Molloy's phrase
is an astonishingly incongruous union of hard and soft textures—a
union by no means unique in Beckett's soundworld. For example:

> [Moran:] But what words can describe this sensation at first all darkness and
> bulk, with a noise like the grinding of stones, then suddenly as soft as water
> falling. (Trilogy 149)

> [Malone:] The rain pelted down on his back with the sound first of a drum,
> but in a short time of washing, as when washing is soused gurgling and
> squelching in a tub. (Trilogy 240)

It is therefore no accident that one of Hamm and Clov's more
perplexing exchanges should concern the sound of the sea.

> HAMM: Open the window.
> CLOV: What for?

> HAMM: I want to hear the sea.
> CLOV: You wouldn't hear it.
> HAMM: Even if you opened the window?
> CLOV: No.
> HAMM: Then it's not worth while opening it?
> CLOV: No.
> HAMM: (*Violently*) Then open it! (*CDW* 124; cf. *ThN2* 33-34)

According to Adorno in "Trying to Understand *Endgame*," Hamm's reasoning amounts to "a belated legitimation of Fichte's free activity for its own sake" (265)—albeit in the form of an ironic *reductio ad absurdum*. The sea, heard by most of us as "soft" in the everyday sense, had been heard as "hard" by some characters in Beckett. Now we find the sea, a "hard" sound in Serres's sense of the word, perceived by Hamm as an aesthetic experience, heard as "soft."

The alarm, too, is received unusually by Hamm and Clov.

> (*Exit* CLOV. <*Brief ring of alarm off.*> *Enter* CLOV *with alarm-clock. He holds it against* HAMM*'s ear and releases alarm. They listen to it ringing to the end. Pause.*) [CLOV:] Fit to wake the dead! Did you hear it?
> HAMM: Vaguely.
> CLOV: The end is terrific!
> HAMM: I prefer the middle. (*Pause.*) (*CDW* 124; cf. *ThN2* 33-34)[8]

While we might consider Clov's praise somewhat exaggerated, it is actually Hamm's more measured response that really strikes us as odd. On one level, "I prefer the middle" could be bitterly sardonic, denying Clov's remark (and attendant pleasure) what small legitimacy it had. On another reading, however, Hamm's comment appears to suggest that he can distinguish amidst the uniformity and insistence of the alarm's hammering some ebb and flow and even, implicitly, the presence of a creating mind which consciously contrived the alarm to stimulate aesthetic discernment and delight in its hearers/listeners. The alarm is the very epitome of a uniform, insistent, hammering, mechanistic sound, whose effectiveness as a tool relies entirely on its being heard as a noise rather than listened to as music. Hamm's almost impossibly sensitive reaction, however, shows that he is treating this manifestly "hard" sound as if it were "soft," this time in Serres's sense of the word. Whereas Malone had jumbled the various noises of the world into one vast continuous buzzing, Hamm seems able to read variation into the uniform. Beckett thus explores the extreme poles of perception: perceiving difference *as* the same, and perceiving difference *in* the same.

3. Hammering, or Sounding-out "Hamm"

Beckett's examination of hard and soft sounds, both in the everyday sense and that of Serres, reveals that such distinctions are entirely arbitrary, not so much black-and-white terms for contraries as relative terms along a continuum. The investigation was continued when Beckett made his directorial debut with *Endspiel* in 1967. Michael Haerdter was struck by Beckett's results:

> It is incredible how many subtle nuances of diction and action Beckett can work out of a few minutes of dialogue exchanged by two unmoving heads in monotone. Here instead of small hammerstrokes of rectification one must rather speak of a watch-maker's technique: the precise adjustment of a miniature movement. (McMillan and Fehsenfeld 211)

Notice that in Haerdter's description the dialogue itself comes to resemble the sound of the alarm, with the "two unmoving heads" taking the place of the stationary bells of the alarm-clock. (Beckett is known to have enjoyed the reverse aspect of this correspondence in the image created when Clov held up the clock between his head and Hamm's, the alarm-clock suddenly taking on the qualities of a third head.) Beckett methods for achieving such fine results, as recorded by Haerdter, are even more incredible:

> "Say it in monotone and rhythmically, please. The words are blows, dry blows. One hammerstroke is like the next one." (225)

Beckett here exhibits attitudes towards hard and soft sounds as complex as those of his fictional creations. Haerdter comes close to recognizing the incongruity, but flinches from the force of his own logic; there is no need to substitute "a watch-maker's technique" "*instead of* small hammerstrokes of rectification", as small hammerstrokes of rectification are precisely the means by which a watch-maker creates his intricate and accurate pieces. They are also the means by which Beckett insists on repetition, thus heightening the audience's sensitivity to a pitch where it is alert to the most minute differences. "Agreed then on monotony, it's more stimulating," said the Unnamable (Trilogy 371). As Hamm's experience of the alarm shows, subtle and nuanced effects can indeed be caused by insistent hammering.

Indeed, the image of Hamm as "hammer," which seems the chief obstacle to a conjunction of *Endgame* and music, could in fact become a tool for establishing more accurately the nature of their relationship. The hammer-interpretation gained authorial approval in 1967, as relayed by Ernst Schröder:

> Speculative requests for interpretation had been put down at the first rehearsal when Beckett, in response to our questions, set out the phonetics of the names of the parts. Anyone who had read Esslin or Adorno had it brought back vividly: Hamm is an abbreviation of the German word *Hammer*, Clov is French *clou*, a nail, and therefore not to be pronounced Clav; Nagg short for German *Nagel* (nail), Nell comes from English *nail*. So it's a play for a hammer and three nails? "If you like!" (McMillan and Fehsenfeld 238)

Beckett's noncommittal shrug has been taken as the definitive answer to the mystery of Hamm's name, and has subsequently formed the basis of numerous interpretations (see Cohn 45, Chambers 79, and Kenner 54, all in Chevigny; Cohn 1980, 113; Kenner 1973, 121; and Brater 82). The hammer symbolises what many consider *Endgame*'s world of fear and intimidation, centred on the tyranny of Hamm. However, far more interesting to me is the extent to which Hamm is *himself* subject to the desires and needs of others, exposing the futility of Hamm's gestures of control.[9] The dependency of Hamm and Clov is *mutual*—a fact that remains largely beyond the grasp of the "hammer and three nails" interpretation.

Only rarely has the hammer-interpretation been wielded with subtlety and sophistication. Ruby Cohn, for example, pointed out that "Latin *hamus* is hook, a kind of crooked nail, so that Hamm may be viewed as another nail" (Cohn in Chevigny 45), so that "Hamm" puns both on "hammer" and "nail." Beckettians might also have pondered Beckett's interest in the phrase "*clavum clavo*" from Robert Burton's *Anatomy of Melancholy*,[10] which he duly entered in his *Dream* notebook (Pilling 114, #801). If Clov is indeed derived from "*clou*" (which ultimately derives from "*clavus*" or nail), this would be an important source; its self-reflexive logic, its image of nails driving out nails, would nip in the bud any simplistic interpretation of Hamm and Clov as binary opposites, one agent and one patient. Critics have tended to be content with the hammer that is closest to hand; Emmanuel Jacquart, however, is a notable exception. In *"Endgame, Master Game"* Jacquart ponders an alternative, as emphasised in a note by his translator: "Jacquart suggests here that the word for hammer (marteau) points toward both hammer and tuning fork" (90 n. 1). Jacquart is poised on the threshold of a new realm of *Endgame* interpretation, which would stem from Nietzsche's subtle deployment of the hammer/tuning-fork to sound out false gods in the Foreword to *Twilight of the Idols* (31—32). Unfortunately, Jacquart reduces the process to a mere smashing of idols (78), thus missing the opportunity to recast the hammer as a potentially soft instrument. (Admittedly, in the "Afterword" in which "The Hammer Speaks" Nietzsche himself loses this delicate balance, advocating that his comrades merely "become hard" [122].) Though an essay could be written on the significance of piano-tuners in Beckett—and would include Hamm's attentive striking of the walls (*CDW* 104; *ThN2* 15)—two other kinds of "soft" hammer strike me as being of particular relevance for *Endgame*: those found in a piano and those found in our ears.

Since Beckett's authorization of the hammer-interpretation carries such weight, we would do well to attend to its details: according to Schröder, Beckett told his actors that Hamm is an abbreviation of the *German* word *"Hammer."* True, Schröder is German, the production was German (at the Schiller-Theater, Berlin), and Beckett was presumably addressing the company in German. Nevertheless, the limiting adjective "German" draws attention to itself by virtue of its very superfluity. As it happens, the German word *"Hammer"* facilitates a transition between *Endgame* and music by way of the hammers of a piano.

Ludwig van Beethoven disliked the name *"pianoforte,"* as it implied that the instrument was an Italian invention; instead, he suggested *"Hammerklavier."* Whereas in English there seems to be a vast gulf between the words "hammer" and "piano," in German *"Hammer"* and *"Klavier"* (piano) are yoked together in the word *"Hammerklavier."* Furthermore, though Beckett derived Clov/*clou* from *clavus* (Latin for "nail"), one might just as convincingly trace it to *clavis* (Latin for "key"). The interaction of hammer and key within a piano might thereby provide a new model with which to think about Hamm and Clov's relationship in *Endgame*, revealing a far more fascinating and complex set of connections.

The pianist's finger—itself a miraculous kind of fleshy hammer—strikes the key, which in turn releases the hammer, having passed through the complex system of levers known as the action: "Of the six thousand pieces in a piano some four thousand five hundred are in the action" (Grover 58). The hammers in a modern piano are intricately crafted and tipped with felt, their dimension and texture varying according to the thickness of the string which they strike (Grover 58-59). The real innovation of the piano is the escapement mechanism, enabling the hammer to rebound instantly from the strings. On earlier keyboard instruments, in order to create the illusion of sustained tone one would have to repeat a note (for example as part of an ornament); the piano's escapement allows for far more rapid repetition, while its action and soundboard produce far greater ability to sustain tone; the hammering of a note is therefore no longer a mere expedience but is emancipated to become a source of compositional innovation in its own right. While it is true that the rise of the piano relative to earlier keyboard instruments is due principally to its greater volume, the advantage brought by its hammer mechanism is more precisely its superior dynamic *range*. It is this capacity to play both loudly *and* softly that is celebrated in the names "fortepiano" and the more familiar "pianoforte" ("loudsoft" and "softloud").

Beethoven would be disappointed to hear that his term *"Hammerklavier"* failed to gain wide acceptance as the instrument's name. Instead, it has become associated with a particular piece for piano: Beethoven's Sonata op. 106 in B-flat major. Parallels between the *Hammerklavier* Sonata and *Endgame* exist on both formal and circumstantial levels; and if one wanted to pursue further the issues raised by Jacquart in "Beckett et la Forme Sonate," the *Hammerklavier* Sonata might be the place to start—even if it strains both "sonata form" and the piano sonata itself almost to breaking point. Rather as Nietzsche's moments of delicate hammering are obscured by the blinding image of Nietzsche as bombastic iconoclast, people attribute the nickname *"Hammerklavier"* to the sonata's stunningly stentorian opening, ignoring its many moments of profound tenderness and lyricism. In an attempt to move beyond our traditional and reductive notions of "Hammer" and *"Hammerklavier,"* one could cite Adorno's "childhood image of Beethoven":

> I thought the "Hammerklavier" Sonata must be an especially *easy* piece, associating it with toy pianos with little hammers. I imagined it had been

written for one of those. My disappointment when I could not play it.
(Adorno 1998, 4 #4 [notebook entry from 1944])

The *Hammerklavier* Sonata is in fact one of the most challenging
pieces in the piano repertoire, by virtue of its delicate as much as its
dramatic deployment of hammers.

Discussing the various overtones of the "hammer"
interpretation, Hugh Kenner pointed out that "a French audience
would hear no such resonances in 'Hamm'"—even though he
continues, "but Beckett has been known to pun across languages
before" (Kenner 1973, 120). But, as we have seen, "Hammer"
resonates differently in German and English ears. The hammers in our
ears play a crucial role in the reception of sound, in its transformation
from physical sensation to meaningful experience, from pulsation to
vibration, from hard to soft.[11]

> The vibratory movement [of the eardrum] is transmitted across the middle
> ear by the three bones (ossicles) [...] known respectively as the hammer
> (malleus), anvil (incus), and stirrup (stapes) [...] The function of the drum
> and bones is to collect the vibrations from a light-weight medium, the
> outside air, and give them enough thrust to set the relatively heavy inner-ear
> liquid into vibration. (Woodworth and Schlosberg 326-27)[12]

The reflexive logic glimpsed by "*clavum clavo*" is exemplified by the
hammers of the ear and the piano, respectively responding to one
another at either end of the sonic process. The physics of sound
production and reception demand the reciprocally-constructed
instruments to serve as transmitter and receiver; each is a mirror-
image of each other. Here truly is an archetypal symbiotic
relationship; polar opposites composed of identical elements
differently arranged. The subtle nature of the process is perhaps most
finely captured by Michel Serres in *Les cinq sens*, where he describes
the cochlea of the inner ear as a kind of coiled-up piano.

> *La boîte reçoit-elle ou émet-elle? Ecouter signifie vibrer, mais vibrer
> consiste à émettre. A déplier la cochlée, par exemple, un piano inversé
> apparaît sur quoi s'étagent aigus et graves, de gauche à droite. Mais un
> piano sonne, il n'entend pas. La même raison ne cesse pas: il faut à l'oreille
> une oreille plus centrale pour l'écoute de ce qui se transmet par les trois
> oreilles externe, moyenne et interne, qui s'entendent successivement.* (151)[13]
> [Does the box receive or transmit? To hear means to vibrate; but vibrating
> means transmitting. If you unfurl the cochlea, for example, you find a

> reversed piano, with the high-pitched notes arranged on the left and the low notes on the right. But a piano makes sounds, it doesn't hear them. So logic requires that for each ear there be yet another, more central ear, to listen to what is conveyed through the outer, middle, and inner ears, which listen to each other in succession.]

The soft hammers in a piano and in our ears, the soft hammers crucial to both the production and reception of musical sound, loom large in *Endgame*.

4. Hard of Hearing

It is curious to note that for all the time spent pondering the possible puns of Hamm's name, no one has seen fit to remark that we never actually *hear* "Hamm."[14] My tentative explanation for this silence will seem especially perverse in the context of an argument for the significance of sound and even music to *Endgame*: could it be that Hamm is hard of hearing? It seems perverse even to consider this possibility, to look beyond Hamm's foregrounded blindness. At work here is an assumption of some automatic sensory compensation, as summed up in the Unnamable's bald assertion that "the blind hear better" (Trilogy 376). "When we are deprived of the sense of sight, the other senses take up the role of sight in some degree," wrote Marshall McLuhan (79)—but there is no natural law that states this should always be the case. For me to wonder whether Hamm might have hearing difficulties is certainly no more perverse than it had been for Beckett/Smeraldina to remark of Beethoven "the poor man he was very shortsighted they say" (Beckett, *Dream* 139). Beckett's writing is frequently indifferent, often callously so, to people's more obvious hardships, devoting excessive attention instead to coincidental features of their situation. While the blind often have excellent hearing and the deaf excellent sight, in the cases of Hamm and Beethoven neither of them seems to have enjoyed such compensations.

Hamm's insistence that the window be opened despite and almost *because of* the fact that he might/would not be able to hear the sea is also testimony to a negative aesthetics (shared by Romantics and Pre-Socratics) whereby "'Heard melodies are sweet, but those unheard / Are sweeter'" (Keats, in Gontarski 124), and "The harmony past knowing sounds / more deeply than the known" (Heraclitus 31 #47). Adorno's suggestion that "senselessness" might be the "key to the play" (265) here takes on a new relevance. By ignoring Hamm's demand and instead "mark[ing] time audibly" (*CDW* 124; *ThN2* 34), Clov renders it impossible for us to know whether his diagnosis of Hamm's condition was correct. All we can say for certain is that Hamm is apparently unaware of Clov's deception, attributing the sea's apparent silence to its supposed calmness. However, the window also remains closed for the audience; we remain in the dark as to the state of the sea but also that of Hamm's hearing.

The latter issue arises again in the episode with the alarm. There is something distinctly incongruous in Clov's asking Hamm if he heard this alarm which he has already said is "[f]it to wake the dead". But perhaps the most incongruous aspect of the exchange is Hamm's eventual answer: "vaguely." Despite this, Hamm says he "prefer[s] the middle" of the alarm; he also, famously, expresses a violent preference for the middle of the room. What has seemed an irrational obsession might, however, have a sound basis. As Oliver Sacks has written, "sensitivity to vibration can become a sort of accessory sense" (7),[15] and Hamm might be more than usually reliant on this "vibration-perception." Hamm resembles the spider discussed in *D'Alembert's Dream*: "[a]t the centre she is conscious of what is going on at any point in the huge mansion she has woven" (Diderot 183).[16] Hamm's outbursts are less the demands of a tyrant than the needs of a victim; Hamm is none the less paranoid, but we now have a potential cause of his paranoia. My intuition is backed up by Beckett's otherwise inexplicable change of stage direction from "[CLOV] *moves chair slightly*" (*CDW* 105) to "CLOV *thumps chair*" (*ThN2* 15-16); thumping is a more violent and frustrated action, but, crucially, produces a sound that vibrates through Hamm's chair, thus giving him at least a chance of gauging whether he is indeed correctly positioned.

In the case of both the sea and the alarm, the audience does not hear quite what Hamm hears; questions are raised about Hamm's perception of "hard" and "soft" sounds; the audience is troubled by the discrepancy between their experience and Hamm's. Many of these issues come together in one of the great unheard sounds of the play, heard all too clearly by the unfortunate Hamm.

> HAMM: (*Pause.*) There's something dripping in my head. (*Pause.*) A heart, a heart in my head.
> (*Pause.*) (*CDW* 100; *ThN2* 11)

HAMM: Perhaps it's a little vein.
(*Pause.*) (*CDW* 101; *ThN2* 12)

HAMM: (*Pause.*) Something dripping in my head, ever since the fontanelles.
(*Stifled hilarity of* NAGG.)
Splash, splash, always on the same spot. (*Pause.*) Perhaps it's a little vein.
(*Pause.*) A little artery. (*Pause.*) (*CDW* 116; *ThN2* 27)

Since Hamm's distracted complaints are our only means of apprehending this phenomenon we might be tempted to respond to it as Nagg does: with hilarity, whether stifled or vented. If the issue of hearing in *Endgame* is broached at all, it tends to be by means of the old music-hall joke "our hearing [...] our what?" (*CDW* 99; *ThN2* 10)—which, according to Ruby Cohn, was only added in the final draft (Cohn 1980, 183-84). However, consider Nagg's sequence of reactions. On the first occasion Nagg asks his wife, "(*Soft*) [d]o you hear him?"; addressed to Nell, this apparently rhetorical question is potentially genuine. Nagg hears Nell's answer all right, pleading "[n]ot so loud!" On the second occasion, though, the literal meaning of Nagg's words raises doubts about his own hearing: "[w]hat was that he said?" However, just because Hamm's experience is not directly perceptible by us does not mean to say it does not exist. Try as Hamm might to put it out of his mind, he cannot, since it is a sound that will exist as long as he has a mind. Through the veil of Hamm's strikingly weird description, we dimly perceive a phenomenon familiar to us all: it is the internal pulsing of blood through the skull and the ears. The dripping or splashing qualities of this sound connect it both with the hammering of the alarm and the washing of the sea. Hamm is describing a kind of internal hearing that strikes us as strange and absurd when externalized. It is a sound that perhaps even the deaf can "hear," so little is it a sound at all, but more a beating, a motion. It is the sound we mistake for that of the soft sea when we clasp a hard sea-shell to our ear: the sound of nothing, attesting to something.

To Michael Haerdter's comments about Beckett's direction of *Endgame*, Beckett responded, "*Oui, c'est pythagoréen*" (McMillan and Fehsenfeld 236). I wonder if Beckett's knowledge of things Pythagorean included the following legend in Iamblichus:

He was once engaged in intense thought about whether he could find some precise scientific instrument to assist the sense of hearing, as compass and

> ruler and the measurement of angles assist the sight and scales and weights
> and measures assist touch. Providentially, he walked passed a smithy, and
> heard the hammers beating out the iron on the anvil. They gave out a
> melody of sounds, harmonious except for one pair. (50-51)

Thus Pythagoras began the experiments in which he would discover
the principles of harmony, the foundation of western classical music.
As Malone lay dying, he remained alive to the musicality of hammers,
remarking, "[t]he hammers of the stone-cutters ring all day like bells"
(Trilogy 288). Hammers remain central both to musical reception and
production, in particular the delicate hammers within our own bodies
and within the body of the piano. The notion of Hamm as "hammer,"
far from reinforcing the disjunction between the worlds of "hard" and
"soft" sounds, actually assimilates them all. The possibility that
Hamm might be hard of hearing only reinforces these links:
Pythagoras's search for hearing aids led to the accidental discovery of
music; at the summit of musical achievement (many, including
Beckett, would argue), one finds a deaf composer, Beethoven.

It is by means of such an unlikely network of relationships
that music resonates throughout *Endgame*. Music does not exist in a
realm apart, untouchably abstract; nor is it accurate to lump it along
with natural bodily emissions of sound. In other works, Beckett
lurches between these two extremes, his ambivalent attitude towards
music representative of a more pervasive ambivalence towards the
intellect and the emotions, mind and body, irony and lyricism (Laws
295-308). As Herbert Blau writes, "the grotesque comedy of Beckett
seems to leak from a defective bypass in the braininess of a bleeding
heart" (94); Hamm's "headheart" thus symbolises the ways in which
in *Endgame* such contrasts are both polarized and fused. With any
dualism, it is not so much the binary terms that are troubling so much
as their shared continuum. In *Endgame*, Beckett explores the
indeterminate zones in which hard sounds merge with soft, noise with
music, groans and howls with song, touch with hearing; the
counterintuitive processes by means of which pitch emerges from
rhythm, quality from quantity, and sublime pleasure from almost
unbearable pain. To begin with noise and end with music would
present an "optimistic" reading, and to present music then noise a
"pessimistic" one; of course, neither shape tells the entire truth. The
message, if any, is not of pain being sublimated into the realm of
music, nor of music annihilated in the horror of suffering, but of the

inevitability and absurdity of both pain and art; humanity inflicting and afflicted by both.

Thomas Mansell, London Consortium

Notes

[1] Samuel Beckett. *Endgame: A play in one act* [1956] in Beckett, *The Complete Dramatic Works*: 89-134. (Henceforward cited in the text as '*CDW*'.) Samuel Beckett. *Endgame* [revised text] in S. E. Gontarski, ed.. *The Theatrical Notebooks of Samuel Beckett. Volume 2:* Endgame. London: Faber and Faber, 1992: 1-42. (Henceforward cited in the text as '*ThN2*'.)

[2] "The action of the play as a whole is composed on two themes, in musical fashion, as double fugues used to be" (Adorno 1991, 269).

[3] Jack MacGowran was puzzled by the passage, and received this response from Beckett during rehearsals of 1964: "'When I wrote it in French, there is a French proverb which is well known, "Everything ends with a song", and I could not translate that proverb which is particularly French into English unless I did it that way.'" (McMillan and Fehsenfeld 175). (MacGowran's reminiscences were originally published in Richard Toscan's interview 'MacGowran on Beckett' in *Theatre Quarterly*, July-September 1973.)

[4] Translations from Serres are my own, with thanks to Mathilde Villeneuve and Steven Connor for their comments.

[5] "*La vie comme telle exploite cette distinction. Elle va de la dureté à la douceur. Son élan se dirige du matériel vers le logiciel, de l'énergie à l'information. Le sensible suit ce sens. Le corps sait cet écart et sa direction, dans et par le sensible.*" (Serres 120). ["Life itself exhibits this distinction. It moves from the hard to the soft. Its momentum takes it from the world of material hardware to intelligible software, from energy to information. The sensible follows this trajectory: sensitivity succeeds sense. The body knows this gap and its direction, in and through the sensible."]

[6] "*Il [le corps] a toujours su sans que le langage ait eu à le dire que le langage est dur et doux, il a toujours su depuis sa naissance que le donné se mélange de dur et de doux, son travail de sensation transforme la dureté en douceur, comment ne connaîtrait-il pas différence et transition?*" (Serres 124). ["It [the body] knew all along, without needing to be told by language, that language itself is both hard and soft. It has always known, from the day it was born, that the sensible world is a mixture of the hard and the soft, and that it is the job of sensation to translate the hard into the soft. How could it have failed to know difference and change?"]

[7] "*La vie devient un équilibre difficile à maintenir entre la nappe musicale et le bombardement chaotique du bruit. Quant l'harmonie se retirera, comme rompt une digue, je mourrai les oreilles crevées sous l'inondation hurlante. La victoire définitive du multiple marque la fin de l'agonie.*" (Serres 113). ["Life becomes a tottering balance between the soft blanket of music and the chaotic battery of noise. As harmony withdraws, the dam is burst; I shall die, my ears destroyed by the howling torrent. The end of the agony is marked by the decisive victory of the multiple."]

[8] The passage in angled brackets was in *CDW*, but was cut at some stage during production and therefore does not feature in the revised text (*ThN2*).

[9] Recall Arsene's speech in *Watt* in which he speaks of a "third person, on whose existence the existences of Ann and Mary depend, and whose existence also in a sense if you like depends on the existences of Ann and Mary" (none of whom in fact exists). (49)

[10] "I was not a little offended with this malady, shall I say my mistress Melancholy, my Egeria, or my *malus genius* [evil genius]? and for that cause, as he that is stung with a scorpion, I would expel *clavum clavo* [a nail with a nail], comfort one sorrow with another, idleness with idleness, *ut ex vipera theriacum* [as an antidote out of that which was the prime cause of my disease]." (Burton 21).

[11] "*Je suis la maison du son, ouïe et voix tout entier, boîte noire et retentissement, enclume et marteau, grotte à échos, cassette à musique, pavillon, point d'interrogation errant dans l'espace des messages doués ou privés de sens, émergé sur ma propre conque ou noyé sous les vagues des ondes, je ne sais que creux et note, je suis tout entier creux et note mêlés.*" (Serres 149-50). ["I am the house of sound, hearing and voice all in one. I am black box and reverberation, anvil and hammer, echoing caves, music cassette, bell-mouth and bell, a question mark wandering around in the space of messages more or less meaningful, rising up from my own conch-shell, or drowned under the rolling waves. I only know hollow and note, I am entirely constructed from a mingling of hollow and note."]

[12] It was Vesalius who in 1543 first "gave an accurate description of, and named, the malleus" (Carterette 20).

[13] I am grateful to Steven Connor for first alerting me to this passage.

[14] Kenner alludes to this fact in a typical aside: "His name, we gather from the program, is Hamm" (Kenner, in Chevigny [1969], 53).

[15] In fact "much of our hearing takes place through the skin itself" (McLuhan 133). As Molloy remarks of a particularly disturbing sound, "[i]t's with your head you hear it, not your ears" (Trilogy 40-41).

[16] That Beckett was indeed thinking of *D'Alembert's Dream* in connection with these matters is established beyond question, to my mind at least, by a related and sustained passage in *Molloy* (Trilogy 49-50).

Bibliography

Primary Texts

Beckett, Samuel. *Dream of Fair to Middling Women* [1932] ed. Eoin O'Brien and Edith Fournier. London: Calder Publications, 1993, repr. 1996.

—. *Embers: A piece for radio* [1959] in Beckett, *The Complete Dramatic Works*: 251-64.

—. *Endgame: A play in one act* [1956] in Beckett, *The Complete Dramatic Works*: 89-134.

—. *Endgame* [revised text] in Beckett, *The Theatrical Notebooks of Samuel Beckett. Volume 2:* Endgame ed. S. E. Gontarski. London: Faber and Faber, 1992: 1-42.

—. *Molloy* [1947] in Beckett, Trilogy: 5-176.

—. *Malone Dies* [1948] in Beckett, Trilogy: 177-289.

—. *The Complete Dramatic Works*. London: Faber and Faber, 1986.

—. *The Complete Short Prose 1929-1989* ed. S.E. Gontarski. New York, NY: Grove Press / Grove Atlantic, 1995.

—. 'The End' [1946] in Beckett, *The Complete Short Prose*: 78-100.

—. *The Theatrical Notebooks of Samuel Beckett. Volume 2:* Endgame ed. S. E. Gontarski. London: Faber and Faber, 1992.

—. *The Unnamable* [1950] in Beckett, Trilogy: 291-418.

—. *Trilogy*. London: Calder Publications, 1994.

—. *Watt* [1945]. London: John Calder, 1976, repr. 1998.

Secondary Texts

Adorno, Theodor W.. 'Trying to Understand *Endgame*' in *Notes to Literature* [1958], Volume One ed. Rolf Tiedemann, translated by Shierry Weber Nicholsen. New York: Columbia University Press, 1991. (241-75) [Also collected as 'Towards an Understanding of *Endgame*' translated by Samuel M. Weber, in Chevigny. (82-114)]

Adorno, Theodor W.. *Beethoven: The Philosophy of Music. Fragments and Texts* ed. Rolf Tiedemann, translated by Edmund Jephcott. Cambridge: Polity Press, 1998.

Blau, Herbert. *Sails of the Herring Fleet: Essays on Beckett*. Ann Arbor, MI: The University of Michigan Press, 2000.

Brater, Enoch. *Why Beckett*. London: Thames and Hudson, 1989.

Bryden, Mary, ed.. *Samuel Beckett and Music*. Oxford: Clarendon, 1998.

Burton, Robert. *The Anatomy of Melancholy* [1621] ed. Holbrook Jackson. New York: New York Review of Books, 2001.

Carterette, Edward C.. 'Some Historical Notes on Research in Hearing' in Carterette and Friedman. (3-39)

Carterette, Edward C. and Morton P. Friedman, eds. *Handbook of Perception. Volume 4: Hearing*. New York and London: Academic Press, 1978.

Chambers, Ross. 'An Approach to *Endgame*' in Chevigny. (71-81)

Chevigny, Bell Gale, ed.. *Twentieth Century Interpretations of Endgame*. Englewood Cliffs, NJ: Prentice-Hall, 1969.

Cohn, Ruby. *'Endgame'* [from *The Comic Gamut* (1962)] in Chevigny. (40-52)

—. *A Beckett Canon*. Ann Arbor, Michigan: The University of Michigan Press, 2001.

—. *Just Play: Beckett's Theater*. Princeton, NJ: Princeton University Press, 1980.

Diderot, Denis. *Rameau's Nephew* [*c.* 1761] *and D'Alembert's Dream* [1769] translated by Leonard Tancock. Harmondsworth: Penguin, 1966, repr. 1981.

Gontarksi, S.E.. *The Intent of Undoing in Samuel Beckett's Dramatic Texts*. Bloomington, Indiana: Indiana University Press, 1985.

Graver, Lawrence and Raymond Federman, eds. *Samuel Beckett: The Critical Heritage*. London: Routledge & Kegan Paul, 1979.

Grover, David S.. *The Piano: Its Story, from Zither to Grand*. London: Robert Hale, 1976.

Harmon, Maurice, ed.. *No Author Better Served: The Correspondence of Samuel Beckett and Alan Schneider*. Cambridge, MA, and London: Harvard University Press, 1998.

Heraclitus. *Fragments: The Collected Wisdom of Heraclitus* translated by Brooks Haxton. Harmondsworth: Penguin, 2001.

Iamblichus. *On the Pythagorean Life* translated by Gillian Clark (Translated Texts for Historians, Volume 8). Liverpool: Liverpool University Press, 1989.

Jacquart, Emmanuel. 'Beckett et la Forme Sonate' in Matthijs Engelberts, Marius Buning, and Sjef Houppermans, eds. *Poetry and Other Prose / Poésies et Autres Proses. Samuel Beckett Today / Aujourd'hui* 8. Amsterdam and Atlanta, GA: Rodopi, 1999. (159-74)

—. "*Endgame*, Master Game" translated by Brian Evenson. *Journal of Beckett Studies*, 4.1 (Autumn 1995): 77-92.

Kenner, Hugh. 'Life in the Box' in Chevigny. (53-60)

—. *A Reader's Guide to Samuel Beckett*. London: Thames and Hudson, 1973.

Knowlson, James. *Damned to Fame: The Life of Samuel Beckett.* London: Bloomsbury, 1996.

Laws, Catherine. 'The Double Image of Music in Beckett's Early Fiction' in Marius Buning, Matthijs Engelberts, and Onno Kosters, eds. *Beckett and Religion. Beckett/Aesthetics/ Politics.* Amsterdam and Atlanta, GA: Rodopi, 2000. (295—308)

McLuhan, Marshall. *Understanding Media: The Extensions of Man* [1964]. London: Sphere Books, 1967, repr. 1971.

McMillan, Dougald and Martha Fehsenfeld. *Beckett in the Theatre: The Author as Practical Playwright and Director. Volume 1: From* Waiting for Godot *to* Krapp's Last Tape. London: John Calder, 1988.

Mehta, Xerxes. 'Beckett's Early Style in the Theatre: *Waiting for Godot'*. Unpublished conference paper presented to the Samuel Beckett Working Group, St Petersburg, 25 May 2004.

Nietzsche, Friedrich. *Twilight of the Idols* [1889] *and The Anti-Christ* [1895] translated by R. J. Hollingdale. Harmondsworth: Penguin Books, 1990.

Oppenheim, Lois, ed.. *Samuel Beckett and the Arts: Music, Visual Arts, and Non-Print Media.* New York and London: Garland, 1999.

Pilling, John, ed.. *Beckett's* Dream *Notebook.* Reading: Beckett International Foundation, 1999.

Pountney, Rosemary. *Theatre of Shadows: Samuel Beckett's Drama 1956—1976.* Gerrards Cross: Colin Smythe, 1988.

Sacks, Oliver. *Seeing Voices: A Journey into the World of the Deaf* [1989]. London: Pan Books [Picador], 1990.

Serres, Michel. *Les cinq sens. Philosophie des corps mêlés – 1.* Paris: Éditions Grasset et Fasquelle, 1985.

Woodworth, Robert S. and Harold Schlosberg. *Experimental Psychology* [1938]. London: Methuen, 1950, rev. edn 1954, repr. 1965.

Re-Evaluating *Endgame*

Colin Duckworth

I have to begin with a revealing confession: I have always found it difficult to like *Endgame* as much as Beckett's other plays. Why is this? In any case, what does *like* mean? Is it the same as *admire*? Or as *consider important*, or *original*, or *entertaining*, or *thought-provoking*? Why is the confession revealing? Because it was Beckett's favourite play,[1] so my lukewarmness must be an indication of my own limitations as a dedicated Becketteer.

The Beckett plays I instinctively compare *Endgame* with are all, I realize, plays I have directed: *O les beaux jours, Krapp's Last Tape, Play, Rockaby, Rough for Theater I, Ohio Impromptu, Waiting for Godot,* and *En attendant Godot.* Not *Endgame.* Why is this even remotely significant? To answer that, I shall try to outline my personal view of the qualities and exigencies of Beckett's drama as theater (not as literature), before applying these concerns to my (I hope) enhanced appreciation of *Endgame.* As Ionesco said (*Journal* 147) of his own *Endgame* play, *Le Roi se Meurt,* I am writing this as a lesson for myself.

Most of the people who have told me they find Beckett boring or unacceptably harsh have, when pressed, admitted they have only read him. Vital though seeing the plays is, it has for many years been clear to me that in order to understand any play thoroughly (I would not dare to say completely) one is in a privileged position if one has either played a major role in it or (preferably) has directed it. This will be a truism unworthy of stating for anyone involved in theater arts, but it has been vigorously contested by many purist literary colleagues who regard the vagaries of performance as impediments to a deep understanding of text. Beckett himself would not disagree with the truism, however, given the many changes he introduced as a result of his hands-on involvement in theater productions of his texts.

Ionesco's *Le Roi se Meurt* is a case in point. In my book *Angels of Darkness* I stated that it is

> less than satisfactory because the kind of enlightenment (based on imaginative speculation) that we need should *begin* at the point of Bérenger's disappearance. [...] This is the matter [Time, Being, Existence, and the Self which either disintegrates or continues in some form or other after death] that forms the ground bass of the richly speculative world of Beckett's novels and plays.

Ionesco's play, I concluded, "leaves one with the feeling of being cheated, as one would [...] if Clov were to open the door and wheel Hamm out into the open spaces beyond their refuge" (30-31). At the time of writing that (1971) I had seen performances of both plays, but since then I have enjoyed the experience of directing *Le Roi se Meurt*. As a result, my deeper understanding of the play and consequent respect for it were so increased that I have translated and adapted it as an opera libretto.[2]

Being an analytical, literary-trained director forces one to come to terms with all the nuances, subtleties, subtexts, hidden motivations (of author and characters), as well as the usual *theatrical* elements such as casting, set, blocking, props, lighting, costume, voice, accent, intonation, cadences, pacing, and tempi. And temperaments; Beckett once said to me, "I simply produce an object," but as Ruby Cohn, in quoting this, has noted,

> the *dramatic* object is pregnant with performance by human skills. Beckett's dramatic roles challenge the actor not only in his craft but in his secret identity. Beckett's plays urge director and designer to drown the ego in disciplined detail. (*Just Play* 11)

Beckett's relationship with his play texts was that of a composer with his scores. (One cannot say he was a frustrated musician, because he was a very competent pianist.) Roger Blin attests to this with specific reference to *Endgame*: "Beckett saw his text in musical terms, with absolutely strict divisions" (308). His approach to directing his plays was very much that of the conductor—or rather, the leader of a chamber ensemble—and reveals that his creative faculties were as much musical as intellectual. This was at once a joy and a curse. A joy because his musical sensitivity enabled him to hear his words as music, with cadences, phrasing, tempi and auditive quality given as much (sometimes more) emphasis than the transmission of verbal meaning. A curse because the enterprise he undertook was flawed from the start (but well worth while trying, if only to "fail again and fail better"). This is because of the obvious and inescapable fact that words have a semantic value or make semantic 'noise' for the receiver even if the writer wishes to exclude it, whereas pure music has none and works on a different area of the brain. In his own directing (and in his stage directions), Beckett often downplayed clarity and comprehensibility (notably in *Play* and *Not I*), or suppressed emotional indicators (for example, Listener's face in *Ohio Impromptu*) in an attempt to eliminate these distractions from the "pure" musicality of speech. Blin records his difference of opinion with Beckett (in 1957) regarding the tragic quality of the ending of *Endgame*. Beckett "didn't want tragedy," and was unperturbed by the fact that his approach meant that "[T]here was no suspense, whether or not Clov left was unimportant." The same word was to be repeated "in exactly the same way, like the same note in music played by the same instrument," even if plot-point and context were quite different (308). Musical values had absolute priority over dramatic ones. Of course, as he became more experienced, Beckett had to compromise.

The status of a Beckett play text, therefore, is closely akin to that of a musical score, both only fully realized when performed. But—before anyone objects that that is true for any script—particular qualities and sensitivities are required of director and actors of a Beckett play which are ideal but not so vital with, say, Shaw, Ibsen or Brecht, for whom plot, action, character, or ideology are of fundamental importance. Those playwrights can be read, or seen in a mediocre performance, and still, to a large extent, understood and appreciated. A Beckett play, just like a Beethoven or Debussy chamber work, can only be fully seized in a very good performance done by practitioners with those intuitive qualities and sensitivities.

Presumably God considered Noah and his family to be worth saving; in Beckett's ark, only Nell and Clov seem to have any moral merit or redeeming qualities (it's a reasonable percentage!). But the play's power to win over is, for me, reduced by Beckett's determination to make the play depend on "the power of the text to claw," to make it "more inhuman than 'Godot'" (Letter to Schneider). This is the result of making the overwhelmingly dominating character an egocentric, hollow, self-obsessed, self-pitying and orotund Prospero-Lear bereft of compassion. Ionesco created a not dissimilar protagonist in *Le Roi se Meurt*, who disintegrates as the extinction of his realm and his own death approach. However, King Bérenger's moral collapse and reversion to infantile dependency are movingly depicted, and there is a broader spectrum of human types in the text of *Le Roi se Meurt* to alleviate the harshness of impending death and the bitterness of the man who has never faced up to the inevitability of death: a warm, loving and sensual Queen Marie, a comic guard, and a couple of very down-to-earth women, the Nurse and Queen Marguerite.

Alleviation, momentary distraction from the growing darkness, is to be found in *Endgame*, but of a different kind, inserted, *plaqué*, rather than growing organically out of the situation on stage: Hamm's soliloquies, Nagg's joke. Above all, it is the physical comedy of Clov's stage business with the ladder and the flea-powder (like Lucky's with all his impedimenta, and the three-hat routine of Didi and Gogo) that lightens the mood. However, it is *in performance* that such important visual elements can really be appreciated. Even after forty years I can recall Jack MacGowran's Clov at the Aldwych (1964), with his slowly growing exasperation and rebellion, spavined gait and meticulously choreographed movements.

In *Endgame* the darkness is relieved at times, on a sit-com level, by the Basil-and-Sybil kind of tetchy verbal feuding—"goings on"—that Hamm and Clov engage in. If we compare this with, say, the second act of the posthumously published *Eleutheria*, which is at times not only like *Endgame* but also a parody of knockabout farce, we can see that it would need only a slight transformation to turn parts of *Endgame* into a parody of *Fawlty Towers*:

SCENE: *The lobby of Fawlty Towers. Basil begins to pick up the objects lying on the ground.*
SYBIL: *(behind counter)*: What *are* you doing, Basil?
BASIL: Putting things in order, dear. I'm going to clear everything away.
SYBIL: *(knowing chaos will result as usual)*: Order!
BASIL: I love order. *(He looks meaningfully at Sybil.)* A world where all would be silent and under the last dust.
SYBIL: *(exasperated)*: What in God's name do you think you're doing?
BASIL: *(straightening up)*: I'm doing my best to create a little order, light of my life.
SYBIL: Drop it!

> BASIL: *(drops the objects he has picked up.)*: After all *(with mock resignation)*, there or elsewhere. *(He stomps off doing a German goose-step.)*
> SYBIL: *(irritably)*: What's wrong with your feet? Tramp! Tramp!
> BASIL: I must have put on my boots.

I have just read in this morning's paper a film review that is curiously relevant. "It is hard to watch two heads bobbing above water for perhaps half the running time of *Open Water*—and to listen to the banal squabbling of this charmless couple [...]"; I knew what was coming next before my eye took it in: "[...] without imagining, from time to time, that it would be better staged as a cryptic Samuel Beckett-style play" (Martin A3).[3] Three key qualities of the *text* of *Endgame*—*banality, squabbling, charmless*—some readers (and spectators of a poor production) would say. They could be applied equally to the text of other Beckett plays, which I have directed, particularly *Play*, *Krapp's Last Tape,* and *Godot*; but in rehearsal director and cast participate in a magical process by which they can transcend these qualities. Would the same be true of *Endgame*?[4]

There is, in *Endgame*, no equivalent to the subtle study of sorely tested friendship, affection, and camaraderie ("Back to back like in the good old days!") of Didi and Gogo, who are far from being "charmless." Conversely, the two women of *Play* are notable for their bitchy barbs,[5] but their bitter monologues can, in *performance*, be imbued with other qualities that raise them above banal and charmless squabbling. My own production brought out the caustic archness of "the other (younger) woman," the resentful vulnerability of the (older) wife, solely on the basis of the age and personality of the actresses. The man became almost endearingly bewildered, beleaguered, and out of his depth, rather than a pleasure-seeking deceitful adulterer, or the suave smoothie of Alan Rickman in the Gate film version. The same actor (Robin Cuming) played "my" Krapp, which brought about a prevailing sad nostalgia for what might have been, rather than the harshness of Pierre Chabert's interpretation. I am not claiming correctness or superiority for any approach (on the contrary, Beckett would not have liked my 'sentimental' approach); I am just emphasizing the additional insights into the multi-dimensional potential of the text afforded by the weeks of textual investigation that result in dramatic incarnation.

Vivian Mercier's famous quip about *Godot* (a play "in which nothing happens, twice" [144-145]) could have been written only by someone who had never been involved in a production of it. Physical happenings—Gogo's struggles with his boot, Didi's walk and responses to nature's calls, Pozzo's blind fumbling, Lucky's manipulation of too many bits of luggage, like Clov's multiple limping ascents up the ladder, Hamm's punting with the gaff, the shock of Nagg's and Nell's first appearance above the rim of their bins, the precise centering of Hamm, the knocking on the hollow wall—assume equal status with the dialogue. Above all, the vocal or musical qualities, which are impossible to realize on the page—intonations, accents, pacing, rhythms, contrasts of voices—were all of paramount importance to Beckett.

Is my experience of having directed *Godot* twice likely to be more relevant to my attempted appraisal of *Endgame*? For instance: What light can be thrown on Hamm by my experience of having "created" two Pozzos? Would I be better equipped to see that Lucky and Clov, despite their both being in the slave position, are utterly different in conception? Only the opportunity to engage in a production of *Endgame* would prove anything.

The suggestive and haunting quality of Beckett's finest plays derives from what might be happening beyond the stage space. I have explored this idea in two essays with reference to *Godot*, *Krapp's Last Tape* and *Play* ("From stage space"; "Beckett's Theater"). Maybe one reason for *Endgame*'s lesser appeal for me lies in the lack of a suggested Elsewhere, of a place where significant action is mysteriously taking place? All we have is a brief reference to the small boy sitting outside in the corpsed world. Otherwise, Nothing. Not only in space, but in time as well: none of the four characters seems remotely interested in what brought them to this dire situation. Harry White comments that:

> As with *Godot* before it, *Endgame* concedes the past, [particularly the] slow disintegration whose final phase is enacted in the present tense. The anterior existence of lives which have come to inhabit the barren terrain of *Endgame* is crucial to Beckett's purpose [which is to] sustain the illusion of realist drama. (160)

His perception is diametrically opposed to that of Julie Campbell, who concedes no attempt at realism in *Endgame*: "Beckett's art is not representational, but abstract" (131). I find White's argument for the play's being transitional more persuasive, as it allows for an evolution in Beckett's art.

However, I find it hard to agree with White's contention just quoted: there is no reference to the immediate past, to the "slow disintegration" that led to the voluntary incarceration of this improbable quartet. This lack of temporal context and the ensuing sense of total isolation in space and time is, of course, essential to Beckett's intention to create situational universality and ambiguity; hence the well-documented process of 'vaguening' the play went through in its various stages. It is this apparent insouciance about the event(s) leading up to their life in the ultimate refuge that makes Hamm and Clov the offspring of Pozzo and Lucky. Certainly, we know more about these two intruders into the dimension of the tramp-clowns than we do about the immediate past of Hamm and Clov: times are getting tough up at the manor, there may be chicken and wine for the master, but he has professional worries, and the servant has to be sold off. The boy gives us more of an inkling about Mr. Godot's estate: he has a farm with sheep and goats, he has a white beard, he employs under-age labor, and may be unjust in meting out punishment.

Didi and Gogo exist on the insignificant periphery of a solar system of which Godot is at the control center, and in which Pozzo's manor is an inner (albeit dying) planet. Didi and Gogo's world extends beyond the small area round the tree to the place where Gogo gets regularly beaten. Krapp anchors his being by referring not just to past events but to people and places in his present world beyond the den: the church where he fell off the pew, the cold late-summer park, Fanny, the bony old ghost of a whore. He presumably has a continuing source of booze too, since there is no suggestion that provisions are near depletion as in *Godot* and (even more so) in *Endgame*. *Rockaby* invokes and evokes a social and human context: the old woman by her window hoping to see another blind up inviting human contact. The Reader in *Ohio Impromptu* conjures up a vivid picture of the world by the river and the Isle of Swans to which he must return. The triangle in *Play* babble eternally in limbo about their bitter relationship as if it all happened yesterday. Man, wife and mistress exude bitterness and hostility, but they can nevertheless become (miraculously, given the static and repressed way they are portrayed in the text) rounded and understandable human beings caught up in a very common situation.

The situation in *Endgame* is, for the time being, uncommon, rarely seen except in science fiction. We are presented with the last humans left on earth. However, it is astounding that the only references to their past concern things that happened long ago: the disastrous bicycle ride of Nagg and Nell, recrimination about childhood cruelties and deprivations. It is as though they have taken to heart the disapproving words of Didi and Gogo about "all the dead voices":

> VLADIMIR: What do they say?
> ESTRAGON: They talk about their lives.
> VLADIMIR: To have lived is not enough for them. (63)

This lack of reference to the immediate past (and therefore of any context that would enable us to explain how and why these four last humans came to this extremity) does not escape Hamm's notice:

> HAMM: Do you know what it is? [...] I was never there. [...] Absent, always. It all happened without me. I don't know what's happened. [...] What has happened?
> CLOV: What for Christ's sake does it matter? (74-75)

It mattered less and less for Beckett from *Endgame* on, right up to *What Where*, in which a framework reference is entirely absent. This determination not to anchor or embed the work results in both universalization (inviting the recipient's urge to impart and impose meaning) and abstraction (which, like pure mathematics and non-programmatic music, resists all attempts to attribute reductive meaning outside itself). The answer to Hamm's question, "We're not beginning to ... to ... mean something?" (32) must be "No," since, ontologically, meaning derives from and depends on context (defined technically as the intersection of time and place) and persistent—not transient—change (if nothing has been changed by the end of this game/play, then there is no becoming, and therefore no meaning). There are two possible triggers of persistent change: the boy, and Clov's departure. Neither is activated.[6]

In between writing *En attendant Godot* and *Fin de Partie* Beckett had his conversations about art with Georges Duthuit, in the course of which Beckett spoke disapprovingly of art that "[strains] to enlarge the statement of a compromise," that "never stirred from the field of the possible," that manages only to "[disturb] a certain order on the plane of the feasible" (*Dialogues* 102-103). There was a constant yearning in Beckett to be a painter of abstractions governed by shades of light and dark, and at the same time a composer of sounds that happen to be words. David Warrilow and Billie Whitelaw both felt the Beckett actor was a musical instrument being played by Beckett (Bryden, "Beckett and Music" 193). The major plays of the 1950s and 1960s, *Godot*, *Endgame*, *Krapp's Last Tape* and *Happy Days*, reveal the compromises he was obliged to make in order to accommodate the demands and practicalities of theater and to be accessible to a public he had never previously sought to please. As Beckett himself realized, "If they did it my way they would empty the theater" (Letter to Schneider). Not only that, the exigencies of narrative are implacable. As H. Porter Abbott has remarked, "Beckett's incorporation of musical form, like his incorporation of pictorial form, must give way in some degree to the vector of story form—that is, to the vector of history—which is the time we are sentenced to live in" (21).

The strain of compromise is evident, above all, in *Endgame*, with which Beckett had much trouble. As a musical structure, *Endgame* is a prototype of the *diminuendo al niente* form, which he slowly perfected from *Come and Go* to *What Where*. It is significant that Peter Szendy's analysis of Heinz Holliger's mini-operas based on *Come and Go* and *What Where*, is entitled *End Games*. Referring to the "semantic networks of Beckett's dramaticules," Szendy states that such an open-ended work "has never before taken as its theme the advent of the end, the process of ending" (128-9). But surely this is precisely the theme of *Endgame*?

"Musical" elements such as rhythm, pacing, vocal quality and intonation are of paramount importance to directors and actors of any Beckett play. Just as Beckett wrote "pour une voix" (Bernold, 107)[7] (like Flaubert with his *gueuloir*), any director who ignored the auditive qualities of his/her production would be failing in a crucial aspect of his job. To "know" a Beckett script is to know or intuit what it *sounds* like. So far as I am concerned, Beckett-directing is not so much conducting as providing a score for the words. From the first read-through, the compromises start: somewhere between the director's ideal performance and what the actors bring of themselves to their rôles lies the production to come.

Important though these musical qualities are, they are not very much help when it comes to the day to day concerns of transforming the text into sounds and actions that are not just musically and pictorially satisfying, but are convincing as the words and gestures and movements of human beings *en situation*, for that is how the public (and most critics) judge a good performance. A *purely* musical performance would sound like a cross between T.S. Eliot reading his own poetry and some ghastly *Sprechgesang*.

In view of the fact that *Endgame* (like *Krapp's Last Tape*) is a transitional structure between the comparatively stable narrative of *Godot* and the abstract plays from *Not I* on, how far is it possible to envisage *Endgame* as a musical structure? John Spurling persuasively analyzes the play by analogy with music, in terms of pitch, timber, tones, colors, instruments, solos, duos, trios, recitative, and cadenza (72-77). However, the musical analogy will manifest itself only in performance.

I stubbornly and romantically persist (even though I know the theories and practice of imaginative creativity) in considering the characters as real people, knowing all the while that they have been dumped there, *in media res* (whatever the *res* may be), just as we have been dumped here by God or chance, without explanation.

Their ignorance about how they came to this dire situation places *Endgame* in the same category as *Happy Days*, in which vital questions are never posed or answered: how and why did Winnie come to be half-buried? Who did it? Why does she never question the injustice of or the reason for her predicament? Winnie talks a lot about her past—but only the distant past. In both cases, an abyss or ignorance or oblivion separates past and present, but there is a difference. With *Happy Days*, one can concur with Clov: what does is matter? Winnie's half-burial is obviously an archetypal, ontological fear, a mythical icon, and a pictorial device representing the decanting from being to non-being we are all heir to. With the situation presented in *Endgame*, one is justified in asking, as Hamm does, what happened? Julie Campbell has no doubts about this: "What happened before doesn't matter. [...] What matters here is the present" (138).

Her argument is sound as part of her defense of socio-political *non-specificity* in production and interpretation, but my argument is about the absence of *individual context*, which is quite another matter.

Is the reason for the lack of even the suggestion of an explanation to be found in Beckett's determination to universalize *Endgame*? If so, to universalize what? The private? Or the public? Given the extreme unhappiness of Beckett's personal situation while he was struggling with *Fin de Partie*—"one of the most terrible times of his life" (Knowlson 400)—it is hardly surprising that his mood was somber and depressed. The devastation caused by the death of his much loved brother Frank explains Beckett's ironic denunciations of God's benevolence, but not the misanthropy and paucity of redeeming human qualities in the characters. Unlike *Waiting for Godot* and *Happy Days*, *Endgame* reveals nothing like the same capacity for warmth, affection, good-natured amusement, companionship, love even.

I am not alone among Beckett *aficionados* in having these reservations. Michael Billington, reviewing the recent production at the Albery Theater in London, confesses that "while *Endgame* meant a lot to Beckett, I increasingly wonder how much it means to the rest of us, especially if we don't share his view of the unalterable absurdity of existence." But then he admits to being won over *by performance*: "My doubts were largely quelled by the heightened theatricality of Warchus's production," with Michael Gambon's "magnificent Hamm, which evokes multiple images: a screaming Bacon Pope, a dying Prospero, a decaying Irish landlord." But wait, there's more: "Yet, while we are royally diverted, I found myself for once questioning the universality of Beckett's despairing vision" (28).

There will be no agreement about how successful the universalizing process was in *Endgame*. Universalizing a personal tragedy and universalizing a personal world-view are quite different matters. Of the first, little or nothing was known until Beckett's biographers latched on to details of his private life many years later. The second could be and was deduced (and traduced) from the start: "pessimism" and "nihilism" were favorites, together with "unrelieved." During the last fifty years, untold thousands of spectators have laughed at the comic stage business of Didi, Gogo and Clov, have been wrily amused by Winnie's misplaced sunniness, deeply moved by Krapp's solitary lament for wasted life, by Didi's anguished questioning of his own humanity ("Was I sleeping while the others suffered?"), and by Pozzo's tormented onslaught on "accursed time." The flow of new resonances, analogies and associations—political, religious, psychological and ontological—never ceases. How does *Endgame* score?

Not well, by comparison; but given the situation (admittedly, no more terminal than Winnie's) such concerns may reasonably be expected to appear less urgent.

My own conclusion, for the moment, is that since bitterness is often a response to grief, Beckett's ability to universalize private grief through vaguening unspecificity in *Endgame* is a tremendous feat of creativity, as powerful as Kafka's in *The Trial*, and more accessible than T.S. Eliot's in *The Waste Land*. That alone would be remarkable, but it seems to me that the effectiveness and originality are compounded by the way Beckett brought together intense private emotion and societal anxiety. The purgatorial and the apocalyptic are inextricably linked in the play—it is hell stinking with corpses, within and without, tenuously separated by a hollow wall—but we are left to conjecture whether the decelerating grind towards the end, longed for and yet subject to Hamm's strategic delays, will ever get to a halt.

The end of what? Is the context merely (merely!) the end of an individual life's journey? The "intense pleasure" with which Beckett listened to a recording of Schubert's song cycle, *Winterreise*, at the very time (summer, 1956) he was battling with *Fin de Partie* (Knowlson 425), is hardly surprising, given that Wilhelm Müller's poems are a mournful but moving evocation of the journey towards longed-for oblivion in a dreary landscape. Clearly, however, Beckett was not going to be content with a re-statement of Romantic *Weltschmertz*.

Nor, surely, would he settle for a lament for the end of the world, this muck-heap? Ruby Cohn states, "*Endgame* is unmistakably about an end of a world" (*Comic Gamut* 231). In the mid-1950s, the Soviet invasion of Hungary and Anglo-American H-bomb tests in the Pacific did not encourage optimism, but—despite his alert interest in world affairs—Beckett was not given (until *Catastrophe*) to using theater for overt political comment. *Endgame* must be something more than a warning tract.

Cohn's statement above reads in full: "Since *Endgame* is unmistakably about an end of a world, there are many recollections of the Book of Revelations." This leads to a more probable interpretation, or at least one that is more consistent with my idea of the level on which Beckett was working: one that takes *Endgame* above and beyond such mundane matters into a more esoteric and truly apocalyptic dimension; one that takes us from Schubert to Messiaen, in fact.

The score of Olivier Messiaen's *Quatuor pour la fin du temps* is prefaced with a quotation from the Apocalypse of John, 10, 6:

> Je vis un ange plein de force, descendant du ciel [...] il leva la main vers le Ciel et jura par Celui qui vit dans les siècles des siècles, disant: Il n'y aura plus de Temps...
> (I saw an angel full of might, descending from the sky [...] he raised his hand heavenwards and swore by the One who lives for ever and ever, saying: There shall be no more Time...)

The idea of the abolition of Time is obviously in the Beckettian mode, and yet it is barely hinted at in *Endgame*, when Hamm, resuming his story, interjects a *non sequitur*: "Moments for nothing, now as always, time was never and time is over, reckoning closed and story ended" (83). How is it that Beckett does not develop this much more profoundly philosophical and poetic image—not just the end of the Hamm and Clov association, or the end of the world, but *the end of Time itself*—especially since it is apparently to be found in this same source, the Revelation or Apocalypse of John?

The answer, I think, is simply that he either possessed or was recollecting a more modern and more scholarly version of the Bible than Messiaen. Older versions, in English and French, use the word *time/temps*, whereas the correct concept is *delay/délai*. "There will be no more delay." "Il n'y aura plus de délai."[8] This is consistent with the previous verse ("Men will seek death and they will not find it; they will long to die, and death will fly from them" [*Revelation* 9,6]), which is central to Hamm's wondering "why it [the end] was so long coming."

Fortunately for music-lovers, Messiaen was misled by an antiquated Bible into being inspired to write some of the most ethereally beautiful (and strikingly titled) music of the twentieth century, but it is nevertheless strange that Beckett did not, apparently, know the quartet, which was written in 1940-41, just before and during Messiaen's incarceration in Stalag VIIA.[9] It may be argued that Messiaen's lush mystical religiosity would have been as alien to Beckett as Beckett's ironic, parodic mockery of biblical themes would have shocked Messiaen. Musically, however, they would surely have understood one another, and there are similarities that would have ensured mutual respect and sympathy: Messiaen was a medical orderly in the French army when he was taken prisoner in 1941; Beckett was Quartermaster and Interpreter at St-Lô hospital in 1945. They both had poor eyesight. They were both fascinated by mathematics and used them in their art forms. In any case, Beckett formed close friendships with religious believers (such as Tom MacGreevy and Dr Arthur Darley), thanks largely to the tolerance inculcated during his schooldays at Earlsfort House (Knowlson 36, 349).

If, then, it is true that music-lover Beckett never heard or knew of the quartet, it remains puzzling. Messiaen scholar Rebecca Rischin wrote to me (29 September 2004), stating that the quartet's title "refers to the end of time, both musical (rhythm) and philosophical (apocalyptic)." How could this not interest the Beckett who wrote: "music is the Idea itself, unaware of the world of phenomena, existing ideally outside the universe, apprehended not in Space but in Time only, and consequently untouched by the teleological hypothesis" (*Proust* 92)? If only Beckett had paid more attention to the (French!) music being written round him in Paris!

It would be another thirty years before Beckett was to bring together the Winter Journey and the End of Time—in *What Where*:

> It is winter.
> Without journey.
> Time passes.
> That is all.
> Make sense who may.
> I switch off.

These are the last words Beckett wrote for theater.

Back to *Endgame*: one mystery, "a major enigma" (Restivo 222), remains, however: "le môme [...] avec les yeux de Moîse mourant"

(The kid […] with the eyes of a dying Moses). The boy is the only mystical element in *Fin de Partie*, and yet his relegation to near banality in *Endgame* has been sufficient for him to be treated by critics as a mere successor to the departing Clov. Let us ignore Beckett's possible embarrassment at having introduced such an overt appeal to salvation from a spiritual dimension,[10] and add to speculation. The boy is obviously not just an ordinary lad waiting for a domestic vacancy; he sits outside without harm even though "it's death out there." He is meditating; Hamm, now the blind seer Tiresias, immediately bestows upon him the eyes of a dying (beardless) prophet. This, then, could in fact be Beckett's familiar reductive technique applied to the angel of Revelation, come to announce that (as the Jerusalem Bible has it), "The time of waiting is over." The polyvalent child, just a messenger in *Waiting for Godot*, has arrived with the good news that Didi and Gogo despair of hearing.

The apocalyptic world's-end situation, captured perfectly by the original but erased Flood inspiration of *Fin de Partie*, has not, alas, ceased to be of immense and growing concern to every thinking person since Hiroshima. Beckett mirrors the macrocosmic self-destructiveness of the human race in the microcosm of the dysfunctional family, tearing each other apart with selfishness, cruelty, and greed, precisely those human qualities that threaten to reduce Gaia to the state of a treeless and waterless desert.

At this point in my re-assessment of *Endgame* another odd coincidence occurred: I was invited to join a group of actors who had formed THE MAYA COMPANY. But not as director. I was to be there as dramaturg: répétiteur, observer and commentator on their decisions: a bit like a chairman of a committee. I hate committees. One of them designed the camel, I seem to recall. I didn't like the idea, but with nothing in the offing and nothing to lose but my chains, I agreed. My contract stipulates that I won't have any decision-making power. I can record rehearsals but not let any outsider hear them or read transcripts without approval of all cast.
    The cast had already chosen itself:

Harry Bolton (Hamm): a large, expansive man with a great voice. Great experience but first time in a Beckett play.

Connor Moyne (Clov): a nervy, wiry Irishman, tense and easily rubbed up the wrong way. I shall have to be careful with him. Has already played Lucky in Dublin, and has seen many Gate productions of Beckett there.

Nathan Worth (Nagg): first experience of Beckett. Was a household name in music hall during the 'fifties before it died the death.

Norma Ritchie (Nell): has played Winnie, so understands a lot of what's going on.

DAY 1

I shall refer in this journal only to moments of major difficulty or enlightenment.

Met in our rehearsal venue for the next week. Odd arrangement and, as it turns out, equally odd venue, but suitably dismal and cold—basement of an old warehouse by the river some way out of the city, with two high windows that are just above ground level. Immediately realize where the play is set, below ground. Had always assumed the windows were high up just for the comic effect of Clov's repeat ascensions, and to let interpreters like Kenner (155) deduce that it's a skull we're in. So, we're on the way down to hell, as Hamm remarks: "Old wall! ... Beyond is the ... other hell" (26).

We first established some ground rules: each actor would be free to comment on the others' approach, interpretation, style, pacing, delivery, accent, rapport ... but final decision would be with the speaker unless another actor felt it was adversely affecting his/her own rôle. I'll be listened to as I'm the only one to see it from spectator's angle. Harry points out that I also know more about Beckett's plays than any of them, to which Connor purses his lips in disagreement and responds: "I don't see why we need a fecking academic here at all." So I say, with what I hope is a humble look, "I was directing *O les beaux jours* before you were born, and *Godot* when you were still in short pants."

Connor still made it pretty clear he didn't think I should be there at all, except to prompt.

Nathan is very wary of being stuck in a dustbin. "Will this be good for my image?" he jokes, then asks, "Why dustbins anyway?"

I hazard a reason: "Beckett wanted to avoid repetition. In *Godot* there's endless space, so in the next play it's a closed space. In *Godot* the supernumerary couple are always on the move, so he made the next ones static."

Connor: "But he didn't avoid repetition. Hamm repeats Pozzo—both landowners, Pozzo has a manor, Hamm had paupers Clov had to inspect on horseback or bike. I remember Alan Stanford at The Gate telling me how hard it was playing Pozzo and Hamm in repertory, stopping the one flowing into the other, keeping their music and mannerisms distinct. And they're both blind. Blindness is a major repetition."

Me: "And a major concern: Beckett was very worried about his eyesight and the double emphasis expresses that fear. Soon after writing *Endgame* he wrote an unfinished play for just two characters: a cripple in a wheelchair and a blind violinist.[11] Hamm split in two. It's a progression, isn't it—authority figure humbled, the mighty fallen, but finally the blind man is the victim-slave figure, helpless. Some of that insecurity Beckett must have felt has to come out in Hamm—in fact, he once said in rehearsal, 'His assurance is always put on'."

Harry: "Yes, that helps. Vulnerability of the bully."

Nathan: "All right, but can we get back to my problem? Why can't we be bedridden instead?"

Norma steps in: "It'd be more comfortable for us, but what a moment when the audience sees those dustbin lids lift up, then the heads peeping over the rims. Brilliant theater, comic and pathetic."

Nathan: "Stand-up comedian to legless cast-off! What a career!"

I am thus alerted to a danger of directorless theater: but for Norma, Nathan would have got his own way, since I have no power other than to point out that the Beckett estate wouldn't allow such a radical departure from script. Glad I didn't have to voice that argument, but time may come.

Harry keeps appealing to me for comments and reassurance. He's taking Hamm's vulnerability to heart!

At end of day, we make an unpleasant discovery. We realize we can't get out. Connor climbs the ladder for the first time to look out of window, and sees nothing but deserted concrete yard surrounded by a high wall. We shout. Useless. It must be a joke. Reactions. They blame me: the only outsider—I must be in on it. "But I'm in the same position as you! I'm a prisoner too." They're not convinced.

Harry suggests, obvious really, summoning help by our mobile telephones. One after the other we try to contact people, but the signal is too weak down there.

Norma: "Somebody's bound to initiate a search when we don't turn up tonight."

With a shock we realize that not one of us is expected back home. My wife is overseas, Norma and her husband are separated, and the others are unattached at the moment. We learn from each other that we were discreetly questioned about close contacts before being cast. This makes us doubly uncomfortable. No one would miss any of us for some time.

Implications: food? In the fridge? But it's secured with a combination lock, like a safe. Someone must have the combination—they couldn't mean us to die. I say, "That would take quite a few days, actually, since we have water." Nobody appreciates this remark.

I look in the file I was given. There's an envelope, addressed to me, marked PERSONAL AND CONFIDENTIAL—TO BE OPENED AT END OF DAY ONE. Open sealed orders when out at sea! In it, a number, with instructions: I have to memorize the number of the fridge combination lock, then throw it (the number) down loo. I have to distribute rations. Not popular. All are dependent on me. Profound mistrust. Connor rushes me, so I chew up the bit of paper, saying I hope I've remembered the number right or we all starve. They turn on Connor. Already we are getting as tetchy as Hamm and Clov.

Nathan asks why doesn't Clov just whisk Hamm away from the cupboard when he's unlocked it? This is the only hold Hamm has over Clov, and he would lose it. They're clearly thinking of doing this to me, so I say I'll refuse to open it while any of them are in the kitchen. Connor glowers: "So you can gorge yourself in secret!"

Norma: "Now wait a minute. If he lets us all know the number, we'll start suspecting each other of cheating during the night.

It'll tear us apart very quickly. We'll soon tell if he's not losing weight like the rest of us."

Connor wants to smoke. Loud protests from all but Nathan: "He should use his own conscience." Connor: "I have none." But he does compromise—the loo always smells of stale smoke. Ah well, he'll soon run out of fags or matches.

Toilet, running water: at least there is one. Sudden realization of what Nagg and Nell's bins must have smelled like. (Hamm remarks on Clov's smell, but this would be overpowered by the bins' stink.) How does Hamm cope? Does Clov have to lift him? No shower or bath. Air getting staler and hotter. So are we. The last refuge of the 4 playing the endgame of earthly existence must be like this.

DAY 2

We agree this must be a test, like reality TV. Search for cameras. None. To make us LIVE the experience of being shut up and likely to die of hunger and thirst. We start rehearsing with this in mind, certain that once we have begun to respond positively, the test will end.

I remind them: "At least we have something positive to do to while away the time—work on the play. Let's get on with it." They agree.

Harry raises the question of the acting style needed. "The whole situation is so surreal and most of the dialogue is unnatural, I feel a very stylized, mannered delivery is what's wanted."

Connor: "I think that's true for Hamm, a real old Donald Wolfit-type ham actor, always with one eye on where the spotlight is. But we others are pretty natural, especially if Clov has an Irish accent."

Harry: "It goes deeper than that. I sense an uneasiness in this play about whether the characters are real or *all* conscious of being actors in a play, in a Pirandello sort of way. Not just Hamm. All those knowing theatrical hints: 'Not a underplot, I hope.' 'What's to keep me here?—The dialogue.' 'Winding up for my last soliloquy.'"

Nathan: "Ah, but only Hamm sees things that way. They're all his words."

Harry: "Then they're infectious, because it's Clov who says 'This is what we call making an exit,' and likens their refuge to a stage, when he turns his telescope on the audience and says 'I see a multitude in transports of joy'."

Connor: "Maybe Clov has seen *Waiting for Godot* and remembers Estragon looking out at the audience and saying 'Inspiring prospects'!"

Me: "At the risk of annoying Connor, can I point out that the original French text doesn't infer that Clov's an actor making an exit. It says 'gagner la sortie,' 'make for the exit,' like a spectator."

Connor: "Thanks for that valuable bit of trivia. What does *the original French text* have for 'It's easy going'? I don't know if it means 'Going is easy' or 'This is plain sailing'."

Ignoring his heavy irony and raised eyebrows, I refer to my copy of *Fin de Partie*. "It has 'Ça va tout seul,' so since Clov is imagining what it will be like walking across that desert out there, it must mean he'll be so happy to be free the journey will be easy."

Nathan wants to know what "pap" means. Is he calling for his father, his pappy? Norma the Earth Mother tells him it's mushy food for babies.

Nathan: "It's still an odd word to use. When I first read it I thought Nagg is calling for his dad, his pappy. If it's baby food, why put it in the mouth of an old man? That word, I mean. He could have said gruel, or porridge."

Norma: "Well, you've got me thinking now. Pap means nipple too, so maybe he's calling for his mother as well. I wonder what the original French was?"

I'm able to oblige, to Connor's disgust. "*Bouillie*. Milky cereal stuff specifically for babies without teeth. Beckett could have used *gruau*, gruel, but obviously wanted to introduce the idea of reversion to toothless infancy by the aged. By translating it as pap rather than gruel he not only keeps the image of return to babyhood, but also introduces these other ambiguities—father, mother's breast."

Nathan is excited by this idea. "Hence the bonnet! And the leglessness! I'm a baby who can't walk. I remember seeing old Moore Marriott in a film playing himself, about 60 looking 80, and his toothless father, about 80 looking 110. In a nightshirt and nightcap, with a cracked high-pitched voice."

Harry: "We'll have to knock a few of your teeth out."

Nathan: "Thanks, mate, no need." He takes his plate out of his mouth, puts on the cracked voice, ages twenty years. He's finding Nagg in himself.

DAY 3

More search for a means of escape. None. Like the inhabitants of the cylinder in *The Lost Ones*.

Violent disagreement between Harry and Connor over Harry's approach to Hamm. He does seem to be taking the vulnerability too much to heart, and has lost some of the domineering quality. "You're not giving me enough to react to," Connor complains, "feed me more contempt! Try saying 'compassion' as if it was an insult."

At last, a deeper discussion—we're getting on. Harry wants to know if we all have to agree about what has happened to the world. "It can't be the biblical flood because there's dry land out there. So is it post-nuclear or global warming or what?"

Nathan: "What strikes me is that nobody talks about what's happened. Wouldn't you think they'd talk about the extinction of every other living creature on earth?"

Harry: "Maybe they've exhausted that topic. They've been there a long time."

Me: "Or maybe they're indifferent, like most people are about the way we're destroying the planet."

Norma: "Or traumatized by what's happened, like returned soldiers don't want to talk about the horrors of war."

Connor: "All right, let's think what *is* going on out there. Perhaps our resident professor can offer an explanation of how it is Clov can still go out to fetch sand from the shore even though it's death out there. No more nature, no more tide, no more navigators. Yet Clov goes out for sand, and togs up at the end in Panama hat and raincoat and umbrella, ready to walk out."

This apparent inconsistency had already worried me, but I pretended to summon up instantaneous enlightenment: "I think there'd be little danger in dashing out in polluted or radio-active air to get more sand, then back in. And the final exit is either sheer bravado, or exasperation, or a case of 'I may be some time,' like Oates leaving the tent and going out into the blizzard to his death. As Beckett once wrote to me, 'How's that for exegesis?'"

DAY 4

Harry is just realizing how difficult the ending is. "It's incredibly courageous, or foolish, of Beckett to put in a long soliloquy when the audience has been alerted to expect the final curtain. The play could end on 'Old endgame lost of old, play and lose and have done with losing,' or on 'Moments for nothing, now as always, time was never and time is over, reckoning closed and story ended.' Beautiful dying fall, that. But then Hamm runs the danger of crawling into bathos, and that's what worries me! Shakespeare doesn't put Lear or Hamlet through this!"

Me: "But he does it to Prospero. Think of Hamm's end-word-game as an anti-heroic parody of Prospero's epilogue, Harry. You must be here confined in this bare island. Your charms are all o'erthrown, your strength is faint, your ending is despair."

Then came a surprising development: we were discussing whether Clov will really leave (and make a closure to the play) or not (leaving it as one of those open-ended structures).

Harry: "The stage instruction says you 'halt by the door and stand there, impassive and motionless till the end.' But why don't you actually turn the handle of the door, and then change your mind?"

Connor was not receptive to the suggestion—he never likes advice if he isn't giving it. Then he thought again: "Well, it's possible, even though it would make it more likely that Clov will leave, and Beckett wanted it to remain unresolved. But I see one point only where I could logically go to open the door, and that's where you say 'And to end up with? ... Discard.' I see this—I mean Clov sees it—as a signal that I no longer have any more services to do here, and I make a move to open the door. But,"—Connor was quite excited by the idea now—"you then throw away that bloody imperious whistle that's been driving me crazy, and it occurs to me that Hamm's going to die, he won't be telling that interminable story, and life might be bearable here from now on."

They then walked the scene from Hamm's "Old endgame lost of old." Clov put his hand on the handle of the metal door on "Discard," pushed it down, and ... *the door opened!*

Instead of being pleased, Connor immediately sowed doubt about whether we had tried the door properly to start with, but my written instructions proved that we'd been imprisoned against our will. After three days, we rise again.

The outcome is that we have all agreed to consider hiring a lawyer and suing the company. At first we were all pretty angry and were just about to take a vote on it when Norma, who'd been very quiet, said something like this:

"Let's just think about this a moment longer. It's been very aggravating, but don't you think we'll do *Endgame* much better? We didn't have to *act* the situation, being cooped up, getting on each other's nerves, being short of food. It was *for real*. Normally, during rehearsals we'd have pretended to be stuck in a refuge, and then gone home to have dinner, watch telly, have a shower and go to a comfortable bed. But we *know* now what it's like for Hamm, Clov, and even Nagg and Nell, though we were spared the dustbins."

This response to our experience reminded me of something: "We're a bit like the convicts in St. Quentin penitentiary. They immediately understood *Waiting for Godot* because it expressed their own situation, waiting without end. They couldn't go home after the performance, and we couldn't leave after rehearsal."

Harry nodded and added, "When Connor accidentally turned that handle this morning, Clov's words rang round my head as they've never done before: 'I open the door of my cell and go.' And we haven't wasted our time—we've covered a few problems. It's been very concentrated, no distractions. And it'll be the end of the production if we sue."

Connor persisted: "We'd have covered those problems anyway, without having our civil liberties trampled on. They wouldn't dare to sack us. We'd take them to the cleaners for unlawful imprisonment *and* unfair dismissal."

Nathan was undecided. We vote tomorrow. I shall value these three days of hell in the cell—but as old Krapp says, "I wouldn't want them back."[12]

Colin Duckworth, University of Melbourne

Notes

[1] Quoted, for example, in McMillan and Fehsenfeld 163. What he actually wrote (to Tom Bishop in 1978) was, "I suppose the one I like the least is *Endgame*," which one takes to be self-depreciative Beckett-speak for indicating a preference. Not for him Mel Brooks' style, "The biggest best thing I ever did" (on *The Producers*).
[2] Production for Melbourne French Theater, 1980, at The Open Stage, Melbourne. Australian composer Michael Easton was working on the music for my libretto, *A*

King No More, when he died in December 2003. The music has only just (June 2007) been composed by Michael Bertram.

[3] In fact Beckett had a very good eye and ear for banality, and knew when to cut it; hence, for example, his steadfast refusal to allow a production of *Eleuthéria*.

[4] The genesis of *Endgame*, admirably summarized and analyzed by Ruby Cohn in *Just Play* (Ch. 9, "The Play That Was Rewritten: *Fin de partie*"), is also a process of purification and de-banalization by excision and revision.

[5] As Barbara Bray (either bravely or in a state of denial) commented in "The New Beckett," her review of the world première performance of *Play*, the three players in this banal love triangle are "people in all their funny, disgraceful, pitiable fragility and all the touchingness, in spite of everything, of their efforts to love one another, and endure" (29).

[6] "Ontology X is entirely based on the principle that meaning derives from context: specifically in our case 'context' is defined technically as the intersection of time and place. To 'exist' an Entity has no meaningful attributes except those that are contextually derived, directly or indirectly, from events at specific times and places" Letter (7 November 2004) from Godfrey Rust, chief data architect of Ontology X, a proprietary 'contextual' ontology used in the development of several recent international media information standards (MPEG21-RDD, ONIX, ISWC, ISTC, DOI).

[7] Beckett also told Jean Reavey that "Drama is following music" and "I never write a word without first saying it out loud" (Lois Oppenheim, in her Introduction to *Samuel Beckett and the Arts*, xv).

[8] See, on these two variants, Glasson 63.

[9] Edward Beckett kindly wrote to me on 4 October 2004, "As far as I know Sam never heard this piece and certainly never spoke with me of Messiaen's music." For a recent well-researched correction of the myths that have grown up regarding the composition of the quartet, see Rebecca Rischin, *For the End of Time: The Story of the Messiaen Quartet*. Professor Rischin informs me (29 September 2004) that she does not know when exactly Messiaen entitled the work, and that he "claimed the title had nothing to do with his imprisonment."

[10] Not the only one, by far. See my "Beckett and the missing sharer."

[11] *Fragment de théâtre I* was written in French in the late 1950s and translated as *Rough for Theater* in *Collected Shorter Plays* 66.

[12] The Maya Company's indefinitive production of *Endgame* is scheduled to begin, possibly, at the Wintergarden Theater, Tuktoyaktuk (N. Canada) in 2070, to coincide with the disappearance of the Arctic Ice Cap.

Bibliography

Abbott, H. Porter. 'Samuel Beckett and the Arts of Time: Painting, Music, Narrative' in Oppenheim (1999): 7-21.

Beckett, Samuel. *Waiting for Godot*. London: Faber, 1956.

—. Letter to Alan Schneider, 11 January 1956. *Village Voice*, 19 March 1958, reprinted in *The Village Voice Reader*. New York: Doubleday, 1962. (183)

—. *Fin de partie*. Paris: Editions de Minuit, 1958.

—. *Endgame*. New York: Grove, 1958.

—. *Proust and Three Dialogues with Georges Duthuit*. London: John Calder, 1965.

—. *En attendant Godot* ed. Colin Duckworth. London: Harrap, 1966.

—. *Fragment de théâtre I* in *Pas—suivi de quatre esquisses*, Paris: Editions de Minuit, 1978.

—. *Disjecta* ed. Ruby Cohn. London: Calder, 1983.

—. *Rough for theater* I in *Collected Shorter Plays*. London: Faber, 1984.

—. *Eleuthéria*. Paris: Editions de Minuit, 1995.

—. *Eleuthéria* translated by Barbara Wright. London: Faber, 1996.

Ben Zvi, Linda ed. *Drawing on Beckett: Portraits, Performances, and Cultural Contexts* (Assaph Book Series). Tel Aviv: Tel Aviv University Press, 2003.

Bernold, André. *L'Amitié de Beckett*. Paris: Hermann, 1992.

Billington, Michael. Review of *Endgame. The Guardian* (11 March 2004): 28.

Blin, Roger." Interview with Roger Blin by Joan Stevens" in Oppenheim (1994): 301-314.

Bray, Barbara. "The New Beckett" in *The Observer, Weekend Review* (16 June 1963): 29.

Bryden, Mary ed. *Samuel Beckett and Music*. Oxford: Oxford University Press, 1998.

—. "Beckett and Music: Interview with Philip Glass" in Bryden (1998): 191-194.

Campbell, Julie. "There is no more …: Cultural Memory in *Endgame*" in Ben Zvi (2003): 127-140.

Cohn, Ruby. *Samuel Beckett: The Comic Gamut*. New Jersey: Rutgers University Press, 1962.

—. *Just Play*. Princeton: Princeton University Press, 1980.

Duckworth, Colin. *Angels of Darkness: Dramatic Effect in Beckett and Ionesco*. London: Allen and Unwin; NY: Barnes and Noble, 1972.

—. "From stage space to inner space in Beckett's Drama: Signposts to Elsewhere" in *Space and Boundaries/Espaces et Frontières: Indicium 3* (1988): 131-138.

—. 'Beckett's Theater: Beyond the stage space' in Stewart (1999): 93-99.

—. "Beckett and the Missing Sharer" in *Beckett and Religion: Samuel Beckett Today/Aujourd'hui* 9 (2000): 133-143.

Glass, Philip. In Bryden (1998): 191-194.

Glasson, T.F. *The Revelation of John*. (The Cambridge Bible Commentary). Cambridge: Cambridge University Press, 1965.

Ionesco, Eugène. *Le Roi se Meurt*. Paris: Gallimard, 1963.

—. *Journal en miettes*. Paris: Mercure de France, 1967.

Knowlson, James. *Damned to Fame: The Life of Samuel Beckett*. London: Bloomsbury, 1996.

Kenner, Hugh. *Samuel Beckett: a critical study*. London: Calder, 1962.

Martin, Adrian. Film review of *Open Water* in *The Age* (14 October 2004): A3.

McMillan, Dougald and Fehsenfeld, Martha. *Beckett in the Theater*, vol. 1. London: John Calder, 1988.

Mercier, Vivian. "The Mathematical Limit" in *The Nation* (14 February 1959): 144-145.

Oppenheim, Lois ed. *Directing Beckett*. Ann Arbor: Michigan University Press, 1994.

— ed. *Samuel Beckett and the Arts: Music, Visual Arts, and Non-Print Media*. New York and London: Garland, 1999.

Restivo, Giuseppina. 'Caliban/Clov and Leopardi's Boy: Beckett and Post-Modernism' in Stewart (1999): 217-230.

Rischin, Rebecca. *For the End of Time: The Story of the Messiaen Quartet*. Ithaca, NY: Cornell University Press, 2003.

Spurling, John (with John Fletcher). *Beckett: a study of his plays*. London: Eyre Methuen, 1972.

Stewart, Bruce ed. *Beckett and Beyond* (Princess Grace Library Series 9). London: Colin Smythe, 1999.

Szendy, Peter. 'End Games' in Bryden (1998): 99-129.

White, Harry. 'Something is Taking its Course: Dramatic Exactitude and the Paradigm of Serialism in Samuel Beckett' in Bryden (1998): 159-171.

Memory and Its Devices in *Endgame*

Jane E. Gatewood

In his first published essay, on Proust, Samuel Beckett meditates, as did Proust, on the function of memory within human consciousness, arguing that humans are imprisoned by Time in a way analogous to Tantalus's imprisonment in the underworld: "There is no escape from the hours and the days. Neither from to-morrow nor from yesterday" (2).[1] Like Tantalus immersed in water, who could neither drink the water beneath him nor reach the fruit above him, human beings cannot attain, even through memory, the past which saturates and informs their present circumstances any more than they can grasp the future hanging before them. But unlike Tantalus, Beckett notes, "we allow ourselves to be tantalized" (3); we strive to remember yesterday, while yearning for what will come tomorrow. And while Beckett stages characters who are tantalized, who strive for the past and anticipate what will come, he ultimately denies these characters the ability to remember unequivocally their yesterdays, leaving them only their future bleakly projected before them. Such circumstances inform most of Beckett's *oeuvre*, including those characters confined to a bunker-type room in *Endgame* (1957).

Before any character speaks in *Endgame*, memory pervades the stage. The stage directions offer a description of a "bare interior" with "grey light"; on the "left and right back, high up, [are] two windows, curtains drawn" (1). Clov enters and stands below each window, looking up. He walks off-stage, re-entering with a ladder, which he uses to help him look out one of the windows. As he moves over to the other window, he forgets the ladder and must return for it. He repeats this process several times, moving back and forth between the windows; but each time the space between forgetting and remembering diminishes, linking the physical space of the stage with the mental space of memory. The initial action of the play foregrounds the function, or dysfuntion, of memory, revealing disruptions and disjunctions which occur when present circumstances are met and aided by memory.

Hamm, a master of sorts, is blind; Nagg and Nell, Hamm's legless parents, are confined to ashbins; Clov, Hamm's helper/servant, wishes to leave but does not. And the entire drama seems to hinge upon Clov's potential departure which would "end" the "game" played between the characters, as Hamm would be unable to care for himself or his parents. But the anticipation of a departure, like the anticipation of an arrival in *Waiting for Godot*, serves to foreground not the action of leaving but the feeling of anticipation, the desire and trepidation for what will come. This fearful anticipation of impending circumstances, though, is accompanied by an anxiety over what has already passed—a decidedly modernist anxiety regarding history and its counterpart, memory. Thus *Endgame* depicts present circumstances which are invaded and informed by yesterdays that cannot be confirmed or substantiated, and, in an attempt to control the flux of the past in order to control the present and future, characters in *Endgame* attempt to rework and reorder memories of the past. But instead of the past being reworked by the remembering subject, the opposite occurs: memory reworks the subject, eliciting a loss of the subject indicative of later works of postmodernism. Looking at *Endgame* in the context of those plays that immediately preceded and followed it—*Waiting for Godot* (French 1952, English trans. 1954) and *Krapp's Last Tape* (1958)[2]—helps to situate the play both in Beckett's *oeuvre* and in the larger context of twentieth century literature, revealing that while *Endgame* displays a modernist anxiety about memory and history, it also projects a postmodernist loss of the subject. Thereby, the play can easily be situated on the cusp between the two movements, further problematizing any clear demarcation between them.

Rather than locate truth and reality externally in the world of outward action, works of literary modernism turn to the inner realm of consciousness. But a knowing, if fragile, subjectivity—a center of consciousness that renders senses and impressions—often facilitates this linking of inner and outer worlds.[3] Likewise, Beckett's *Endgame* seems a similar retreat to the interior: its bunker-like room evokes a sense of retreat to the core of the earth, and the ashbins that contain Nagg and Nell and their memories further this sense of interiority. But breaking from this modernist interiority, with its desire for knowledge and its reliance upon an interpreting subjectivity—a Prufrock of Eliot or a Conradian Marlow—*Endgame* anticipates moves characteristic of late-modernism or postmodernism. Gradually, the modernist concern with knowing or epistemology ultimately resigns itself to a fractured knowledge, redirecting its efforts to a concern with the nature of the fractured state itself and what constitutes such an existence—epistemology gives way to ontology. Works of literary postmodernism thus negate the knowing subject and re-focus their attention on this reconstituted subject and its environs.[4] *Endgame* displays a loss of the coherent, knowing subject along with projecting a concern about an ontological status of being, rather than an epistemological state of knowing.

Writing about memory and the histories and subjectivities it produces, James Olney asserts, in "Memory and the Narrative Imperative," that the "justification, validation, and necessity of writing one's life are established in [St. Augustine's] *Confessions*" (858-59). He charts the compulsion to narrate "a life" using St. Augustine and Samuel Beckett as touchstones to demonstrate that narrative, as a constructor of identity, is invariably linked to memory and has undergone changes of approach in the modern era. According to Olney, narrative for Augustine is capable of rendering the past through present memory. Furthermore, order of narrative is crucial for it represents a "continuity of identity" (866). To achieve an ordered telling, past events are remembered in "reverse chronological order" and narrated in "forward chronological order" (866). For Augustine, the form of the narrative, its ordered telling, is not separate from that which it tells, the narrative itself. And the narrative reveals a coherent, and chronological, life: the centered, unitary self is retrieved from and revealed through such narrations of memory. As such, this form of narration is recuperative as it seeks to restore, to create via memory, the idea of the self.

Yet Beckett's characters do not engage in "ordered tellings" or narrations of their lives, however they may try. Such a telling would allow the creation of an understandable line of causality for present situations and identity—a process and result Beckett saw as antagonistic to his project, which was increasingly concerned with what he termed "the mess" and the tension between mess and form in art. As the twentieth century saw a decline of traditional formalizing structures in art, Beckett found himself faced with a quandary as an artist: he desired a form which accommodated the mess. According to Tom Driver, Beckett noted that art traditionally "withstood the pressure of chaotic things [...] but now we can keep it ["the mess"] out no longer 'it invades our experience at every moment. It is there and it must be allowed in'" (23).[5] Thus as Beckett saw it, traditional form in art necessarily excluded chaos and remained largely unquestioned; however this traditional form was no longer workable. In Beckett's view, art had to reject form that excluded chaos. Again according to Driver, Beckett went on to note that such a responsibility

> does not mean that there will henceforth be no form in art. It only means that there will be new form, and that this form will be of such a type that admits the chaos and does not really try to say it is something else. The form and the chaos remain separate. The latter is not reduced to the former. To find a form that accommodates the mess, that is the task of the artist now. (23)

Beckett took this task upon himself, incorporating characters into his dramas who, while they desire to narrate their lives and establish coherent and cohesive subjectivities, are trumped both by an inability to remember and an inability to say "I." Thus while Beckettian characters possess a modernist desire to locate a tangible and cohesive past to serve as a mythos for the present, their quest for ballast confuses the past with memory of the past; rather than locate an objective history upon which to base their current subjectivities, they locate a subjective memory, which renders a greater unreliability to their present circumstances and facilitates a dissolution of the cohesive subject.

    Nonetheless, as Olney aptly notes, Beckett's characters are overcome by the same impulse as Augustine to narrate their lives. Olney views the *Confessions* as an attempt by Augustine to confess what he is: "It is a confession of himself, not of his actions, not even of his thoughts, but confession of his very self that Augustine undertakes in Book Ten, and it is altogether significant how immediately he comes to memory in this confession of himself" (870). In an odd sort of circularity, narrative, as the product of memory, attempts to encompass memory within narrative in order to know the self, and this process of memory production is capable of rendering a knowable self for Augustine. But while Augustine claimed identity of the self through memory, Olney notes that Beckett will not permit "the easy claim of 'I remember' or the secure identity that such a claim entails" (863).

Olney asserts that Augustine's question in Book Eleven of the *Confessions*—"why then do I put before you [God] in order the stories of so many things?"—becomes for Beckett, "why should I try to put in order, time after time, the stories of so few things, my old stories, my old story, as if it were the first time?" (857-58).[6] For Beckett, Augustine's question of necessity becomes one of futility paired with necessity, for he once noted "there is nothing to express, nothing with which to express, nothing from which to express, no power to express, no desire to express, together with the obligation to express" ("Three Dialogues" 17). This articulation of Beckett's modernist obstacle outlines the quandary faced not only by Beckett but also by his stage characters in *Endgame*, as well as in *Waiting for Godot* and *Krapp's Last Tape*. Additionally, the paradox of a lack of expression combined with the obligation to express creates an opposition that Beckett sought to incorporate into his work.[7] These plays are constructed with reference to such an opposition and embody his concern with form and his skepticism regarding language. By creating characters who ultimately cannot remember, or if they can, immediately undermine memory's validity, Beckett constantly draws attention to the problem of memory: that "reference [in memory narrative] is never to events of the past but to memories of those events" (Olney 863).

The past for Beckett's dramatic characters proves irretrievable and ultimately unknowable; the "yesterday" Beckett discussed in his early essay, *Proust*, becomes an irrecoverable memory. Vladimir and Estragon, in *Waiting for Godot*, know where they are "going"—nowhere, they will continue to wait for Mr. Godot—but they do not know where they have been. Early in Act I, Vladimir and Estragon attempt and fail to establish what they did yesterday, demonstrating that for Beckett's characters the past is unverifiable and irretrievable. And if they can't remember, they cannot claim or reconstruct a past. The future of *Godot* is certain, not the past. As a result, present location, since it is derived from the past, becomes as elusive as are past activities. In Act I, Vladimir and Estragon have difficulty pinpointing their current day and the day on which they are to wait for Mr. Godot:

> ESTRAGON: You're sure it was this evening?
> VLADIMIR: What?
> ESTRAGON: That we were to wait?
> VLADIMIR: He said Saturday. (*Pause.*) I think.

ESTRAGON: You think.
VLADIMIR: I must have made a note of it. [...]
ESTRAGON: (*very insidious*). But what Saturday? And is it even Saturday?
    Is it not rather Sunday? (*Pause.*) Or Friday?
VLADIMIR: (*looking wildly about him as though the date was inscribed on
    the landscape*). It's not possible!
ESTRAGON: Or Thursday?
VLADIMIR: What'll we do? (15)

This passage highlights and extends the importance and problem of the past and its memory: if the characters cannot remember the past, they cannot establish the present. Here, the unknowable past has extended itself into the present, displacing certainty of time and place and uncovering the significance of the play's nonspecific setting: "A country road. A tree. Evening" (7). *Waiting for Godot* seems to occur outside time and place and signals the lack of temporality the characters experience, as they are unable to understand themselves via cause and effect—via past and present.

While Vladimir and Estragon attempt to create reality through recalling a past they cannot remember, their attempts always prove futile. In the following exchange in Act II, Vladimir attempts to shake a realization from Estragon that things have changed since yesterday, but again Estragon cannot remember yesterday.

VLADIMIR: The tree, look at the tree.
Estragon looks at the tree.
ESTRAGON: Was it not there yesterday?
VLADIMIR: Yes, of course it was there. Do you not remember? We nearly
    hanged ourselves from it. But you wouldn't. Do you not remember?
ESTRAGON: You dreamt it.
VLADIMIR: Is it possible that you've forgotten already?
ESTRAGON: That's the way I am. Either I forget immediately or I never
    forget.
VLADIMIR: And Pozzo and Lucky, have you forgotten them too?
ESTRAGON: Pozzo and Lucky?
VLADIMIR: He's forgotten everything! (60-61)

Here, as Olney suggests, the characters deny the absolute statement of "I remember." Didi attempts to coax Gogo into such a statement, but Gogo hesitates. Eventually, Gogo states that he remembers being "kicked in the shins" by "a lunatic who played the fool" (61) but establishing when and where the occurrence took place results in futility. So, we are left with an occurrence without specific relation to time or place; the lack of verifiable memory thereby denies its causality or origin.

The unremembered yesterdays of *Godot* serve to contextualize those that occur in *Endgame*. *Endgame* can be read as a form of a third act for *Godot*, and when viewed in this manner, it offers a winding down of that play's action which consisted of waiting for the future; moreover, the lack of memory surrounding what has passed in *Godot* foregrounds the lack of causality regarding *Endgame*'s dramatic situation. The characters in the latter play are confined to a room, presumably in post-apocalyptic circumstances. Things are winding down; "something is taking its course" (Beckett, *Endgame* 13). But we don't know why or how the characters or their circumstances came to be, and in Aristotelian terms, such things wouldn't matter: all that would matter is what comes next. But plays like *Endgame* suggest we already know what comes next; what we don't know is what is actually happening, nor do we know what came before. So, just as Didi and Gogo's unremembered yesterdays serve to undermine the present circumstances in *Waiting for Godot*, the nostalgia for the past by Nagg and Nell in *Endgame* conflates that past with fictional stories, furthering its questionability. Extending this dubiousness, Hamm and Clov render questionable present circumstances, while also reworking that past, leaving only the future undisputed yet perfectly tensed.

But unlike those in *Godot*, the yesterdays of *Endgame* aren't simply unremembered; they are longed for by Nagg and Nell and denied or reconstructed by Hamm and Clov. The distinct character pairings of *Endgame*, which Beckett sought to emphasize visually with red and white faces,[8] serve to reveal and to stress memory's dual and tantalizing function of evoking nostalgia for the past along with a simultaneous desire to control it in order to avert, or at least delay, a certain future demise. During Nagg's and Nell's only exchange of dialogue with one another, Nell repeats, "Ah yesterday!" whenever Nagg refers to "yesterday" (15, 20). The stage directions note that Nell is to utter the line in an "elegiac" tone, emphasizing nostalgia for the past. But more importantly, Nell, although prompted by Nagg's seemingly innocuous reference to a specific day, mourns the conceptual space that precedes their current confinement to their bins. She doesn't literally mourn the day that came before; rather, she mourns the concept of the past. And that Nagg utters the phrase that tugs her chords of nostalgia proves telling, for the evocation of yesterday "nags" her.

Also tugging at them are their differing accounts of the past, for Nagg and Nell disagree about different versions of memory. Following her second elegiac lament of "yesterday," Nell attempts tears.

> NAGG: [...] Are you crying again?
> NELL: I was trying. (20)

To cheer her, Nagg offers to tell "the story of the tailor," which Nell declines, asserting "[i]t's not funny" (20-21). This declaration produces a squabble between intimates, eliciting a shared memory of Lake Como.

> NAGG: It [his tailor story] always made you laugh. (*Pause.*) The first time I thought you'd die.
> NELL: It was on Lake Como. (*Pause.*) One April afternoon. (*Pause.*) Can you believe it?
> NAGG: What?
> NELL: That we once went out rowing on Lake Como. (*Pause.*) One April afternoon.
> NAGG: We had got engaged the day before.
> NELL: Engaged!
> NAGG: You were in such fits that we capsized. By rights we should have been drowned.
> NELL: It was because I felt happy.
> NAGG (*indignant*): It was not, it was not, it was my story and nothing else. Happy! Don't you laugh at it still? Every time I tell it. Happy!
> NELL: It was deep, deep. And you could see down to the bottom. So white. So clean. (21)

Nagg and Nell manage to evoke a shared memory, but the circumstances of each one's version of the memory differs: Nell remembers the depth and color of the water and her emotional state of happiness; Nagg remembers their boat capsizing resulting from Nell's excitement following his "tailor story," which he retells in the play. This instance demonstrates that memory attempts to evoke a past real scenario, and narrative attempts to establish the credibility of that scenario; but their differing accounts of the past undercut one another, thereby subverting the event's causality and coherence and distancing Nagg and Nell from a concrete past as well as from one another.

Vladimir and Estragon make a similar move in *Waiting for Godot* when they attempt but fail to remember and recount what they did "yesterday"; likewise, Nagg and Nell in *Endgame* attempt to evoke a shared past in order to unify their current, and separate, confinement. But their evocation of the past through memory serves an opposite end: rather than unite, the remembrance emphasizes the individuality of memory, revealing that it is always personal and never shared. Attempts to bridge it only create a breach.

Nagg and Nell are described as having "very white faces" (9, 14), serving to emphasize, visually, the faded quality of memory, and to embody the washed-out, retreating quality of the past. Clov checks Nell's pulse shortly after Nagg and Nell's shared memory of Lake Como, reporting that she lacks a pulse; she is pushed into her bin and heard from no more. No longer Nagg's wife or Hamm's mother, she becomes death's (k)Nell—an omen of impending death which remains throughout the play. Although Nagg remains "alive" in his bin, he comes to signify the past that "nags" and tugs the other characters.[9] While they remember their past in *Endgame*, this past is intermixed with fictional stories that serve as touchstones for their memories. This mode of remembering, mingling real occurrences with fiction, serves to undercut the credibility of the evoked memories rather than provide them with greater contextualization and believability. Further, Nagg's mingling of the fictional story of the tailor with the memory of Lake Como serves to equate memory creation with fiction, thus emphasizing that memory never refers directly to the past, but only to a memory of the past, which is always already a fiction.

While this past clings to the present, Hamm and Clov both deny and rework their past in order to control their present and thwart the future. And like other Beckettian character pairs—Vladimir and Estragon; Nagg and Nell—Hamm and Clov also evoke and question "yesterday." Midway through *Endgame*, Hamm asks Clov when he last oiled the castors on the chair, to which Clov responds, "I oiled them yesterday" (43). Hamm exclaims, "Yesterday! What does that mean? Yesterday!" prompting a "violent" reaction from Clov: "That means that bloody awful day, long ago, before this bloody awful day. I use the words you taught me. If they don't mean anything any more, teach me others. Or let me be silent" (43-44). Thus for Hamm, yesterday lacks meaning and provides no guiding point of reference for current circumstances. But when contextualized with other statements,

Hamm's skepticism regarding the past reveals a greater fear concerning the function of the past within the present, as well as a desire to control this function through memory and its narration.

Throughout the play, Hamm speaks in a series of questions about the past, expletive statements and inquiries about the present, and declarations regarding the future.[10] This suggests that he wonders about what has come before, explains and enquires for confirmation about what is, and declares what will come to pass. But his sustaining effort involves retelling the story of his life, which also seems to be the story of Clov's life, and Nagg's earlier conflation of memory with his fiction of the tailor anticipates Hamm's "story." This tale concerns a specific day on which a man came to ask the narrator, who is presumably Hamm, to take in his son. Hamm gives an elliptical narration, repeatedly revising and commenting on his own story as he narrates it, and this fictional biography proves a clever move by Hamm, in that it self-consciously renders memory as a fiction. But this self-consciousness doesn't allow Hamm the control over the past he would like. Consider, for instance, the following portion of Hamm's story:

> HAMM: (*Narrative tone.*) [...] It was a glorious bright day, I remember, fifty by the heliometer, but already the sun was sinking down into... down among the dead.
> (*Normal tone.*) Nicely put, that.
> (*Narrative tone.*) Come on now, come on, present your petition and let me resume my labors.
> (*Pause. Normal tone.*) There's English for you. Ah well ...
> (*Narrative tone.*) It was then he took the plunge. It's my little one, he said. Tsstss, a little one, that's bad. My little boy, he said, as if the sex mattered. Where did he come from? He named the hole. A good half day on horse. What are you insinuating? That the place is still inhabited? No, no, not a soul, except himself and the child—assuming he existed. Good. I enquired about the situation at Kov, beyond the gulf. Not a sinner. Good. And you expect me to believe you have left your little one back there, all alone, and alive into the bargain? Come now! (*Pause.*)
> It was a howling wild day, I remember, a hundred by the anemometer. The wind was tearing up the dead pines and sweeping them... away. (*Pause. Normal tone.*)
> A bit feeble, that. (51-52)

If Hamm's story presents his memory of Clov's coming to live with him, it foregrounds memory's fictional nature by presenting the retelling as a story, and this self-conscious move by Hamm suggests a desire to control and order the past. Hamm's narration interweaves details of his story with commentary on the form and style of the rendering, and while his changes in tone, from "narrative" to "normal" and back again, serve to distinguish the teller from the tale and the past from the present, the distinction is perhaps as feeble as Hamm considers his description of the wind to be. These moves not only interweave the past with the present, but also stress that while Hamm seeks an ordered telling, stories from the past evade such order. The elliptical nature of the telling, its starts and re-starts—"It was a ____ day..."—demonstrate that, rather than encompass memory within a cohesive and coherent narrative, memory eludes such narrative forms, obscuring its own origin. Moreover, the story's details change according to the mode of rendering, for the descriptions of the day on which the story takes place change according to the measuring device used.[11] This suggests that no individual telling or rendering can be comprehensive or all-encompassing. Hence, the story is not only a retelling, but an emergent creation, only just coming into being; past and present dovetail into a new formation, revealing that memory can never encompass or recreate the past, but that it necessarily informs and is informed by the present. Rather than render a knowable past by assembling it into a cohesive narrative, Hamm's attempts to retell his story serve to rework him. As he builds his narrative, he establishes the possibility that he has taken in Clov, lending greater credibility to his earlier statement that he "was a father" to Clov (38). But Hamm hesitates to complete his tale, even under Clov's prodding. He knows how the tale will finish, and this knowledge lends a greater fearfulness to Hamm's statements. Thus rather than account for, reconcile, and contain the past in narrative, Hamm's story serves to work him over, revealing not the story of his life to others but disclosing to himself the tale of how his life will end.

In *Company*, Beckett notes that "the greater part of what is said cannot be verified" (7). As plays like *Endgame* suggest, the past is irretrievable and ultimately unknowable. The unknowability of the past offers an important temporal inversion that Beckett extends to his dramas: the past, although it has already been lived, cannot be known; the future, even though it is unlived, remains certain—we will die. Thus although memory attempts to establish a bridge between the known and the unknowable, the known and unknowable do not exist temporally as one might think. Beckett's plays reveal that the known is not what has already taken place, the past, and the unknowable is not what lies ahead, the future. Rather the known is that which will come—future, death—and the unknowable is that which came before—past, birth—for the most important event of human experience, birth, is beyond personal memory.[12]

In an attempt to control the present through the past, characters in *Endgame* attempt to rework and reorder the past. But rather than create a "continuity of identity" from a narrative constructed from memory, the reworked and reordered story undermines the speaking subject. Hamm changes the story's details by changing the day's measuring devices, each time beginning again the story he does not want to end. He returns to the story's beginning in an effort both to return to his own origins and to stave off his story's end, and, by extension, his own. But each return to the story's beginning, and each different beginning, emphasizes his own impossibility of locating and returning to his origin, and his resistance to ending highlights his desire to stave off death. Hamm finishes narrating his story before it is fully completed, stating "I'll soon have finished with this story" (54)—one of the only statements in the play whose verbal structure is in future perfect tense.[13] This telling shift in verb tense further suggests that the future is already known. Thus, although he and Clov both allude to the fact that "it must be nearly finished," he resists finishing his "chronicle," even though he knows how it, and he, will end (1, 50, 58).

Hamm's attempts to rework the chronicle of his life anticipate similar moves to catalog and store memory in *Krapp's Last Tape*,[14] which portrays a man on his sixty-ninth birthday, dramatizing his birthday ritual of making an audio tape of the year's events after listening to recordings of past years. Krapp literally has the past stockpiled under lock and key, as the tapes of the past are locked in a room to the rear of the stage. Nonetheless, the past eludes him. Before Old Krapp begins this year's annual listening, he searches first through the desk's drawers and then through entries in a ledger to find the tape he seeks. As he reads the particular entry he seeks in the ledger which one could assume was written to help him recall the events recorded, he cannot remember the reference points of many of the words.

> KRAPP: The black ball... [*He raises his head, stares blankly front. Puzzled.*] Black ball?... [*He peers again at the ledger, reads.*] The dark nurse... [*He raises his head, broods, peers again at ledger, reads.*] ... Memorable...

> what? [*He peers closer.*] Equinox, memorable equinox. [*He raises his head, stares blankly front. Puzzled.*] Memorable equinox? (331)

As the words in the ledger fail to signify meaning, the recordings on the tape fail to provide an unquestionable past upon which Krapp can continue to build. Here, again, Beckett denies his characters the claim of "I remember," as Krapp cannot remember events that previously occurred. Like Hamm, Krapp's attempts at capturing the past prove futile, as the memory of the event fails to mirror or reinstate the origin of the actual occurrence, and Krapp's retellings, or replayings, fail to establish a "continuity of identity," for they are unordered. Old Krapp forwards and rewinds the tape to locate the memory he seeks.

> TAPE: [...] What I suddenly saw then was this, that the belief I had been going on all my life, namely—[KRAPP *switches off impatiently, winds tape forward, switches on again*]—great granite rocks the foam flying up in the light of the lighthouse and the wind-gauge spinning like a propeller, clear to me at last that the dark I have always struggled to keep under is in reality my most—[KRAPP *curses, switches off, winds tape forward, switches on again*]—unshatterable association until my dissolution of storm and night with the light of understanding and the fire—[KRAPP *curses louder, switches off, winds tape forward, switches on again*]—my face in her breasts and my hand on her. We lay there without moving. But under us all moved, and moved us, gently, up and down, and from side to side. (316)

Here Krapp has found the memory he seeks, and he again switches off the tape and winds it back to hear the full segment about the two in the boat on the lake.[15] Such disorder in the memory-telling does not foster any vestige of "continuity of identity." Rather, the disorder emphasizes that memory can never return or reinstate the past; the past remains inaccessible even through memory. Moreover, the staging device of the tape recorder serves to demonstrate that rather than ordering memory and the past for self-knowledge, memory and its devices for cataloging the past rework the self, dispelling any possibility for coherent and cohesive subjectivity. Rather than rework the past through memory, the self is reworked by memory. This reworking exhibits Beckett's anxiety concerning history and memory, while revealing more fully the existential crisis begun in *Waiting for Godot*: the self can never know the past, and history is always conditional, contingent upon one unknowable—the inability of the self to be sure of its own existence.

Waiting for Godot culminates in the image of two tramps on a country road in the evening, the same image with which the play began. This final view, together with Beckett's stage directions, undercuts the dialogue that precedes it, for Vladimir and Estragon have once again decided to leave: Vladimir asks, "Shall we go?" and Estragon replies, "Yes, let's go," but the stage directions note that "*They do not move*" (94). Thus, the play ends at a metaphoric crossroads: the interior words and worlds of the characters are undercut by their exterior actions and circumstances, presenting a rupture between word and action—between the interior realm of language and the exterior world of action. This final breach in *Godot* signifies a larger rupture indicative of literary modernism: a disruption, facilitated by technological and scientific advances latent in the Industrial Revolution, between interior human consciousness and the exterior world. In his essay "The Metaphysical Poets" (1921), T. S. Eliot located this "dissociation of sensibility" as a disruption between thought and feeling (241-50).

Hamm projects a similar sort of rupture as he renders his impressions of the external world and the past, for he always undercuts them, revealing a modernist anxiety regarding externality, interiority, memory and history. But this anxiety is problematized by a negation of the knowing subject. Hamm's first verbal utterance in *Endgame* employs an anti-grammatical structure, following the syntax of a chess move: "Me—(*he yawns*)—to play" (2), states Hamm, situating the objective case first-person pronoun as the operational subject followed by the infinitive form of the verb "play." The subject, the subjective form, is quite literally negated or subverted by Hamm's insertion of himself into the "play." The infinitive form of the verb foregrounds the "play," or game, to carry on *ad infinitum*, without end. But the negation of the subject is not unequivocal, for Hamm's "playing" involves a cat-and-mouse game between memory, history, and the present, allowing Hamm both to assert and to deny his, as well as Clov's, subjectivity, history, and past. Such a move allows Hamm the illusion of control over his subject position while he avoids the play's ultimate certainty, the only fact that Hamm leaves unquestioned—his negation, death.[16] Nothing in *Endgame* is left unquestioned except the certainty of the end. For instance, Hamm asserts that he is blind, but he also notes that his eyes have gone white (4, 36)—a fact that would require him to have vision to discern. He also notes that "outside of here it's death"; but Clov has a vision of a boy on the horizon, and vermin, in the form of rats and fleas, seem to penetrate the bunker with ease (9, 78, 70, 33).[17] Moreover, the tale of the exterior world also becomes the tale of the interior one, told and rewoven by Hamm; midway through the drama Hamm notes, in seeming self-referential fashion:

> I once knew a madman who thought the end of the world had come ... I used to go and see him, in the asylum. I'd take him by the hand and drag him to the window. Look! There! All that rising corn! And there! Look! The sails of the herring fleet! All that loveliness! (*Pause.*) He'd snatch away his hand and go back into his corner. Appalled. All he had seen was ashes. (*Pause.*) He alone had been spared. (*Pause.*) Forgotten. (*Pause.*) It appears the case is ... was not so ... so unusual. (44)[18]

Hamm qualifies his verb tense in the final sentence of this passage, relegating the present (is) to the past (was) in an attempt to dispel the possibility that this phenomenon might have some application to his current circumstances. But if such cases were not so unusual, such a statement raises the possibility that the outside world is not dead and ashen, but alive and lovely. Hamm also suggests this latter prospect to Clov:

> HAMM: Did you ever think of one thing?
> CLOV: Never.
> HAMM: That we're down in a hole. (*Pause.*) But beyond the hills? Eh? Perhaps it's still green. Eh? (*Pause.*) Flora! Pamona! (*Ecstatically.*) Ceres! (*Pause.*) Perhaps you needn't go very far. (39)

But neither scenario presents itself as certain or unquestionable, and "the mess" of a world which resists definition and formalization emerges. As Hamm and Clov's words create the concept of the dead and ashen outside world, they also subtly call into question the validity of such a world. Such moves raise the question of textual stability and the authority of language, as the text and the characters call their own authority into question. Hence, the rupture between the interior and exterior realms in *Endgame* is not a straightforward one, for both areas are rendered questionable, albeit in different fashions. The facts of the external world are undercut, but only by the subjectivities who discern them; yet the facts of the past and the function of memory compromise the knowablility of these subjectivities. Thus, the interior consciousness proves as troublesome a terrain as the past.

The characters of *Endgame* "play" at life, with variations, until the end. The point of *Endgame* is not that any of these variations or interpretations is supremely valid, but that none of them is sustainable. No certainty exists, neither for the critic nor the characters. The drama, like life, will end before we or the characters know what has passed. Rehashing it doesn't clarify the event, but it does illuminate the process of constructing meaning and creating narrative. As can be inferred from Hamm's discourse in *Endgame,* the only certainty the characters can rely upon is not that they exist or that their pasts serve as reliable ballast for the present, but that they will die. Such a move suggests that the certainty of existence lies not in the past of memory and history but in the absence of the self promised by the future. With its existential shifts, bleak turns on the function of memory and history, and its skepticism regarding the import of both, *Endgame* anticipates the loss of the subject and the culmination of history evident in later works of postmodernism. But while such turns give a nod to emerging postmodernist tendencies, they effect a modernist despair, leaving plays such as *Endgame* at a literary-historical crossroads similar to that at which we find many of Beckett's characters.

Jane E. Gatewood, University of Georgia

Notes

[1] Samuel Beckett, *Proust* (New York: Grove Press, 1931). Beckett begins this line of discussion by reference to "Proust's creatures," but discussion quickly expands to the larger humanity with the inclusion of first person plural pronouns, "we" and "us," rather than remaining with the third person "they" or "them." For the Tantalus analogy, see 3.

[2] *Waiting for Godot* was first produced in Paris 1953 as *En Attendant Godot*; its first English production occurred in London in 1955. Written in English, *Krapp's Last Tape* was first produced in London in 1958; an English publication and French translation both appeared in 1960.

[3] For extensive historical analyses of literary modernism see James Longenbach, 3-28; Michael Levenson; and Paul De Man, "Literary History and Literary Modernity," 142-65. See Levenson in particular for a discussion of modernism's reliance upon a knowing and "animating" subjectivity, 2-8.

[4] See Fredric Jameson, 1-54, in which Jameson juxtaposes two artworks—one by van Gogh, the other by Warhol—of similar subject matter (shoes) in order to demonstrate the different subject matter produced at different historical moments. Van Gogh's shoes, Jameson argues, following Heidegger's lead in "The Origin of the Work of Art," evoke a specific subject (the peasant wearer), whereas Warhol's *Diamond Dust Shoes* efface the subject, calling attention only to their reproducibility, which is made ever more apparent by their materiality as a gelatin print.

[5] Especially relevant for this article, the quotes are Driver's, not Beckett's, recreated from his memory of talking with Beckett: "I [Driver] reconstruct his [Beckett's] sentences from notes made immediately after our conversation. What appears here is shorter than what he actually said but very close to his own words" (22).

[6] This question is formulated for Beckett by Olney.

[7] See Driver, 23. Driver noted that, for Beckett, the presentation of opposites forsakes clarity, quoting him thus: "If life and death did not both present themselves to us, there would be no inscrutability. If there were only darkness, life would be clear. It is because there is not only darkness but also light that our situation becomes inexplicable. Take Augustine's doctrine of grace given and grace withheld: have you pondered the dramatic qualities in this theology? Two thieves are crucified with Christ, one saved and the other damned. How can we make sense of this division? In Classical drama, such problems do not arise. The destiny of Racine's Phedre is sealed from the beginning: she will proceed into the dark... Within this notion clarity is possible, but for us who are neither Greek nor Jansenist there is not such clarity. The question would also be removed if we believed in the contrary—total salvation. But where we have both dark and light we also have the inexplicable."

[8] Maurice Harmon, 27-29. In a letter dated 5 January 1958, Alan Schneider asked Beckett for clarification regarding the reason for Clov's and Hamm's red faces if they were eternally indoors. Beckett replied in a letter dated 10.1.58, "Actually illogical that H and C living in confinement, should have red faces. Scenically it serves to stress the couples and keep them apart."

[9] Telling, too, is Nagg's first appearance on stage, which juxtaposes him with Clov's reference to a horse; while this reference certainly extends the drama's many chess references, suggesting that Nagg is a knight, whose moves forward must also necessarily move to the side, the Nagg-horse metaphor contains further implications for the function and import of memory: Clov and Hamm are engaged in a brief, shared remembrance regarding Clov's desire for a bicycle. Clov tells Hamm that he did his rounds "sometimes on horse," but never on bicycle. As Clov says, "sometimes on horse," the stage directions note that "the lid of one of the bins lifts and the hands of Nagg appear, gripping the rim. Then his head emerges." Hence, the stage directions serve to juxtapose Nagg with reference to a horse, suggesting metaphorically that he is a former workhorse who has ceased to be useful, an "old nag," further implying that the past has ceased to have import in the present. Additionally, since Hamm and Clov are engaged in memory, this stage metaphor also suggests that re-hashing the past is akin to "beating a dead horse."

[10] *Endgame*, 3, 7, 13, 36. See for instance, Hamm's past-tense questions to Clov regarding the color of his eyes: "Did you ever see my eyes? [...] Did you ever have the curiosity, while I was sleeping, to take off my glasses and look at my eyes?" He asks repeated present-tense questions regarding the time for his pain killer—"Is it not time for my pain killer?"—and expletive statement-questions regarding the state of the day: "This is not much fun. (*Pause*). But that always the way at the end of the day, isn't it, Clov? [...] It's the end of the day like any other day, isn't it, Clov?" His future-tense statements regard Clov's future: "One day you'll be blind, like me. You'll be sitting there, a speck in the void, in the dark, forever, like me."

[11] *Endgame*, 51-53. Hamm describes the day as "extra-ordinarily bitter," "glorious bright," "howling wild," and "exceedingly dry"; the day is also measured variously by a thermometer, heliometer, anemometer, and hygrometer.

[12] Olney, 861-62, discusses Beckett and the problem of remembering one's own birth.

[13] Hamm speaks frequently in future tense, particularly to Clov, but rarely does he shift to future perfect.

[14] Likewise, *Endgame* displays similar attempts to store and bottle memory: Nagg and Nell, old and full of nostalgia for the past, exist in bins that can be capped and sealed. After Nagg and Nell engage in their shared memory of Lake Como, Hamm asks if they have been "bottled" and demands that their lids be "screwed down," suggesting an attempt to restrict and contain the past (24).

[15] Notably, the lake reference is reminiscent of Nagg and Nell's shared memory of Lake Como in *Endgame.*

[16] Following the play's chess analogy, Hamm also defers his end by remaining in the center of the room, since as a "king" he can only move one square at a time, the center allows him more avenues of retreat than would the edges or the corners.

[17] The flea in particular, via an allusion to John Donne's "The Flea," causes Hamm alarm, for he notes, "But humanity might start from there all over again! Catch him, for the love of God!"

[18] See also Martin Esslin, 45, for more analysis of this passage and Hamm's own characterization.

Bibliography

Beckett, Samuel. *Company*. New York, NY: Grove, 1980.

—. *Endgame.* New York, NY: Grove, 1958.

—. 1960. *Krapp's Last Tape* in John P. Harrington, ed. *Modern Irish Drama*. New York, NY: W. W. Norton, 1991. (311-18)

—. *Proust*. 1931. New York, NY: Grove Press, 1957.

—. 1949. 'Three Dialogues [with Georges Duthuit]' in Esslin (1965): 16–22.

—. *Waiting for Godot*. 1955. London: Faber & Faber, 1965.

De Man, Paul. *Blindness and Insight*. New York, NY: Oxford University Press, 1971.

Driver, Tom. "Beckett by the Madeleine" in *Columbia University Forum* 4.3 (Summer 1961): 21-25.

Eliot, T. S. *Selected Essays, 1917-1932*. New York: Harcourt Brace & Co., 1932.

Esslin, Martin. *Samuel Beckett: A Collection of Critical Essays*. Englewood Cliffs, NJ: Prentice-Hall, 1965.

—. 'Telling It How It Is: Beckett and the Mass Media' in Joseph Smith, ed. *The World of Samuel Beckett*. Baltimore: The Johns Hopkins University Press, 1991. (204–216)

—. *The Theatre of the Absurd*. New York: Doubleday, 1969.

Harmon, Maurice, ed. *No Author Better Served: The Correspondence of Samuel Beckett and Alan Schneider*. Cambridge, MA: Harvard University Press, 1998.

Jameson, Fredric. *Postmodernism, or the Cultural Logic of Late Capitalism*. Durham, NC: Duke University Press, 1991.

Knowlson, James. *Damned to Fame: The Life of Samuel Beckett*. New York: Simon & Schuster, 1996.

Levenson, Michael. *A Genealogy of Modernism*. New York: Cambridge University Press, 1984.

Longenbach, James. *Modernist Poetics of History*. Princeton: Princeton University Press, 1987.

Olney, James. "Memory and the Narrative Imperative: St. Augustine and Samuel Beckett" in *New Literary History: A Journal of Theory and Interpretation* 24.4 (Autumn 1993): 857-80.

Paul Ricoeur and Watching *Endgame*

Michael Guest

In light of Paul Ricoeur's *Time and Narrative*, the possibility arises to augment the phenomenological approach to *Endgame* with a consideration of the role of the watcher.[1] The action of narration in its complex relation to time is the crucial aesthetical dynamic of *Endgame*. The characters of the play subsist in a process of narration. It is not quite as though they create and recount their chronicles, jokes and reminiscences in order to pass the time as such—in something like the way words are given to puppets to utter, as though their narratives are appended to them. Rather, their very existence is by virtue of and subject to a complex and paradoxical temporal "action" of narration that manifests itself in the audience's perception of their action and dialogue.[2] The dramatic themes and action of *Endgame* focus specifically upon issues of time and narrative in an assault upon traditional mimesis. In pursuing the implications of Beckett's writing, it is necessary to broaden the idea of narration beyond an exclusive identification with the objective text. Phenomenological readings tend to restrict their attention to philosophical ideas insofar as these are expressed or encoded as objective thematic properties of the text, implying traditional mimesis. Lance St John Butler describes Beckett's works as "literary correlatives of ontological insight" (5) and "ontological parables" (148), descriptions based on an idea of the work as an objective entity. Similarly, while drawing on the hermeneutics of Hans-Georg Gadamer and Ricoeur, Jonathan Boulter sees in *Endgame* "a precise *thematization* of some of the central concerns of a philosophical hermeneutics" (40, my emphasis), proposing a "supplementary role" (48, 50) for the audience, which fills in a "semiotic void" (50) produced by the dialogue.

Contrarily, Ricoeur's is a theory in which the watcher is seen as integral with the work, rather than in any sense ancillary or supplementary to it. Ricoeur's accomplishment in *Time and Narrative* places him at a leading edge of critical theory and provides a riposte to recent hegemonic modes of reading that focus on Beckett's negative action of undoing or unsaying as a purely deconstructive manifestation. In considering the work primarily as a process that unfolds within a temporal experience, Ricoeur is thoroughly in keeping with theoretically oriented features of Beckett's writing. Considered as a succinct allegory and simulacrum of reading, for example, the prose piece *The Lost Ones* (1972) may seem on the one hand to endorse the deconstructionist implication that the world arises illusorily in text that refers to nowhere outside itself; but on the other, it intimates the possible existence of a trapdoor that opens up to the outside (Guest 29-31). *Endgame* is the ancestor of this creative scenario, which Beckett distills to minimalist dimensions in a number of later works, in an exploration of the artistic work as indeterminately closed and open. Beckett presents a hermetic, doomed world, while simultaneously configuring the work to be *open* specifically by virtue of the watcher's engagement with it. Beyond linguistic issues, this interaction depends upon a complex play of time, involving the historical existence of the work itself, time as configured explicitly within the work, and the temporality that a watcher brings to the work's realization. To appreciate this dimension of *Endgame* requires what I would call a *lateral* as opposed to a *thematic* perspective.

1. Positioning the watcher

Leo Bersani and Ulysse Dutoit's essentially phenomenological reading exemplifies a lateral approach to *Endgame*, in their emphasis upon the play as unfolding in time for an observer. In their introductory reading of Beckett's negative comments about artistic "expression" in his "Three Dialogues," they propose the need to understand "how something that Beckett calls the failure to express can renew what we can, after all, only designate as artistic expression" (17). In other words, Beckett's denial of *expression* as such turns on a particular, traditional implication of the word itself, a scenario in which A constructs an objective representation that is then *expressed* to B. Beckett disavows this as traditional, rationalist baggage. He identifies this commonsense scheme of expression with the "plane of the feasible" and the "dreary road" of the traditional:

> D. – What other plane can there be for the maker?
> B. – *Logically* none. Yet I speak of an art turning from it in disgust, weary of
> its puny exploits, weary of pretending to be able, of being able, of doing a
> little better the same old thing, of going a little further along a dreary road.
> (Beckett 1983, 139; my emphasis; see Bersani and Dutoit 17)

Beckett's perspective is explicitly that of the "maker" as poet or artist, but he projects a point of view that receives and responds to the work, a point of view from which he articulates his critique of tradition. To incorporate the coincidence of the moments of conception and reception in a creative act, however, would be to contradict the traditional logic of expression.

Referring to Clov's opening lines, Bersani and Dutoit observe that the play is not merely "nearly finished," but rather, it *is* finished in the sense of being a finished work by the time it has reached the stage. The play is "at once over and perhaps about to be over" (39), a paradox that manifests itself in one's experience of the play:

> Our experience of *Endgame* as a text in time, a text already finished and
> therefore condemned from the very start to be no longer taking place in time,
> repeats the biological and psychological truth of Hamm and Clov's lives.
> (42)

From this point of view, the play's web of signification focuses upon the instant occupied by the watcher, rather than upon an objective structural scheme of climax and resolution comprehended from a removed, objective point of view (40). At the same time, here Bersani and Dutoit move us away from conventions of characterization that have evolved in concert with such a scheme: the behavior of characters in *Endgame* "is derived not from observation of the real but from premises about the structure of being in time" (47).

I refer to Bersani and Dutoit's phenomenological perspective as lateral in the sense that it incorporates within its interpretive focus the moment of the watcher's response to the aesthetic work. Phenomenological readings of the play do not, however, necessarily demonstrate this characteristic purely by being phenomenological. It is possible and valid to restrict oneself to reading phenomenological themes as represented objectively in the work or text. Coining the slogan "To the things themselves!" Heidegger describes the phenomenological method of philosophy as "primordially [...] rooted in the way we come to terms with the things themselves" (50); but in criticism, the term "the thing itself" is liable to be assigned exclusively to the work as object. Conversely, a perspective that incorporates the response of the watcher is almost automatically phenomenological in identifying itself with the watcher's experience. Wolfgang Iser's theory of reader response, for example, is inherently phenomenological and draws explicitly on phenomenological philosophers such as Edmund Husserl, Roman Ingarden, and Hans-Georg Gadamer. In applying phenomenological hermeneutics to literature, Mario J. Valdés insists that a literary text "is available only through an immersion in the text-reader relationship, which relegates the author-text relationship to the historical event of composition" (29).[3]

Departing from this perspective tends to inhibit the dynamics of the narrative of *Endgame* and skew it towards the objective and commonplace. It is, in fact, not much easier to tell the story behind *Endgame* than it is to paraphrase other, later pieces by Beckett that more obviously flout traditional grammar and structure. When Martin Esslin himself attempts to do so on one occasion, he inadvertently circumvents inherent interpretive possibilities. Esslin proposes that a cataclysmic event has placed the characters in their present situation: "Some great catastrophe, of which the four characters in the play are, or believe themselves to be, the sole survivors, has killed all living beings" (22). As circumspectly as Esslin sketches the extended narrative, he cannot help but present the fictional world of the characters as a parallel to the historical reality within which the reader exists. There is no mention in the play of such a catastrophe having occurred, but Esslin clearly wants to bring the play into the comprehension of the uninitiated. Thus he invokes a traditional notion of mimesis, according to which the temporality of the play ought to extend into its own past and future, beyond what the spectacle of the play gives us—as though the world of the play ought necessarily imitate the linear temporality assumed by its watcher in the real world. Hence the apocalyptic scenario that one finds in production:

> A bare room. The world outside is dead, as if destroyed by an apocalyptic event. Inside are the survivors [...] Bunkered down inside their shelter they tell stories to keep the dark away and play out the last moves of their civilization.[4]

This scenario may be calculated to appeal to the popular imagination but is at the expense of the play's immanence, its unfolding in the moment. The play is thrust into the objective flow of time at the expense of its subjective engagement with the watcher. What tends to be lost in the process is the sense of a particular disjunction between the representational orders of the characters' world and ours: a disjunction that Beckett indexes by hanging the room's single painting with its face to the wall. One might characterize the distinction plainly—for an argumentative reason that will become clear—in terms of the fictionality of the world of *Endgame* and the reality of ours. The past and future of that world is imputed to it by words, whereas ours is an experienced fact of existence. At the same time, however, their own particular "fictive experience of time" (Ricoeur 1988, 100-1) reflects and impinges upon our own.[5]

As brief as it is, Esslin's sketch immediately invokes traditional assumptions about how the world of the drama imitates the temporal order of our own, assumptions that later plays of Beckett clearly work to undermine. In *Ohio Impromptu* (1984), for example, Beckett expressly contravenes the principle of temporal unity, in such a way that, from the position of the watcher, the temporality of a narrated story is seen to catch up with and overtake the character narrating it. In the same period that Beckett wrote *Endgame*, recognized critically as one of "impasse," *Molloy* exploits the non-contiguity between its reader's reality and its own fiction in the famous concluding lines: "Then I went back into the house and wrote, It is midnight. The rain is beating on the windows. It was not midnight. It was not raining" (Beckett 1980, 162). Such a gesture undermines the claims to truth that have been expressed within the narrative. The same principle of the unreliable narrator holds equally for *Endgame*. While there is no tangible narrator (indeed, in *Not I* [1984], Beckett represents a silent auditor into the spectacle, an anticipatory intrusion of the watcher's position) the expressions made by the characters are just as subservient to a singular point of view through which the action unfolds.[6] Just because the characters may agree independently upon events that "happened" in the past or may occur in the future, this does not necessarily impute an extensive, exclusive temporality to the world of the play. On the contrary, Beckett calculates such gestures to interrogate the conventional presumptions the watcher brings to the work. There are indeed intimations that the duration of the play is one section of an apocalyptic narrative, that it possesses its own hermetic linearity—as well as antithetical intimations that the action occurs within a detached instant. The play appears to vacillate reflexively between modes of being closed and open, or is simultaneously both. As shall be shown, Ricoeur's comprehensive idea of mimesis explains the contradiction: "a work may be closed with respect to its configuration and open with respect to the breakthrough it is capable of effecting on the reader's world" (Ricoeur 1985, 20).

This is the point of Nagg's and Nell's references to actions projected to have occurred in the real world. Their memories imply that they inhabit the same historical temporality as the watcher, because of the reference they borrow from our reality:

> NAGG: Do you remember –
> NELL: No.
> NAGG: When we crashed on our tandem and lost our shanks.
> *They laugh heartily.*
> NELL: It was in the Ardennes.
> *They laugh less heartily.*
> NAGG: On the road to Sedan (*They laugh still less heartily.*) (Beckett 1958, 18-9)

Their "remembered" image provides them with a past that they *ought* to possess, insofar as we recognize them as imitating human figures in the real world. That recognition is, however, in a certain respect purely conventional, with the characters' references to our naturalistic reality serving to highlight their incongruity with it.[7] Beckett's references to the "real world" project a physical continuity between the characters' world and ours, and a temporal continuity between their present and past. To perceive the characters as existing implicitly in the dramatic genre is to fracture these tenuous physical and temporal continua. Nagg's and Nell's voices are subjugated to the progress of the narration, to a singular narratorial "voice" or point of view that narrates it through them. Beckett counterpoints Nagg's and Nell's interdependent articulation of the "memories" with the artificially diminuendoed strain of their laughter—a stylistic manifestation of voice and point of view. The dialogue stands in formal opposition to Nell's extensive moment of concentrated, introspective remembering. Her further comments disengage her from the artificial dialogue, attributing to her an other-worldly, subjective perception of the nothingness that contains their "shared" remembrance, just as a state of

"zero" encloses the moment represented on stage: "It was deep, deep
[...]" (21); "You could see down to the bottom" (22); "So white" (22);
"Desert!" (22).

    Nell's flat denial of memory—"No"—conveys a nuance that,
as a fictional character playing a role in the fictional narrative, she is
entitled to recite the words of the narrative without remembering any
actual incident to which the words refer (as an actor does, and bearing
in mind that fictional incidents have, by definition, not occurred as
such in *reality*). Alternatively, she may voice the fictional narrative of
their shared memory at the instant of its conception. The "utterance" of
their memory moves us further through the duration of the play toward
its end, while its "statement" (see Ricoeur 1985, 61), its narrative
content, creatively projects its own past. Nagg's and Nell's polarized
recitations of the past intersect with each other in the instant of the
play's conception and realization. The characters are, in a certain
respect, confined to articulate the moment of their own conception, a
moment that happens to be reiterated in the instant of the drama's
realization. Beckett activates the formal possibility of a fictional past,
but rather than reflect an objective timeframe, his technique works to
highlight the fictionality of the world projected by the play. The
watcher's role encompasses but is not limited to the recognition of an
objective temporal scheme and the sequential unfolding of narrative
events within that, following the pattern: *This happened, then this, and
now we have arrived here*. Rather, the watcher is positioned at a
subjective moment of purchase on the array of diverse worlds and
timeframes of the play's narration, its narrative action. Hence, Nagg
and Nell's references manifest their vacillating conjunction with and
disjunction from the world of the watcher.

2. Issues of time and narrative

Co-opting the reader-based theories of Wolfgang Iser and Hans Robert
Jauss, Paul Ricoeur formulates a sophisticated hermeneutical
phenomenology—in its way, a kind of *post*-phenomenology (see
Ricoeur 1984, 77; 1988, 171). Ricoeur's work offers an invaluable
framework for considering Beckett's evolved exploration of dramatic
art in *Endgame*, a framework that lends a particular prominence to the
role of the watcher and to Beckett's complex treatment of time in
relation to plot and narrative. According to Ricoeur, the "temporal

character of human experience" is invariably what is "at stake" in any narrative, and "[t]he world unfolded by every narrative work is always a temporal world" (1984, 3). The action of the narrative implicates the reader at a crucial point in a cycle of time and narrative. Ricoeur aims "less at restoring the author's intention behind the text than at making explicit the movement by which the text unfolds, as it were, a world in front of itself" (81) to a reader. He articulates a hermeneutic phenomenological perspective, according to which our "being-in-the-world" is intrinsically an interpretive or "hermeneutical experience" (Venema 29-31): *"time becomes human to the extent that it is articulated through a narrative mode, and narrative attains its full meaning when it becomes a condition of temporal existence"* (Ricoeur 1984, 52; his emphasis). Ricoeur rejects the idea of mimesis as a copy of appearances—its "weakest function" (1985, 14)—and the related dualistic conception that opposes an "inside" to an "outside" of the text, with meaning inhering entirely in internal structures.[8] Instead, Ricoeur thinks of the text as having transformative "sides." He proposes a "threefold mimesis" (1984, 52-71), a "'mimetic arc' of narrative representation" that moves from the world of human experience, through a structural state of representation and "back again" (Venema 97). Ricoeur refers to the three mimetic "operations" involved as mimesis$_1$, mimesis$_2$, and mimesis$_3$, or "prefiguration," "configuration," and "refiguration" respectively. By a process of emplotment (defined after Aristotle as the poet's selection and arrangement of incidents) (Ricoeur 1984, 64-5), in mimesis$_1$ the narrative configures elements that are prefigured and "preunderstood" in the world of experience, because of the structural, symbolic and temporal features of action in the world (54). This operation is the first or "prior side" of composition, distinct from mimesis$_2$, "the mimesis of creation—which remains the pivot point" (46). At its other "side," mimesis$_3$ (46), the text intersects with the world of the reader (76); this is the "intersection [...] of the world configured by the poem and the world wherein real action occurs and unfolds its specific temporality" (1984, 71; and see 1988, 159).

Ricoeur's ideas of (i) the reciprocal nature of time and narrative (1984, 3) and (ii) the cyclical "stages of mimesis" (1984, 76) hold excellent potential for unlocking *Endgame*.[9] Beckett depicts in *Endgame* a state of hermetic interiority, which yet moves paradoxically toward an exterior that exists in moments of creation and reception. At the same time as the play marks its progress through extensive time, it describes a contradictory instant in which the moments of its creation and reception coincide in a paradoxical present. There is an effect of three disjunct orders of time resonating simultaneously: i) the temporality of creation—that of the unmistakable voice of the writer in the line "Finished, it's finished, nearly finished, it must be nearly finished" (mimesis$_1$); ii) the temporality contained within the configured work as a hermetic entity; and iii) the time of the play's interpretive engagement with the reality and temporality of the watcher (mimesis$_3$). The play's two fundamental dynamics are narration—the narrative action as a whole, encompassing the various narrations of its characters—and the perceived, enigmatic action of the various orders of time, including the play's movement toward the watcher and the temporal world within which the watcher exists. According to Ricoeur's account, narrative is "the privileged means by which we re-configure our confused, unformed, and at the limit mute temporal experience" (1984, xi; see also Venema 92). Narrative brings coherence to an inchoate experience of time, not after the fashion of an objective parable or allegory, but through one's engagement with narrative. Beckett's affinity with Ricoeur's theory is demonstrable in *Endgame* in terms of the play's exploration of its nature as an aesthetic experience.[10]

Beckett's and Ricoeur's mutual interests in Aristotle and St Augustine reinforce the intriguing pertinence of Ricoeur's theory to watching *Endgame*. Ricoeur calls Aristotle the first "cosmologist" and St Augustine the first "phenomenologist," with reference to their antithetical accounts of time (1988, 262). According to Ricoeur, St Augustine's "stroke of genius" is to conceive of the present as "threefold" rather than as a singular instant, and to identify this threefold present with the nature of the human mind, which distends into what we call the present and the past: "in [Augustine's] wake will follow Husserl, Heidegger, and Merleau-Ponty" (1984, 16). St Augustine's idea flies in the face of a compelling received perception of time. "Behind Aristotle," Ricoeur writes, "stands an entire cosmological tradition, according to which time surrounds us, envelops us, and dominates us, without the soul having the power to produce it" (1988, 12). Aristotle thinks of time in terms of a "movement" from one instant to the next, by which one may perceive "before" and "after" yet without being able to affirm the direction of the movement between them, which is future and which past.[11] Alternatively, St Augustine's idea of time turns on subjective perception: "the future and the past exist only in relation to a present, that is, to an instant indicated by the utterance designating it" (Ricoeur 1988, 19). The crux of Ricoeur's theory is that there is no overcoming the impasse between these cosmological and "psychological" accounts of time: "they mutually occlude each other to the very extent they imply each other" (1988, 14). This innate irresolvable openness regarding the question of time precludes one from abstracting a coherent objective representation of a world from the narrative text or work as such. Rather, the work provides a pivot for a process by which one's temporal experience is reconfigured through interacting with narratives. For Ricoeur, Aristotle's poetics of narrative (1984, 14) "respond" to St Augustine's "aporetics of time" (1988, 23, 273), which are those "aporias of time brought to light by phenomenology" (1988, 99 and 103). In other words, the phenomenology of time—"the pure reflection on time" (1984, 6)—is intrinsically "aporetical" and hence ultimately self-defeating as a logical discourse. Ricoeur presents narrative and temporal experience as archetypal modes of action and thought that bear fundamentally upon human existence. It is impossible to reduce these modes to a single discourse (including, of course, a phenomenological discourse):

> [...] speculation on time is an inconclusive rumination to which narrative activity alone can respond. Not that this activity solves the aporias through substitution. If it does resolve them, it is in a poetical and not a theoretical sense of the word. (1984, 6)

The aporias of time are inherent in the measurement of a thing that exists in a state of continual passage from one state of non-existence (the future) into another (the past), and the present state of which is an indivisible point with no duration (Ricoeur 1984, 7-8, 13; St Augustine 269). Ricoeur argues that the temporal aporias that propel St Augustine's speculation also ultimately undermine his conclusion that time exists as a purely subjective phenomenon: "Where Augustine fails is precisely where he attempts to derive from the distension of the mind alone the very principle of the extension and the measurement of time" (1988, 12). The response of narrative to the aporias of time is founded in the process of plot making, in which, by selecting incidents, the poet configures the objective passage of time into a sequential narrative. It is essentially on this basis that Aristotle determines that a tragic plot requires a beginning, middle and end, effectively defining plot as a structure in sequential time (Aristotle 65). Clov's scene with the toy dog he is making (the term *poiesis* originally meant 'to make') alludes to Aristotle's *Poetics*. As poet or maker, Clov dramatizes the emphasis Aristotle places on the imitation of "life" and action, and the further, derivative principle of dramatic composition, that character should be subordinated as secondary in importance to action:[12] "But he isn't finished. The sex goes on at the end"; "But he isn't finished, I tell you! First you finish your dog and then you put on his ribbon!" (Beckett 1958, 30).

In *Endgame*, the opposition between narrative and temporal aporia is present in the characters' experience of progress and stagnation in the sequence of events that constitutes their world-as-narrative: "We're getting on" (18), as opposed to "What time is it?" "The same as usual" (13). Hamm's "The end is in the beginning and yet you go on" (44) short-circuits the Aristotelian idea of plot, reflecting upon the coincidence of contrary temporal conditions of progress and stasis. There is, on the one hand, a temptation to read Beckett as deriding Aristotle's view of time and concomitant recommendations in the *Poetics*—embodiments of traditional views against which Beckett is radically opposed—and to refer Beckett's form to an alternative conception of time implicit in the key pre-Socratic image of the "impossible heap" (Beckett 1958, 12, 45): "the characters are aware of being engaged in a temporal process comparable to the infinite divisions or doublings dear to Zeno" (Chambers 76). The upshot of the paradox is that time ought not progress (any more than Achilles ought to overtake the tortoise) if it is given that time may be reduced to a present instant, though it demonstrably does: "there's a heap, a little heap, the impossible heap" (Beckett 1958, 12). An implication is that the action of the play occurs beyond time, within a finite hermetic instant, and is inexorably slowing to a halt as the limit of the instant approaches, a scenario that may be aligned with the solipsistic scenario of "existence in the skull." On the other hand, however, each delivery of a narrative implies Aristotelian structure; and indeed, the action of *Endgame* consists of one narrative after the next within the play's own narrative scheme, be this dramatized to occur within a static instant. There is no need to view the instantaneous temporality as final or meant to be final; on the contrary, the play's greater aesthetic potential depends on the non-resolution of the two antithetical, objective and subjective, temporal modes.

Endgame resonates richly with St Augustine's enquiry into the nature of time. Prefiguring Hamm's and Clov's famous opening soliloquies, St Augustine laments:

> in my misery I kept crying 'How long shall I go on saying 'tomorrow, tomorrow'? Why not now? Why not make an end of my ugly sins at this moment? (177)

A further index is the business in which Clov sets off the alarm clock against Hamm's ear, *"They listen to it ringing to the end,"* followed with the comments "The end is terrific!" and "I prefer the middle" (34). The sequence alludes ambiguously to Aristotle's *Poetics*[13] and to St Augustine's illustration of the paradoxes involved in measuring time by referring to "a noise emitted by some material body":

> The sound begins and we continue to hear it. It goes on until finally it ceases. Then there is silence. [...] In fact, what we measure is the interval between a beginning and an end. (275)

Beckett shows a brilliant philosophical sense for comedy, turning St Augustine's "material body" into an alarm clock.

Of course, Beckett's debt to St Augustine is well established in works predating *Endgame*, especially in *Dream of Fair to Middling Women* and *Waiting for Godot*.[14] Book 11 of St Augustine's *Confessions*, the focus of Ricoeur's interest in St Augustine's "phenomenology" of time, contains ideas that help Beckett shape the aesthetic world of *Endgame*. St Augustine strives to understand God's creation of the world within mutually exclusive terms of time and eternity beyond time:

> You are the Maker of all time. If, then, there was any time before you made heaven and earth, how can anyone say that you were idle? You must have made that time, for time could not elapse before you made it.
> But if there was no time before heaven and earth were created, how can anyone ask what you were doing 'then'? If there was no time, there was no 'then.' (263)

Beckett assumes these Augustinian dimensions in his role as artist-creator, his created world enclosed in a temporal "zero," in the same way that St Augustine's temporal human existence is enclosed within God's eternity, a non-place outside time: "before he made heaven and earth, God made nothing" (St Augustine 262).[15] Co-opting St Augustine's thought, Beckett supplies a constant source of irony for his characters' narratives and language. Beckett's parody of St Augustine dictates that the world of *Endgame* exists within itself, that what we see is absolutely what we get, so to speak—except that there exists no *we* to perceive it. On this basis, Beckett closes the watcher out of the play, according to St Augustine's model of a world outside which *nothing* exists. Thus, as we watch *Endgame*, we become aware of a certain attitude of parody that the play adopts toward our assumed purchase upon it as watcher, incorporating the precept that no watcher exists to whom to refer. As the work unfolds within the watcher's temporality, however, this precept is revealed as a duplicitous rule of irony that governs all that is being said and done within the play. We know that we are there, but in the very act of referring its action, language and temporality to us, *Endgame* seems to deny that anyone outside the characters themselves may perceive them. Most evidently, the objective perception that the play or text possesses the Aristotelian characteristics of a beginning, middle and end seems implicitly disavowed as illusory.

St Augustine's thinking about time is further identifiable with the rationale of Beckett's "impossible heap" in its opposition to continuous, objective, cosmic time: "In fact, the only time that can be called present is the instant"; and having derived the instant: "[w]hen it is present, it has no duration" (St Augustine 266). St Augustine attempts to answer the problem: "I begin to wonder whether [time] is an extension of the mind itself" (274). He proceeds to illustrate the phenomenon of time as experienced when reciting a psalm, defining the passage of time in terms of the faculties of expectation and memory: "As the process continues, the province of memory is extended in proportion as that of expectation is reduced, until the whole of my expectation is absorbed" (St Augustine 278; see Ricoeur 1984, 19-22). (The refrain in *Ohio Impromptu* "Little is left to tell" [Beckett 1984, 285] strongly evokes this idea.)

The incompatibility of cosmic and phenomenological temporalities motivates telling sequences in Beckett's narratives, from the *Unnamable*—"[...] you must go on, I can't go on, I'll go on" (1980, 382)—to *Worstward Ho*—"On. Say on. Be said on. Somehow on" (7). *Endgame* dramatizes the same irreconcilable opposition between temporal movement and stasis, between the self-secure attitude assumed in telling a story and the angst-ridden realization of the self's non-existence in the terms preordained by the act of narration.

3. Time and the running gag

The running gag, a staple technique of broad comedy, depends upon the watcher's reference to the progress of time. In *Waiting for Godot*, the running gag periodically reiterates the point that there is no point: "We're waiting for Godot"—but Godot never comes. In *Endgame*, the running gag "There are no more [such and such]" plays on enigmas of time and reference and on the static interiority of the configured work conceived as limited to mimesis$_2$. At the same time, the play refers to itself contradictorily, as a work projected to be finished; to the moment of conception, overlapping with Ricoeur's stage of prefiguration (mimesis$_1$) and to the moment of reception and refiguration (mimesis$_3$). Although the running gag is a distinct feature of the dialogue in its own right, the temporal implications of its theme (the issue of linguistic reference) and form (as comic technique subsisting in time) associate it integrally with a "secondary" running gag consisting of repeated references to "yesterday." This secondary gag is integral, in turn, with the metatheatrical dimension of the play, a framework that further implies and implicates the temporality of an actual watcher.

3.1. "Turkish Delight [...] no longer exists."

If conceived of as a "finished," hermetic structure, the play appears to be detached from the things to which its words "once" referred. But paradoxically, upon this conception, time and reference themselves are not permitted to escape into an exterior temporality; the past ceases to exist—as though it never was. From this perspective, the work is apprehended not to re-present objective reality, though it depicts a state of representation, so far as one may conceive of this state as an aesthetic condition completely distinct from any reality of *things*. Here, language itself and, by implication, acts of narrative take on a heavy ironical loading, in the sense that words are significant only in themselves. They are thus condemned to implode to zero. So, for example, when Nagg asks for a sugar-plum, Hamm promises then denies him because "There are no more sugar-plums" (38). While the interaction exemplifies Hamm's thematic cruelty, as an instance of the gag it takes up a comic absurdity inherent in the connotations of the specific request, given the abysmal state of things *here and now* as defined in the hermetic world of *Endgame*. Words such as "sugar-plums" and "bon-bons" are permitted to exist within the instant of the play, but the things themselves do not and, in a sense, never have, in accordance with a rule underpinning Beckett's pastiche of St Augustine that refutes *a priori* the possibility of exterior reference. For Augustine, all creation occurs within the Word of God (258), which is the conceptual basis for what I describe as a rule for the design of *Endgame*. At one instant, in *Endgame* the *word* seems to exist purely in order that the *thing* be denied (with the implication of an exquisitely cruel creator: Beckett's self-representation as the creator of the play, say, such as we see caricatured in Hamm as God or as Clov as *maker*). In watching the play with Ricoeur in mind, one recalls St Augustine's attempt to grasp the reality of God's creation—thereby to know God through his aporetic, ultimately futile reflection upon time (Ricoeur 1984, 6-7). Indeed, Ricoeur describes the limits of phenomenology in much these terms, but he co-opts too the Aristotelian mode of thought, as founded antithetically upon a conception of time as cosmically extensive. We may use this idea to account for the contradictory instant in *Endgame* by which utterances and actions in themselves acknowledge the presence of the watcher.

The play's comedy of cruelty inheres not so much in the characters' thematic portrayal of the trait of cruelty, as in an underlying denial of any possibility of extension (in particular, that of time, narrative, or linguistic reference) beyond the present internal, implosive reality with which the play identifies itself (paradoxically, by means of its unfolding within the watcher's temporality, which is external to the work). The play's action of preempting the thematic order of cruelty is beautifully instanced in Clov's comment, "If I don't kill that rat he'll die" (44), where the axiom of non-extensibility short-circuits his projection of the possibility of a temporally extensive narrative act. Similarly, the poignancy of Nagg's request for a sugar-plum lies in his saying of the word. An abysmal foil encloses and immediately suffocates the word's evocative connotations in the very utterance. It is not exactly that sugar-plums are lost in the past or have ceased to exist, but that the utterance of the word specifically precludes the word, in this case *sugar-plums*, from existing or *ever having existed* as a thing.

In the world of *Endgame* conceived as a hermetic world, the characters are unjustified to speak for another existence outside the present one as figments of fiction, though they do so repeatedly. The "no more ..." running gag gestures toward literal statements of an alternative state of words detached from things, from objective referents:

> CLOV: There are so many terrible things.
> HAMM: No, no, there are not so many now. (33)

This exchange refers both to the projected plot in continuous, objective, Aristotelian time, in which things are subject to a temporal process of ceasing to exist and to the instantaneous, subjective scenario in which "things" are of a separate order from the "now" referred to in the configured work. The context is Hamm's story about the mad painter who in the face of the world's "loveliness" could see only ashes (32). Clov extends the aesthetical theme of this story, with a connotation that the artistic work transcends the material world of "terrible things" (in the sense that "things" are as such generically "terrible" *as things,* as opposed to their aesthetic representations—an ironic reference to art as idealization). The same dualistic relation appears in the gag's allusion to the watcher's reality:

> HAMM: Nature has forgotten us.
> CLOV: There's no more nature.
> HAMM: No more nature! You exaggerate.
> CLOV: In the vicinity. (16)

The "vicinity" of the world of *Endgame* is a morass of temporal, spatial and representational oppositions. Memory and forgetting imply a temporality of succession and continuity ("Why this farce, day after day?" [18]) that underlies the process of ceasing to be (of nature having "forgotten us" or of nature itself having ended). The world passes through the present and into the past, where it ceases to exist except as a trace in the memory.[16] Clov further evokes Aristotle and St Augustine by spatializing the relation between the continuous flow of time and the instantaneous present. Bringing temporal existence and non-existence into simultaneity, he places the "vicinity" of the world of *Endgame* outside the world of nature and beyond its objective temporality, in the Augustinian realm of divine eternity: "Your [God's] years are completely present to you all at once, because they are at a permanent standstill" (St Augustine 263). This paradoxical coincidence of Augustinian and Aristotelian temporalities is further reflected in the relation between the worlds of the play and the watcher, which both occupy the physical "vicinity" presented by the stage and auditorium yet are distinct temporally and in the representational sense of "fiction" versus "reality." (Bear in mind, too, that the world of the present watcher has entered into existence since the play was "finished" objectively, in the sense explained by Bersani and Dutoit.) Clov's words gesture, like his telescope, toward the instantaneous "now" of reception (mimesis$_3$), in which the compounded narrative paradoxes are presented to the experience of the watcher, an experience that is itself bound up in the aporias of time.

From Ricoeur's perspective, to say that Clov gestures toward the *possibility* of the moment of reception would be to remain within the structural confines of the configured work, or mimesis$_2$. Ricoeur refers to this pivotal phase of the configured work, in which the work "projects a world outside of itself" (1985, 5 and 76), as "transcendence in immanence" (1988, 101), a penultimate state of the aesthetic process of the work considered as bordering on but not crossing over into mimesis$_3$, the refigurative experience of a real watcher (1985, 101).

3.2. "Yesterday."

Even when the running-gag does not extend into dialogical business expounding the paradoxes of time, as in the innocuous instance "There are no more rugs" (43), it demonstrates a schism between words uttered and the things to which they refer (or referred), as well as the illusory status, the non-existence, of the fictional past. Clov refuses Hamm's periodic request for painkiller because "It's too soon" (23) or "not time," a sequence that culminates in the punch line, "There's no more pain-killer" (46). Here again the schism between word and referent short-circuits the logic of successive time; this specific instance of the running-gag, moreover, gestures distinctly toward a fictional past assumed to be temporally continuous with the onstage present. In anticipating his daily dose of painkiller, Hamm reflects St

Augustine's emphasis on expectation and memory. That is, Hamm remembers there was still painkiller "yesterday," in keeping with the naturalistic apprehension that the action of the play reenacts a daily ritual.[17] The fictionality of the world of the play, however, enables Beckett simultaneously to prohibit the word "yesterday" from denoting such a past (thinking of the referred past as the non-realm that gathers all the non-referents that are considered "no longer" to exist, but which, in respect to the play's fictionality, literally never did). Hence the deep ambiguity that attends instances of the word "yesterday." Nell twice repeats Nagg's utterance of the word with an *"elegiac"* tone (18, 20); on one of these occasions, her theatrical and poetic emphasis invokes the word's metaphorical connotation of *the past*, contrasting Nagg's commonplace statement:

> NAGG: I've lost me tooth.
> NELL: When?
> NAGG: I had it yesterday.
> NELL: (*elegiac*). Ah yesterday!
>   *They turn painfully towards each other.* (18)

The incremental loss in the everyday temporality of succession is opposed to a more profound sense of loss: a tooth as opposed to transcendent attributes such as youth, love, beauty, life. The disjunction between the levels of signification to which Nagg and Nell direct the word "yesterday" corresponds to the two alternate temporal perspectives, Aristotelian and Augustinian. In respect to the *non-past* of the fiction, however, the word loses its referential function altogether in a paradoxical breakdown of the ability to apprehend and signify time. The word "yesterday" implies the objective passage and measurement of time; however, from the subjective view, the past no longer exists. This is one of the temporal conundrums with which St Augustine grapples: how may one measure what no longer exists (St Augustine 275; see Ricoeur 1984, 8)?

Hamm and Clov's dialogue surrounding the word "yesterday" further demonstrates its breakdown as a meaningful signifier of time in terms of the fiction:

> HAMM: Yesterday! What does that mean? Yesterday!
> CLOV: (*violently*). That means that bloody awful day, long ago, before this
>   bloody awful day. I use the words you taught me. If they don't mean
>   anything any more, teach me others. Or let me be silent. (32)

Clov inserts an indeterminate gap into the flow of time, with his reference to "that day long ago" implying the passage of many days. Moreover, here Clov explicitly associates the breakdown of temporal reference to that of language generally. After a pause, Hamm tells his story of the mad painter, ending with a pointed adjustment of tense, "It appears the case is ... was not so ... so unusual" (32), that foregrounds the narrative procedure of configuring time and projecting a past. In his reply to Clov's next question, "A madman? When was that?"—a question with no apparent motivation other than to present an opportunity to continue articulating the enigmatic theme of time—Hamm echoes Clov's lines on "yesterday": "Oh, way back, way back, you weren't in the land of the living" (32). References to time, "yesterday" as opposed to "long ago" and "way back" have lost their function to quantify time and to compare different orders of time, the recent as opposed to the distant past. These multiple spatial metaphors for time work against the very sense of time's extensiveness, as though the greater the effort made to project a sense of vast continuous time, the more immanent the realization of the moment. In this sequence, once again the spatial metaphor encompasses the theatrical occasion with the phrase "the land of the living" serving to invoke temporal, spatial and representational oppositions between the worlds of the play and the watcher, worlds in immanent confrontation.

3.3. Existing in metatheater

At base, the running-gag is integral with the metatheater of *Endgame*: it is a structural outgrowth of the play's constant preoccupation with its aesthetic nature. *Endgame* is comparable in its metatheatrical aspect to Luigi Pirandello's *Six Characters in Search of an Author*, except that Beckett does not make a metatheatrical scenario overt, with characters performing roles specific to theatrical production. Rather, the metatheater of *Endgame* is implicit in the irony of the dialogue, an irony derived from continuous reference to philosophical and aesthetical questions and paradoxes. The most literal expression of Beckett's metatheatrical irony is the exchange between Clov and Hamm: "What is there to keep me here?" "The dialogue" (39). The naturalistic sense that they stay for the sake of dialogue with each other is undercut by the sense that they exist as characters purely as a contingency of the written dialogue—and also by their metatheatrical dialogue with the watcher in the "land of the living," where life is not preordained in the same *literal* sense as theirs.

Time in the world of *Endgame* is forever "[t]he same as usual" (13), a perpetually repeating, impossible fragment of time:

> HAMM: This is not much fun. (*Pause.*) But that's always the way at the end of the day, isn't it, Clov?
> CLOV: Always.
> HAMM: It's the end of the day like any other day, isn't it, Clov?
> CLOV: Looks like it. (17)

The finitude of the script preordains an endlessly repetitive existence, to which the characters allude constantly:

> CLOV: [. . .] All life long the same questions, the same answers. (13)
> . . .
> NELL: Why this farce, day after day? (18)
> . . .
> NELL: [. . .] Have you anything else to say to me? (18)
> . . .
> CLOV: You've asked me these questions millions of times.
> HAMM: I love the old questions. (*With fervor.*) Ah the old questions, the old answers, there's nothing like them! (29)

These and many similar comments allude ambiguously to the play as representing a world in which the characters repeat much the same words and actions day after day, and to an antithetical order of temporality, according to which only the specific words and actions that comprise the script ever occur. In keeping with the former sense, the play's physical and temporal limits project a conventional frame, beyond which the character's lives are imagined to continue. In keeping with the latter, the characters exist only in the specific terms laid down in the play, which are repeated over and over again, as many times as the work is enacted, read or watched. They only ever exist specifically as the work dictates; they are dormant, so to speak, until the instant a watcher brings presence and temporality. (One apprehends this presence and temporality as *exterior* insofar as one apprehends the work, and equivalently, the world of the work, as objective. From Ricoeur's reader-response oriented perspective, however, such presence and temporality are considered as integral rather than supplementary—as a necessary condition for the work to exist.)

Beckett uses essentially the same strategy in depicting the hermetic cylinder of *The Lost Ones*, where the characters commence their preordained system of actions only ever in coincidence with the onset of a mysterious omnipresent light. This strategy or structural principle, recurrent in Beckett's *oeuvre*, itself ensues from an aporetic reflection on time and constitutes, if not a *reductio ad absurdum*, a paradoxical rendering of the Christian idea of all things existing entirely within the Word of God, which is the starting point for Augustine's investigation of time (see especially 258-9): "[…] *your eyes looked upon me, when I was yet unformed; all human lives are already written in your record*" (St Augustine 237; see Psalms 138: 16).

In *Endgame*, numerous apparently innocent statements are loaded with ironic reference to existence within the script, contributing to a pervasive metatheatrical echo. When Clov declares his desire to sing, Hamm's rejoinder "I can't prevent you" (46) refers to his physical disability, but also to the absolute power of the script to predetermine, to dictate any action. Similarly, Hamm's and Clov's repeated line "don't we laugh?" (16, 25) ambiguously demands a laugh for the comic line just delivered, and their reflection suggests an action something like that of an actor checking to see whether a stage direction indicates one:[18]

> CLOV: […] That's what I call a magnifier. […] Well, don't we laugh?
> HAMM: (*after reflection*). I don't
> CLOV: (*after reflection*). Nor I. (25)

Again recalling St Augustine's recitation of the psalm as a tool to demonstrate the measurement of time, allusions to the future impart an ambiguous impression of prescience:

> HAMM: It'd need to rain.
> CLOV: It won't rain. (13)

> HAMM: […] Well! I thought you were leaving me.
> CLOV: Oh not just yet, not just yet. (15)

> HAMM: […] I'm warming up for my last soliloquy.
> CLOV: I warn you. I'm going to look at this filth since it's an order. But it's the last time. (49)

It is, indeed, the ambiguous character of Beckett's indicators of metatheatricality that projects the hermetic temporal condition of *Endgame* as tenuous and ambiguous. The watcher thus experiences an effect of flicker,[19] of vacillation between mutually exclusive apprehensions of linear and instantaneous, objective and subjective time: Ricoeur's state of the work at the point of "transcendence in immanence."

4. Motion and mimesis₃

> Temporality is then the articulated unity of coming-towards, having-been, and making present [. . .] (Ricoeur on Heidegger, 1988, 70)

> The "right" distance from the work is the one from which the illusion is, by turns, irresistible and untenable. (Ricoeur 1988, 169)

Ricoeur's theory of time and narrative mandates reading through the interaction between the work and the reader/watcher, as he demonstrates with readings of Virginia Woolf, Thomas Mann and Marcel Proust (1985, 101-152)—writers who all, like Beckett, engage consummately with the issue of time. With *Endgame*, one point of access is this effect of flicker, with its numerous compounded sources in dramatic action and philosophical ideas. The visual flickering effect between figure and ground is crucial to the field of Gestalt psychology, in which Beckett displays a deep interest (Knowlson 211, 375). The Gestalt psychologists used such visual effects to demonstrate the function played by the mind in ordering perceptions of the world.[20] In a literary or dramatic work such as *Endgame*, while the structures that propagate the effect originate in text and action, to speak about the effect itself is one way to begin to consider the stage of mimesis₃, concerning the watcher's "refigured experience of time" (Ricoeur 1985, 63).[21]

    A subtle, perhaps subliminal aspect of the stage illusion generated by *Endgame* is an impression of motion, which co-opts the watcher's experience of time as the reading or performance ensues. There is no direct reference to this impression, but rather, it is potential in a complex of textual structures, at once referred to and obliquely motivated by dialogue such as "What's happening, what's happening?" "Something is taking its course" (17) and "We're not beginning to ... to ... mean something?" "Mean something! You and I, mean something!" (27). These comments allude to the metatheater and to the watcher; moreover, their referent in mimesis₃ is an impression of motion that gathers up immanent effects of flicker from the play's aporetic presentation of time in relation to the production of meaning through narrative. The impression of motion is given thematically to a "refiguration of time" (Ricoeur 1985, 103), incorporating an impression that the characters *move* in time toward the watcher. As Aristotle observes, time "has to do with movement" (*Physics*, qtd in Ricoeur 1988, 13); the perception of time is inextricably tied to the perception of motion.

McMillan and Fehsenfeld remark that, in directing *Endgame*, "'Hold back' is Beckett's *ceterum censeo*" (216). It is no paradox that overt appearances of stasis in both physical and narrative action serve to generate an impression of motion. By so severely retarding movement and progression in the objective frame, Beckett plays against deeply ingrained expectations and conventions received from traditional genre, such that the action strains to break out from the paradigm of instantaneity in which it is constrained. This technique of Beckett's in *Endgame* prefigures techniques that evoke the perception of motion and residual images in minimalist plays such as *Not I*, *That Time*, and *Catastrophe*. In *Not I*, for instance, the absence of visual referents in the darkness apart from Mouth and the auditor facilitates a dynamic subjective experience of flux and relativity, which is such that the central component of the dramatic "action" becomes an impression of motion generated by one's continual subjective orientation to the position of the actors. There is a clear link in *Endgame* between the retardation of physical action—two steps forward, one back—and psychological subjectivity in Clov's opening business, in which he appears to lack the power of memory sufficient to accomplish complete, continuous actions in the service of a dramatic progression. Clov's periodic return to the ladder—"*He gets down, takes three steps toward window left, goes back for ladder* [...]*" (11)—gives an impression that his memory is impaired, purely through alternations in the advancement, interruption and repetition of his physical action. Subsequent dialogue characterizes his impaired memory as existential rather than neurological in nature, with memory associated with the action of narrative in the context of an aporetic temporality. Absolute containment within the instant would pre-empt the possibility of narrative and memory. The play's framing within a "*brief tableau*" with Clov standing *"motionless by the door, his eyes fixed on Hamm"* (11, 51-2) further signifies that the entire action of the play, experienced in extensive time, is configured to occur within the compass of an instant (cf. McMillan and Fehsenfeld 214).

The naturalistic set functions similarly, eliciting expectations of naturalistic temporality and action that founder in an obsessive stasis, for the sake of the refigurative impression of motion. In naturalistic drama, the "fourth wall" functions conventionally as a one-way window upon the dramatic world, for the benefit of the watcher's exterior point of view. The world of the play is projected to extend beyond the wings, in a conceptual parallel to the watcher's reality. In contrast, in *Endgame* the exterior world of spatial and temporal "zero" is projected as a state of nothingness that surrounds the realities of the characters and the watcher, with the watcher submerged in the darkness of the auditorium or the imagination. The "fourth wall" of *Endgame* intensifies the focus of confrontation between two subjective worlds, surrounded by nothingness. Gadamer's idea of a "fusion of horizons" (qtd in Ricoeur 1984, 77) of the work and the watcher holds true in either case, but in *Endgame* the combination of Beckett's thematic scenario and radical stage technique undermines the traditional mimetic reference to objective reality and the traditional position of the watcher. As Guicharnaud puts it: "An immobile eye is fixed on the characters—that of the spectator" (117). By precluding exterior points of reference, Beckett frees an impression of motion that traditional conventions, built on overt manifestations of action, would prevent.

Maritime objects and references—such as "glass" for telescope (24, 48), "gaff" (50) and "navigators" (43), along with several ambiguous references to the sea and land outside—allow the indeterminate possibility that their "shelter" is afloat or perhaps a sinking or semi-submerged vessel run aground (Cavell 138). One example of this is when Clov applies the maritime female pronoun, under the misperception that they are sinking: "Christ, she's under water!" (47). Beckett was, indeed, reading about the Biblical Flood when he wrote the first draft of the play (Knowlson 406), and as it is often noted, the name of Noah's youngest son is Ham. Stanley Cavell demonstrates how the play draws on the narrative of the Flood, and proposes that to understand the reasoning of the characters we need to place them in the situation: "The shelter they are in is the ark, the family is Noah's, and the time is sometime after the Flood" (137).

Strictly speaking, however, the validity of the proposition is limited to the objective, allegorical mode of reading; it contains an "objective fallacy" tantamount to identifying Godot as God. From the lateral perspective of the engaged watcher, one emphasizes, rather, the indeterminacy of the nautical references. Rather than project a particular scheme, the references work to undermine the sense of a solid grounding for the stage illusion. In this respect, the nautical scheme of reference works in opposition to the oppressiveness of the set, the retarded physical action, and the point of view locked obsessively on this spectacle of immobility. Prefiguring the theatrical experience of *Not I*, the watcher's imaginative engagement with the play's projected world is dislocated from objective reference, from the realm of traditional mimesis, and metaphorically set adrift. The set is thus not a house, not a boat, but embodies a reflexive attitude to representation in the fashion of René Magritte's painting "The Betrayal of Images" ("*Ceci n'est pas une pipe,*" 1928-9). In this spirit, Hamm "*strikes the wall with his knuckles*": "Do you hear? Hollow bricks! (*He strikes again.*) All that's hollow!" (23).

Thematic allusions to the sea convey a desire for motion, for escape from the static universe of the instant. Hamm wants Clov to build a raft: "the currents will carry us away, far away" (28). He articulates the paradoxical relation of the instantaneous and the eternal: "Get working on that raft *immediately*. Tomorrow I'll be gone *forever*" (28, my emphasis). When Hamm tries to propel himself on his chair, he uses his gaff, "*wielding it like a punt-pole*" (32). His potential trajectory is at once pathetically confined to the instant yet circumnavigates the cosmos, godlike: "Right around the world! (*Clov pushes chair.*) […] I was right in the center, wasn't I?" (23). Similarly, Clov's business with the telescope invokes a chain of associations and impressions extending from the proximate to the cosmic. The telescope connotes a collapsing of space, a bringing closer, and motion—specifically, the motion of the Earth itself and other cosmic bodies, and the movement of ships. Beneath the stasis of the set, beneath the pre-Galilean stasis of the earth, which is like Hamm placed in the "center," beneath the watcher's stable physical reality, exists a reality of imperceptible, perpetual motion. More than merely evoking a semiotic connotation, the telescope is poised to stimulate a sense of motion, however potential or subliminal, due to its historical nautical and astronomical associations. Thus when Clov uses the telescope to look out the windows, he resembles the mariner surveying the horizon and also the astronomer, orientating human perceptions to an infinite cosmos of relativity and motion.

Beckett has Clov turn the telescope toward the auditorium, transposing this complex theme to the metatheater of Beckett's reflexive examination of the work of art and its engagement with the watcher. More precisely, the gesture is a focus for this reflexive awareness, which is at play throughout. The telescope's function of bringing closer conveys an impression of distance, in contrast to the nearness of the characters and the watcher in "real" space, underlining the temporal "distance" that the work traverses in its instant of convergence with the watcher. The concentrated implicit theme of motion is reified in an impression of motion in which the spectacle *comes* to the watcher, an impression of temporal motion reverberating in the appearance of static physical beings. It is a dramatic effect of the "refiguration of time" in Ricoeur's terms:

> The effects of fiction, effects of revelation and transformation, are essentially effects of reading. It is by way of reading that literature returns to life, that is, to the practical and affective field of existence. (1988, 101)

The "shelter" of *Endgame*, not-house, not-boat, but an aesthetic vehicle nonetheless that moves out and returns in time, exhibits a form similar to Ricoeur's "mimetic arc"—perhaps not to put too fine a point on the homophonic resonance with Noah's ark. Hamm's comment on the possibility of their meaning something to someone implies a journey of departure and return: "Imagine if a rational being *came back* to earth, wouldn't he be liable to get ideas into his head if he observed us long enough?" (27, my emphasis). As the line is usually read, the term "rational being" alludes backhandedly to the audience, who is trying to make meaning out of the play; but the line also reflects a characteristically egotistical conviction on Hamm's part in the significance, the substance, of his world. That is to say, from the watcher's perspective, it is conceived to be *they* who are returning to *our* present world, with Hamm reflecting back to us our own delusions about our own nature. The ambiguity of the line thus implies the action of two mutually exclusive worlds at the point of confrontation, each projecting itself into the other in a process that generates an infinitely regressive play of echoes and reflections. Ricoeur's theory provides us with an immensely useful and timely critical vantage point on

Endgame. It enables us to observe the hermetic, limbo-like, *structural environment* of mimesis$_2$, which is perfectly cognate with the scenario of the hermetic world that Beckett depicts in the play, open out into a *refigurative temporal experience* of mimesis$_3$, which is implicit in *how* Beckett configures the play. This latter condition is in keeping with anticipatory gestures Beckett makes toward the play as achieving a *finished* state, a state in which its narrative will have, indeed, *ended* in this respect, just as the play manifests itself anew within the substance of the receptive imagination. Critically speaking, this instant of transformation presents a starting point for appreciating the depth of human significance that informs *Endgame*'s self-referential allegory of aesthetic transmission, a narrative that works in concert with the play's focused exploration of the specific issues of time and narrative.

Michael Guest, Sydney, Australia

Notes

[1] I use the term *watcher* to encompass *reader* and *spectator*, having in mind Ricoeur's explicitly unresolved attitude toward the specific nature of differentiating the theoretical difference between literary and dramatic work: he clearly leans toward the idea that a narrative-theoretical concentration upon the novel "represents simply a de facto restriction" (1985, 154; see too 1985, 69).

[2] Ricoeur justifies the generic use of the term "narrative" in both dramatic and non-dramatic modes with recourse to the mimesis of action (1985, 153).

[3] A comment of Ricoeur's, distinguishing the "hermeneutical experience," prefigures my thematic/lateral opposition: "to understand a text, we shall say, is not to find a lifeless sense which is contained therein, but to unfold the possibility of being indicated by the text" (qtd in Venema 30).

[4] Flyer from Sydney Theater Company's *Endgame*, dir. Benedict Andrews, Sydney Theater Company, December 28, 2002 (Sydney Festival). See also Cohn: "*Endgame* is unmistakably a play about an end of a world" (44).

[5] See Ricoeur (1988), Chapter 5 "Fiction and Its Imaginative Variations on Time," Chapter 6 "The Reality of the Past," and Chapter 7 "The World of the Text and the World of the Reader" (1998, 127-179).

[6] See Ricoeur on voice and point of view in fiction (1985, 91-96) and on their relation to drama (154).

[7] Cf. Ricoeur on novels by Woolf, Mann and Proust: "we would be sorely mistaken if we were to conclude that these dated or datable events draw the time of fiction into the gravitational field of historical time. What occurs is just the opposite. From the mere fact that the narrator and the leading characters are fictional, all references to real historical events are divested of their function of standing for the historical past and are set on a par with the unreal status of the other events" (1988, 129).

[8] Ricoeur remarks on "the prejudice that opposes an 'inside' and 'outside' of a text": "The notion of a structuring activity, visible in the operation of emplotment, transcends this opposition" (1984, 76).

[9] "[T]he hermeneutic circle of narrative and time never stops being reborn from the circle that the stages of mimesis form" (1984, 76).

[10] See, for example, Kenner on *Godot* as "theater reduced to its elements in order that theatricalism may explore without mediation its own boundaries" (49); and Brienza on *Endgame* as "a play about composing" (246).

[11] This is because "[t]he past is before and the future after only with respect to this present possessing the relation of self-reference, attested to by the very act of uttering something" (Ricoeur 1988, 19).

[12] "The Plot, therefore, is the first principle, and, as it were, the soul of tragedy: Character holds the second place [....] Thus tragedy is the imitation of an action, and of the agents mainly with a view to the action" (Aristotle 63). It is interesting to note that Ricoeur's single reference to Beckett in *Time and Narrative* is in this very context of Aristotle's valuation of action and character. Ricoeur points out their extended definitions in modern literature, alluding to Beckett's "unnameable" (sic) characters as limiting figures regarding the modern novel's representation of "beings similar to us" (1985, 10).

[13] It is the precise allusion to aesthetic structure that invokes Aristotle.

[14] See, for example, Knowlson 109, 379.

[15] See Ricoeur on St Augustine and the "aporia produced by the very thesis of eternity" (1984, 25).

[16] Cf. Ricoeur's references to St Augustine (1984, 10 and 232 n. 14).

[17] The dialogue echoes the skeptical idea of time that motivates "the impossible heap": "But the little round box. It was full!" "Yes. But now it's empty" (46).

[18] Cf. Adorno 107-8.

[19] Brian McHale refers to a "flickering effect" as one of "ontological oscillation," or after Roman Ingarden, "an effect of 'iridescence' or 'opalescence'" (32).

[20] The most famous is the figure first shown by Edgar Rubin in 1914, of goblet and faces. Wolfgang Köhler considers figure and ground "two very concrete and phenomenologically real modes of existence [*Daseinsweisen*] of the optical" (qtd in Ash 179-80).

[21] Ricoeur explains the action by which an experience brought into language is conveyed to another person: "Reference and horizon are correlative as are figure and ground. All experience both possesses a contour that circumscribes it and distinguishes it, and arises against a horizon of potentialities that that constitutes at once an internal and an external horizon for experience" (1984, 78). The "gestalt of a text" is an important concept, furthermore, for Iser's reader response theory (284).

Bibliography

Primary Texts

Aristotle. *Poetics* translated by S.H. Butcher. New York: Hill and
        Wang, 1961.
Beckett, Samuel. *Beckett Trilogy.* London: Picador, 1980.
—. 'Three Dialogues' in Ruby Cohn, ed. *Disjecta.* London: John
        Calder, 1983.
—. *Collected Shorter Plays.* London: Faber, 1984.
—. *Complete Short Prose, 1929-1989* ed. S.E. Gontarski. New York:
        Grove, 1995.
—. *Endgame.* London: Faber, 1958.
—. *Worstward Ho.* London: John Calder, 1983.
Heidegger, Martin. *Being and Time* translated by John Macquarrie and
        Edward Robinson. Oxford: Blackwell, 1962.
Iser, Wolfgang. *The Implied Reader: Patterns of Communication in
        Prose Fiction from Bunyan to Beckett.* Baltimore: The Johns
        Hopkins University Press, 1974.
Pirandello, Luigi. *Six Characters in Search of an Author* translated by
        Mark Musa. London: Penguin, 1995.
Ricoeur, Paul. *Time and Narrative* Vol. 1 translated by Kathleen
        McLaughlin and David Pellauer. Chicago: University of
        Chicago P,ress 1984.
—. *Time and Narrative* Vol. 2 translated by Kathleen McLaughlin and
        David Pellauer. Chicago: University of Chicago Press, 1985.
—. *Time and Narrative* Vol. 3 translated by Kathleen McLaughlin and
        David Pellauer. Chicago: University of Chicago Press, 1988.
St Augustine. *Confessions* translated by R.S. Pine-Coffin. London:
        Penguin, 1961.

Secondary Texts

Adorno, Theodor W.. 'Towards an Understanding of *Endgame*' in
        Chevigny. (82-114)
Ash, Mitchell G.. *Gestalt Psychology in German Culture 1890-1967.*
        Cambridge: Cambridge University Press, 1998.
Bersani, Leo, and Ulysse Dutoit. *Arts of Impoverishment: Beckett,
        Rothko, Resnais.* Cambridge: Harvard University Press, 1993.

Bloom, Harold ed. *Samuel Beckett*. Modern Critical Views. New York: Chelsea House, 1985.

Boulter, Jonathan. "'Speak no more": The Hermeneutical Function of Narrative in Samuel Beckett's *Endgame*' in Jennifer Jeffers, ed. *Samuel Beckett*. Casebooks on Modern Dramatists Vol. 25. New York: Garland, 1998. (39-61)

Brienza, Susan D. *Samuel Beckett's New Worlds*. Norman: University of Oklahoma Press, 1987.

Butler, Lance St John. *Samuel Beckett and the Meaning of Being*. London: Macmillan, 1984.

Cavell, Stanley. 'Ending the Waiting Game: A Reading of Beckett's *Endgame*' in *Must We Mean What We Say?* Cambridge: Cambridge University Press, 1976. (115-162)

Chambers, Ross. 'An Approach to *Endgame*' in Chevigny. (71-81)

Chevigny, Bell Gale ed. *Twentieth Century Interpretations of* Endgame. Englewood Cliffs: Prentice-Hall, 1969.

Cohn, Ruby. '*Endgame*' in Chevigny. (40-52)

Esslin, Martin. 'Samuel Beckett: The Search for the Self' in Chevigny. (22-32)

Guest, Michael. 'Beckett versus the Reader' in Angela Moorjani and Carola Veit, eds *Samuel Beckett: Endlessness in the Year 2000*, *Samuel Beckett Today/Aujourd'hui* 11. Amsterdam and New York: Rodopi, 2001. (228-236)

Guicharnaud, Jacques. 'Existence Onstage' in Bloom. (103-123)

Kenner, Hugh. 'Life in the Box' in Bloom. (27-49)

Knowlson, James. *Damned to Fame: The Life of Samuel Beckett*. London: Bloomsbury, 1996.

McHale, Brian. *Postmodernist Fiction*. London: Methuen, 1987.

McMillan, Dougald and Martha Fehsenfeld. *Beckett in the Theater* Vol. 1. London: John Calder, 1988.

Valdés, Mario J. *Phenomenological Hermeneutics and the Study of Literature*. Toronto: University of Toronto Press, 1987.

Venema, Henry Isaac. *Identifying Selfhood: Imagination, Narrative, and Hermeneutics in the Thought of Paul Ricoeur*. Albany: State University of New York Press, 2000.

Endgame's Remainders

Russell Smith

HAMM: "Old stancher! You ... remain." (Beckett 1976, 52)

1. On handkerchiefs

The last words of Samuel Beckett's *Endgame*, in which Hamm addresses his bloodstained handkerchief, are, even for this ham-actor, an unusually bathetic last gasp before the final tableau. This is not *Othello*, so why so much fuss about a handkerchief? It's one of those moments, so common in Beckett, where an object or gesture is apparently called upon to bear a weight of symbolic significance that it stubbornly refuses to shoulder.[1]

In presenting the last human survivors of some ill-defined catastrophe, who prolong their meager existence in a shelter among dwindling supplies, *Endgame* is a play about remainders, about the fact of remaining, about the awkward being-there of "remainderhood." Remainders are not the same as ruins or fragments, which might metonymically gesture towards a totality to be imagined, and thereby hint at the sublime. Instead, the relation of the remainder is one of purely serial subtraction, a residue that bears no indication of the original magnitude. To extrapolate a totality from such remainders would be as absurd as trying to guess from a single grain of millet the size of the original heap. So too, the situation of the characters in *Endgame* does not allow re-inscription into any prior narrative of redemptive teleology. Just as the indivisible lump of the mathematical remainder stubbornly re-emerges from all processes of calculation, so too, in narrative terms, the remainder is, literally, unaccounted for.

In this essay I will argue that *Endgame* addresses itself in particular to the historical situation of Europe after the Second World War, and to the problem of loss and of what to do with what remains. While many critics have been reluctant to attribute a specific context to

Endgame's post-apocalyptic world, Theodor Adorno is insistent on its historical singularity:

> In *Endgame*, a historical moment unfolds, namely the experience captured in the title of one of the culture industry's cheap novels, *Kaputt*. After the Second World War, everything, including a resurrected culture, has been destroyed without realising it; humankind continues to vegetate, creeping along after events that even the survivors cannot really survive, on a rubbish heap that has made even reflection on one's own damaged state useless. (1991, 244)

Adorno argues that *Endgame*'s remainders resist incorporation even into the thematics of existentialist absurdism:

> Instead, the absurd turns into forlorn particulars that mock the conceptual, a layer composed of minimal utensils, refrigerators, lameness, blindness, and the distasteful bodily functions. Everything waits to be carted off to the dump. (252)

Hamm's characteristically florid name for his handkerchief bears an interesting history. According to the *Oxford English Dictionary*, the oldest meaning of the verb *stanch* or *staunch* is "to stop the flow of water," or by extension tears, a sense that is glossed as rare and poetical. The second, more common and contemporary meaning is "to stop the flow of blood" (OED Online). There are three moments in the play where Hamm holds the handkerchief spread out before him. The first time, after removing it from his face at the beginning of the play, and the last time, before replacing it over his face for the final tableau, Hamm addresses it as "old stancher." But on the second occasion, near the end of the play, the handkerchief seems momentarily to recall to him stanching's older, rarer, more poetical meaning: "You weep, and weep, for nothing, so as not to laugh, and little by little ... you begin to grieve" (44).

What is remarkable in this play—a play that depicts the aftermath of catastrophe—is that this is the only specific verbal reference to grief or mourning. At the end of the play Hamm successively discards everything but this bloodstained handkerchief, which he retains not to stop the flow of tears, and certainly not because it has begun to "mean something," but because it functions as a provisional bandage.

What I wish to argue here is that Hamm's gesture of discarding involves a profound ethical argument about historical trauma and the acceptance of loss, an argument that turns on the distinction outlined by Freud between mourning and melancholia (Freud 1991b), and that specifically concerns the historical situation of post-war Europe.

The essay is in two major sections. In the first I survey the contemporary discourse of "trauma studies" and its model of historical trauma, and examine Jonathan Boulter's contention that, through its deconstruction of subjectivity, Beckett's work calls into question the viability of the concepts of trauma and mourning. I also review Freud's distinctions between trauma, mourning and melancholia, and particularly his argument that melancholia involves a deliberate prolongation of attachment to the lost object.

In the second half of the essay, I argue that the greater part of *Endgame* can be read as dramatising the "melancholic stratagem" described by Slavoj Zizek (2000, 661), in which attachment to the lost object is preserved through fidelity to the remainder, in a comic parody of the tragic process of mourning. However, the ending of the play brutally cuts off this melancholic attachment: Hamm's gesture of discarding, rather than comically undermining the concept of mourning, tragically enacts it. The acceptance of loss involves a callous betrayal of the lost object, a callous betrayal that is inseparable from the callous task of going on living. Hamm's imperative "Discard" constitutes the essence of Beckett's ethical critique of post-war European culture.

2. Trauma studies

The history of the word *trauma* travels in the opposite direction to the word *stanch*: originally referring to "a wound or external bodily injury," in the twentieth century the word comes to denote "a psychic injury, especially one caused by emotional shock the memory of which is repressed and remains unhealed" (OED Online).

During the 1990s there was an explosion of interest in the subject of trauma, to the point where "trauma studies" became a recognised cross-disciplinary area of study, drawing on a range of methodologies from historiography, literary theory, psychoanalytic theory and cultural studies. Trauma studies concerns itself in particular with the relationship between trauma and memory, and the role of bearing witness to past traumas as a process of healing. Its concerns range from personal traumas such as childhood sexual abuse to historical traumas such as US slavery and South African apartheid, but its pre-eminent object of study is undoubtedly the Nazi genocide of Jews and other defined groups, usually referred to as the Holocaust or Shoah. In her introduction to a special issue of *Cultural Critique* dedicated to "Trauma and its Cultural Aftereffects," Karyn Ball provides a brief critical history of the field and its characteristic themes: the "hermeneutics and politics of memory" (8); the question of the "moral uniqueness of the Final Solution in the annals of European history" (10); the "trope of unrepresentability" (10), especially in relation to the Holocaust, and a concomitant tendency towards a sacralizing discourse of the sublime; and a later backlash "triggered by the institutionalization of Holocaust studies in the 1980s and 1990s" (13).

Though Beckett criticism tends to resist explicitly historicist readings of his work, *Endgame* clearly bears some kind of relationship to this defining historical trauma of the mid-twentieth century. However, to my knowledge there is no reading of *Endgame* that considers the play in the light of current discourses of historical trauma. This is surprising given the centrality of Adorno in the discourse of trauma studies, and particularly the ongoing controversy over his notorious claim that "to write poetry after Auschwitz is barbaric" (1981, 34). Adorno's endorsement of *Endgame* as an exemplary response to the problem of "art after Auschwitz" suggests that the silence about *Endgame* in "trauma studies" is in fact symptomatic of a broader problem.

This is the conclusion reached by Jonathan Boulter in his essay "Does Mourning Require a Subject? Samuel Beckett's *Texts for Nothing*," the only instance I can find of a sustained reading of a Beckett text in relation to contemporary trauma studies. Boulter comments that Beckett's work is "rarely analyzed in the major theoretical writings on trauma" (345), and speculates that this may be because of a "larger recognition," namely, "that Beckett's work, in its continual interrogation of the workability of the concepts of trauma and mourning, may in fact be read as a generalized critique of the use of trauma and mourning as interpretive tropes" (345).

Boulter's argument can be characterized as a conventional post-structuralist reading, in which he claims that the process of mourning—discovering, narrating, and working-through an originary loss—presupposes a stable, unified subject as the goal of the recovery process, a goal which, for Boulter, betrays what Derrida calls a "nostalgia for origins" (292). By contrast, Boulter argues that "because the Beckettian narrator is unable to present itself as a stable, unified (or potentially unified) subject" (333), the *Texts for Nothing* effectively undermine the preconditions for mourning, and "may in fact call into question the viability of the concepts of trauma and mourning" (345).

I will return to Boulter's argument in a moment, but first it is worth turning to the original Freudian texts on which these "concepts of trauma and mourning" are based.

3. Mourning and melancholy

Freud's controversial and highly speculative essay "Beyond the Pleasure Principle" was written in 1920 in the wake of recent psychoanalytic work with victims of shell shock. What particularly preoccupied Freud was the fact that "dreams occurring in traumatic neuroses have the characteristic of repeatedly bringing the patient back into the situation of his accident, a situation from which he wakes up in another fright" (1991a, 282). This contradicted Freud's theory of the wish-fulfilment character of dreams, leading him to speculate on the existence of a psychic "compulsion to repeat" more fundamental even than the pleasure principle.

Freud famously connected this "compulsion to repeat" in war neuroses with his observation of a game played by his 18 month old nephew, in which the child alternately threw away and recovered a wooden reel attached to a piece of string, announcing the reel's disappearance and return with the words *fort* ("gone") and *da* ("there"). The so-called *fort/da* game (which often involved only the motion of discarding) becomes exemplary of a psychic process in which a traumatic event (in this case, the painful sense of loss caused by the child's temporary separation from the mother) is repeated in symbolic form in order, Freud speculates, to gain mastery over the experience of loss or to enact symbolic revenge on the lost object (283-287).

The "compulsion to repeat" is at the heart of post-traumatic experience. *Nachträglichkeit*, or belatedness, refers to a time-delay in the experience of trauma, in which the traumatic event—a breach in the mind's protective shield—does not fully register in consciousness but returns in the form of nightmares or repetitive actions: the sufferer "is obliged to *repeat* the repressed material as a contemporary experience instead of, as the physician would prefer to see, *remembering* it as something belonging to the past" (288). This process is sometimes described in Freudian theory as "acting-out," as opposed to the therapeutic process of "working-through," in which the subject recognises and comes to accept the reality of the traumatic event as a result of the analyst's interpretation of the post-traumatic symptoms.

It is this model of post-traumatic experience, structurally similar to Freud's earlier theories of hysteria (1991a, 281) which occupies particular prominence in trauma studies. Thus, for Cathy Caruth:

> the wound of the mind [...] is not, like the wound of the body, a simple and healable event, but rather an event that [...] is experienced too soon, too unexpectedly, to be fully known and is therefore not available to consciousness until it imposes itself again, repeatedly, in the nightmares and repetitive actions of the survivor. (3-4)

While this model may be applicable to certain kinds of individual trauma, it is not straightforwardly applicable either to the ordinary process of mourning, in which the nature of the loss is fully known (even if temporarily disavowed), or to historical traumas which are collectively witnessed and remembered. Moreover, in the context of the individual psyche, some models of post-traumatic recovery rely on a crude "storage and retrieval" model of memory that Freud himself later rejected, and, in certain circumstances, have a dangerous tendency to generate phantasmal "recovered memories" through the transference relation in therapeutic practice.[2]

However, it is this model of trauma that Jonathan Boulter uses as the basis of his critique of "the concepts of trauma and mourning." Thus, in his discussion of Caruth, he quite rightly takes exception to her reading of Freud, "which seems too insistent that the subject has no perception of the originary trauma as it occurs" (336). However, Boulter himself comes close to performing the same operation of "collapsing all trauma into the same ontology" (348 n11) when he fails to maintain a rigorous distinction between trauma and mourning, arguing, for instance, that it is "the acknowledgement and eventual recognition of these memories that constitutes the process of mourning" (336).

For there is one significant difference between trauma and mourning: while the trauma survivor struggles to remember, the mourner struggles to forget. While the trauma sufferer repeatedly "acts out" a traumatic experience that eludes consciousness, the mourner consciously "works-through" the loss of a loved one through having constantly to confront the remainders and reminders of their presence.

Thus Boulter continues, "This brief sketch of the Freudian paradigms of mourning and trauma indicates one thing with certainty: both processes require a subject" (336). Although it constitutes the crux of his argument, Boulter doesn't elaborate further on this highly problematic claim, as if it could be casually assumed as a given. The attribution to Freud of an unsophisticated notion of the unified subject is one of the more unfortunate solecisms of orthodox poststructuralist thinking; it is difficult to think of a twentieth-century thinker who did more to undermine the supposed Enlightenment model of the rational, autonomous, humanist subject. The following passage from "Beyond the Pleasure Principle" will have to stand as brief rebuttal:

> It may be difficult, too, for many of us, to abandon the belief that there is an instinct towards perfection at work in human beings, which has brought them to their present high level of intellectual achievement and ethical sublimation and which may be expected to watch over their development into supermen. I have no faith, however, in the existence of any such internal instinct and I cannot see how this benevolent illusion is to be preserved. The present development of human beings requires, as it seems to me, no different explanation from that of animals. (Freud 1991a, 314)

Freud discusses "the normal affect of mourning" in the 1917 essay "Mourning and Melancholia," where he defines mourning as "the reaction to the loss of a loved person, or to the loss of some abstraction which has taken the place of one, such as one's country, liberty, an ideal, and so on" (1991b, 252). In ordinary circumstances, "reality-testing" confirms that the loved object no longer exists, and the ego demands the withdrawal of libidinal attachment from the lost object, a process that is gradual and painful because people "never willingly abandon a libidinal position, not even, indeed, when a substitute is already beckoning to them" (253). This withdrawal of attachment from the lost object, and its transfer to new objects in the decision to go on living, inevitably takes on the character of a betrayal.

Thus the key element of the process of mourning—defined as the successful acceptance of a loss—is not the resurrection, narrative re-enactment and mastery of the traumatic experience of loss, as implied by Boulter, but the act of betrayal of the lost object in the decision to go on living.

Significantly, Boulter outlines Freud's theory of mourning in "Mourning and Melancholia," but does not even mention his discussion of melancholia. Melancholia involves all the same symptoms as mourning—painful dejection, loss of interest in the outside world, loss of capacity to love, inhibition of activity—with an important addition: the lowering of self-regard to the point of "self-reproaches and self-revilings" (252). For Freud, this indicates that, where mourning involves a loss in regard to an object, melancholy involves a loss in regard to the ego. The self-criticisms are the result of a narcissistic ego berating itself for its choice of an unworthy loved object: "An object-choice, an attachment of the libido to a particular person, had at one time existed; then, owing to a *real slight or disappointment* coming from this loved person, the object-relationship was shattered" (257). Whereas mourning involves the death or physical loss of the object, with melancholia the object has been lost "as an object of love" (253). Melancholia is a kind of deliberate prolongation of an ambiguous attachment to the lost object, a "self-tormenting [...] which is without doubt enjoyable" and that signifies "a satisfaction of trends of sadism and hate which relate to an object, and which have been turned round upon the subject's own self" (260).

Freud observes that it often happens that in melancholia,

> one cannot see clearly what it is that has been lost, and it is all the more reasonable to suppose that the patient cannot consciously perceive what he has lost either. [...] This would suggest that melancholia is in some way related to an object-loss which is withdrawn from consciousness, in contradistinction to mourning, in which there is nothing about the loss that is unconscious. (253-54)

Boulter argues that in the *Texts for Nothing*, even though "the symptomatology of some traumatic loss is in place" (342), the narrator's memory, and therefore his self-identity, no longer seems to function: "my past has thrown me out" (Beckett 1995a, 132). This absence of memory creates "a fundamental and aporetic paradox" whereby "the narrator cannot recall his past and therefore cannot forget it" (Boulter 342). For Boulter, the narrator's "lack of history" creates "a subject whose ontology denies the viability of mourning and trauma" (337).

However, what Boulter is describing here—this form of utterance that subverts the process of mourning through evocation of an absence where memory and the subject should be—is more akin to melancholia, a lingering fascination with absence that displays the "symptomatology of traumatic loss" without the supposed preconditions of mourning: a subject, an object, and a memory of their relation.

For Boulter, the *Texts for Nothing* "work to articulate mourning in the expression of its impossibility" (344); but this insistence on the impossibility of mourning is, precisely, the expression of melancholia. While leaving aside the question of the melancholic nature of the *Texts for Nothing*, I wish to argue that, in *Endgame* at least, Beckett is concerned to move beyond the impasse of melancholia and, I think, demonstrate the ethical necessity of the work of mourning.

4. What's happening?

To some extent *Endgame* can be seen as a traumatized acting-out in the wake of a catastrophic event. Certainly, Hamm and Clov appear to be unable to escape a mechanism of compulsive repetition:

> HAMM: Have you not had enough?
> CLOV: Yes! (*Pause.*) Of what?
> HAMM: Of this ... this ... thing.
> CLOV: I always had. (*Pause.*) Not you?
> HAMM: (*gloomily*). Then there's no reason for it to change. (13)

So too, as indicated by Hamm's designation of "this ... this ... thing," both the repetition compulsion itself and the originary trauma that gave rise to it remain obscure. Adorno makes this point repeatedly: "The violence of the unspeakable is mirrored in the fear of mentioning it" (1991, 245); "The name of the catastrophe is to be spoken only in silence" (249); and of Nagg and Nell, "But even the memory of their particular misfortune becomes enviable in view of the vagueness of the general disaster" (266).

At first sight, this silence would appear to accord with the model of post-traumatic neurosis in which the originary event has escaped registration by the conscious mind: Hamm claims that "It all happened without me. I don't know what's happened" (47). But in fact, as Adorno points out, "the reason why the catastrophe may not be mentioned" is not because it is unknown, or obscure, or unfathomable, or unrepresentable, but because "Hamm himself is vaguely responsible for it" (1991, 245).

> HAMM: That old doctor, he's dead naturally?
> CLOV: He wasn't old.
> HAMM: But he's dead?
> CLOV: Naturally. *(Pause.) You* ask *me* that? (23)

So too, although Clov accuses Hamm of responsibility for the death of Mother Pegg, who died "of darkness" after Hamm had refused her oil for her lamp (48), an earlier dialogue reveals Clov's own culpable indifference to her fate:

> HAMM: Is she buried?
> CLOV: Buried! Who would have buried her?
> HAMM: You.
> CLOV: Me! Haven't I enough to do without burying people? (31)

But if Clov is reluctant to bury people, he is a more-than-willing executioner. He can be seen in some ways as the archetypal fascist factotum, whose zeal to exterminate all remaining forms of life exceeds even his master's. When Hamm orders Nagg and Nell to be asphyxiated in their bins—"Screw down the lids"—Clov immediately goes to carry out the task, only to be halted by Hamm's weary afterthought, "Time enough" (22). So too, when Clov reports the sighting of the boy, he immediately sets off to exterminate him with the gaff, only to be halted once again by Hamm, at which Clov protests: "No? A potential procreator?" (50). And it is Clov who utters the play's most chilling formula of political rationality: "If I don't kill that rat he'll die."[3] Clov is a sentimental fascist who is at a loss to explain why he obeys every order, no matter how nonsensical or cruel, but who doesn't disagree when Hamm suggests an explanation: "Perhaps it's compassion. [...] A kind of great compassion" (48).

Each time that Hamm asks "What's happening?" Clov calmly replies that "something is taking its course," as if the word "something" were a sufficient designation. It is clear from the play that something *is* happening, but that this something is happening in a way that defies representation in terms of conventional narrative. The important thing is that a course is being taken: the cycle of repetition is not eternal and immutable, but contains within itself an element of constant but infinitesimal change, like the grains of millet that one day form, not the impossible, but in fact the *inevitable* heap:

> CLOV: Then one day, suddenly, it ends, it changes, I don't understand, it dies, or it's me, I don't understand that either. I ask the words that remain—sleeping, waking, morning, evening. They have nothing to say. (51)

Hamm's and Clov's incapacity to name the "something" that takes its course needn't necessarily surprise us; however, it would be facile to suggest that because it cannot be named it has not happened. Nevertheless, because the final tableau is a near carbon-copy of the opening, and because the play begins with the word "finished" and ends with the word "remain," far too many critics make the assumption that the play describes an endless, hellishly circular repetition.[4] This would be depressing, of course, but reassuringly depressing: a melancholic stasis, a kind of devil-you-know of all possible worlds.

But there are various indicators in the play that time moves, not in a serenely infernal circle, but a kind of mangled, terrestrial spiral. Inside the shelter supplies are dwindling: there's no more pap, no more sugarplums, no more Turkish Delight. So too, the characters are dwindling, subject to the law of entropy, which for Hamm proves that Nature hasn't forgotten them: "we breathe, we change! We lose our hair, our teeth! Our bloom! Our ideals!" (16). Finally, as if to confirm that it can't go on forever, Nell dies, and probably Nagg too. But in any case it all happens too late, because "there are no more coffins" (49).

As most theorists of trauma would agree, the process of working-through is often preceded by a phase of acting-out, and the process of "normal" mourning is preceded by a phase of "pathological" melancholy. It is something like the acting-out of a pathological melancholy that the play presents. The action of the play, the "something" that is "taking its course," can be seen as the passage from melancholy to mourning, from melancholic fidelity to the lost object, to its betrayal in the work of mourning, in the decision to go on living or, in this instance, to die. This is not to say that the play is "about" melancholy and mourning, as if it were simply an elaborate psychological allegory. Rather, in its presentation of its stubborn remainders, *Endgame* critically examines the relationship between absence and loss, such that it can be read as an ethical critique of melancholy.

5. The Melancholic Stratagem

Hamm and Clov are bound in a melancholic relationship to each other, in which the prospect of their separation becomes the premise on which the relationship continues. As Giorgio Agamben puts it: "melancholia offers the paradox of an intention to mourn that precedes and anticipates the loss of the object" (20).

Thus, by the time Clov asks, "What is there to keep me here?" and Hamm responds, "The dialogue" (39), we are able to observe the tautology of this remark: the dialogue has always been about whether or not Clov will ever leave. Clov says "I'll leave you" eleven times in the play, almost always after the dialogue has sputtered to a standstill. "I'll leave you" becomes the paradoxical formula for renewing the relationship.

This bears an uncanny resemblance to the melancholic stratagem described by Slavoj Zizek:

> The melancholic's refusal to accomplish the work of mourning thus takes the form of its very opposite, a faked spectacle of the excessive, superfluous mourning for an object even before this object is lost. [...] Insofar as the melancholic mourns what he has not yet lost, there is an inherent comic subversion of the tragic procedure of mourning at work in melancholy. (2000, 661)

In the play this comic spectacle of excessive or superfluous mourning takes concrete form in the shape of Hamm's dog. Giorgio Agamben compares the melancholic stratagem of possessing the object through its loss with the structure of the fetish, which is "at once the sign of something and its absence" (21). Hamm's dog, clearly, is such a sign: a faithful servant imploring its master, who acts as a surrogate of the unfaithful and independent Clov. The fetish simultaneously denies and asserts the reality of loss: loss is disavowed through libidinal attachment to the signifier of the lost object ("Good doggy!"), and acknowledged in the knowing assumption of a perverse symptom ("Look at what I've been reduced to!"). Clov even makes clear his awareness of this relationship when he hands the dog to Hamm with the announcement "Your dogs are here" (30).[5] In keeping with the general character of the fetish, which often takes a metonymic form such as a wig or a shoe, Hamm's dog is radically incomplete, not only lacking a leg, in which it resembles the limping Clov, but also its "sex," indicating its destiny as a surrogate son, and its ribbon. The temptation might be to psychoanalyze these deficits, but in fact such imperfections are only incidental. As Agamben argues, the "nonfinished," which depends on the fetishistic character of metonymy, is "one of the essential stylistic instruments of modern art" (32). The essence of the fetish is not its physical wholeness but rather that absence of which it is the sign.

Thus when Hamm throws away the dog at the end of the play, it is a decisive moment of refusal: a refusal of melancholy, of the fetish, of the metaphysics of absence. It is the betrayal of the lost object that is the essence of the work of mourning.

Here it is necessary to measure carefully the distinction between absence and loss.

In "Trauma, Absence, Loss" Dominick LaCapra makes the distinction between absence and loss the cornerstone of an ethical argument about the differences between mourning and melancholia, acting-out and working-through. For LaCapra, absence tends to be non-specific and ahistorical, a kind of logical or even ontological category, whereas losses are always specific, historical events. "Absence is not an event and does not imply tenses (past, present, or future). By contrast, the historical past is the scene of losses that may be narrated" (1999, 700).

LaCapra repeatedly underscores the ethical importance of this (non-binary) distinction, arguing that "the difference (or nonidentity) between absence and loss is often elided, and the two are conflated with confusing and dubious results" (700). For instance, the absence of divinity is converted into loss in the Christian mythology of the Fall, and the absence of political harmony is converted into loss in the mythology of a golden age, displacements which give rise to a "misplaced nostalgia or utopian politics in quest of a new totality or fully unified community" (698). Indeed, as LaCapra speculates, "one might ask whether the conversion of absence into loss is essential to all fundamentalisms or foundational philosophies" (702).

So too, the conversion of loss into absence can displace the concrete specificity of historical losses into a kind of generalised rhetoric of absence, in which "one faces the impasse of endless melancholy, impossible mourning, and interminable aporia" (698). This latter would appear to mirror the structure of Boulter's argument, in which the notion of history as the scene of "losses that may be narrated" is seen as fatally dependent on normative categories that Boulter insists are always-already lacking. For Boulter, texts such as Beckett's suggest that "trauma and mourning are deeply nostalgic concepts and processes that presuppose categories (self, history, memory) that themselves no longer have any operational validity" (345).

Boulter's reading of Beckett's *Texts For Nothing* thus articulates quite clearly a melancholic stratagem whereby what is lost is converted into a generalized absence, a kind of "mourning for nothing" which becomes "an extended expression of pity for a self that never was; a self that mourns a self that never was" (343). What Boulter reads as a "work to articulate mourning in the expression of its impossibility" (344) might equally be read as refusal to accomplish the work of mourning: the subject which is required to acknowledge the reality of historical losses evades this demand by denying the reality of its own subjecthood; in so doing, it maintains a melancholic solidarity with the lost object by occupying the structural position of absence.

Boulter's position is characteristic of what Slavoj Zizek describes as a generalized "rehabilitation of melancholy" in contemporary critical theory:

> With regard to mourning and melancholy, the predominant opinion is the following: Freud opposed normal mourning (the successful acceptance of a loss) to pathological melancholy (the subject persists in his or her narcissistic identification with the lost object). Against Freud, one should assert the conceptual *and* ethical primacy of melancholy. In the process of the loss, there is always a remainder that cannot be integrated through the work of mourning, and the ultimate fidelity is the fidelity to this remainder. Mourning is a kind of betrayal, the second killing of the (lost) object, while the melancholic subject remains faithful to the lost object, refusing to renounce his or her attachment to it. (2000, 658)

A similar argument is the basis of Zizek's critique of deconstruction, which he sees as a profoundly melancholic stratagem consisting of a fidelity to an Otherness that "never acquires positive features but always remains withdrawn, the trace of its own absence" (664). This "melancholic, postsecular thought," according to Zizek, "finds its ultimate expression in a certain kind of Derridean appropriation of

Levinas" (663). As an example, Zizek cites Derrida's melancholic fidelity to "a certain *spirit of Marxism*," a standpoint which rejects Marx's particular historical analyses and revolutionary measures in favour of an always-to-come messianic promise of emancipatory liberation, such that "the messianic promise that constitutes the spirit of Marxism is betrayed by *any* particular formulation, by *any* translation into determinate economic and political necessity" (664).

So too, this structure of melancholic fidelity to absence is not just characteristic of deconstruction, but, as Dominick LaCapra notes, is prevalent in a variety of modern theoretical and philosophical systems, from Marx and Heidegger to Lacan and Derrida:

> a similar conflation of absence and loss occurs with respect to the passage from nature to culture, the entry into language, the traumatic encounter with the 'real,' the alienation from species-being, the anxiety-ridden thrownness and fallenness of *Dasein*, the inevitable generation of the aporia, or the constitutive nature of melancholic loss in relation to the genesis of subjectivity. (1999, 703)[6]

What is at stake in such theoretical positions, ultimately, is the ethical capacity to confront historical loss. It would seem that, as Boulter argues, mourning *does* require a subject, and it is just such a confrontation with loss that *Endgame* stages.

6. There's no more pain-killer

In *Endgame* Beckett is always careful to maintain the distinction between absence and loss, and especially between the melancholic form of loss, which is only a paradoxical means of claiming possession of an absence, and the tragic form of loss, the kind of loss that, as LaCapra insists, is a historical event that may be narrated.

Interestingly, LaCapra mentions Beckett several times in the course of "Trauma, Absence, Loss," praising him as a "novelist and dramatist of absence and not simply loss" (714). For LaCapra, Beckett's "nonconventional narratives [...] tend not to include events in any significant way and seem to be abstract, evacuated, or disembodied" (701), thereby preventing their reinscription within the quasi-mythical narratives of loss such as the Edenic or oedipal scenarios.[7] While this may be true of much of Beckett's fiction (and here LaCapra's reading of Beckett's dismantling of ontological categories seems broadly to accord with Boulter's), I would argue that *Endgame* is a play of *losses*, not just absences: historical losses that take the form of events that may be narrated, that in fact are repeatedly narrated through the formula "There's no more..."

Thus we might, in a paradoxical way, draw up an inventory of the play's losses. First, there are no more bicycle wheels (15), then no more pap (15) or sugar plums (38) or Turkish delight (38), no more nature (16), no more tide (41), no more navigators (43), no more rugs (44), no more coffins (49) and finally, in what is perhaps the play's climactic moment, "no more painkiller" (46). Moreover, Hamm has lost his sight and the use of his legs, while Nagg and Nell have lost their legs entirely. Most importantly, of course, it seems there are no more living beings, human or otherwise; all is "corpsed" (25).

But if the play presents what remains after these losses, the nature of these losses and their relationship to the catastrophe is frustratingly unclear: was it a sudden event, or a drawn-out decline?

Evidence points to the latter: Hamm's chronicle records the last survivors of a declining human population, presumably dying as the result of there being "no more nature."

If the play is unclear about how these losses occurred, what is finally of more significance is how the characters deal with these losses. Nell, perhaps the most far gone, has practically renounced the reality of her current circumstances in favour of nostalgic reminiscences of "yesterday." Nagg, on the other hand, is tormented by the experience of *Nachträglichkeit*, the simultaneous acting-out of two temporalities. For instance, his use of the present tense in his discussion of Turkish delight might be read as a melancholy enjoyment of possession through loss:

> Turkish delight, for example, which no longer exists, we all know that, there is nothing in the world I love more. And one day I'll ask you for some, in return for a kindness, and you'll promise it to me. One must live with the times. (38)

Clov appears to enact a similar melancholic stratagem, converting the absence of bicycle wheels into a sense of loss for the bicycle he never had: "When there were still bicycles I wept to have one. I crawled at your feet. You told me to go to hell. Now there are none" (15). So too, he laments that "the earth is extinguished, though I never saw it lit" (51).

Finally, for Hamm too, the dog as fetish plays the role of surrogate son, allowing a kind of melancholic subversion of the tragic process of mourning through an anticipatory possession of the lost object.

If melancholy is a parody of mourning, there are, as I noted above, very few references to mourning in the play. Hamm's apostrophe to his handkerchief—"You weep, and weep, for nothing, so as not to laugh, and little by little ... you begin to grieve" (44)—is the only explicit verbal reference. But Hamm at least observes with punctilio the gestural formalities of grieving: he raises his toque in memory of the painter and engraver (32), and again when Clov announces the death of Nell (41), and provisionally raises his hand to his toque a third time until it is confirmed that Nagg is still living (42). At the end of the play, when Hamm raises his hat a fourth time with the toast "Peace to our ... arses" (52), it is unclear exactly to whom Hamm intends to pay his disrespects: perhaps Clov, perhaps his father, perhaps himself. In any case, whereas Clov's melancholic refusal to mourn extends even to a refusal to bury, Hamm's offence against mourning seems rather one of excessively expeditious formality, a kind of subversion of the law of respect for the dead through an emptily formulaic observance.

But if the greater part of the play consists of parodies of mourning, particularly in the form of melancholy, in which lost objects are preserved through narcissistic attachments to their remainders, the *dénouement* consists of a sequence in which Hamm discards these remainders in a confrontation with the reality of loss, an ethical act of betrayal that constitutes the accomplishment of the tragic work of mourning.

As already noted, the turning point in the play, carefully prepared by Clov with sadistic forestalling, is the moment in which he triumphantly announces that there's no more painkiller:

> HAMM: Is it not time for my pain-killer?
> CLOV: Yes.
> HAMM: Ah! At last! Give it to me! Quick! *(Pause.)*
> CLOV: There's no more pain-killer. *(Pause.)*
> HAMM *(appalled)*: Good...! *(Pause.)* No more pain-killer!
> CLOV: No more pain-killer. You'll never get any more pain-killer. *(Pause.)*
> HAMM: But the little round box. It was full!
> CLOV: Yes. But now it's empty. (46)

Clov even rubs salt into the wound by adapting the same phrase Hamm earlier used to torment his father, "You'll never get any more pap" (15). And as if this were not enough, he immediately tries to lure Hamm into a repetition of the gag:

> CLOV: Is your throat sore? (*Pause.*) Would you like a lozenge? (*Pause.*) No? (*Pause.*) Pity. (46)

It's impossible to be certain what happens from here to the end of the play. Does Clov decide to leave in an act of autonomous agency, or is he dismissed by Hamm, or do they mutually negotiate the terms of their separation through the mediation of the alarm-clock? Does the final tableau suggest that Clov will remain after all? If these issues are undecidable, the one thing that is accepted as fact by Hamm, certainly above Clov's more dubiously credible sighting of the small boy, is the fact that there is no painkiller. The little round box that was full and is now empty is a harrowing disproof *a contrario* of Zeno's paradox of the millet grains.

   Hamm greets this announcement with an anguished determination to put a brave face on it: "Good!" It's a formula he repeats several times in the final moments of the play, as a kind of moral imperative that accompanies the ethical imperative of mourning, "Discard." "Good," a little like Freud's nephew's "*fort*," becomes Hamm's formula for acknowledging the inevitability of loss, and severing attachment to the remainders that have hitherto functioned as "pain-killers."

   First, Hamm dispenses with Clov: "I don't need you any more" (50). Then, finding himself to be alone, he progressively discards a series of objects that function as melancholic metonyms of his losses. The gaff is tested and proven to be useless as a surrogate for his lost powers of independent motion: "Good. (*Pause.*) Discard" (52). So too, after an initial hesitation, he discards the dog, the melancholic fetish of the lost son. Finally, after whistling twice to check that Clov has really gone, he throws the whistle towards the auditorium "with my compliments" (52).

   All that remains is the handkerchief, which he unfolds with theatrical deliberation and drapes over his face for the final tableau. If Hamm retains his "old stancher," it is neither as a melancholic keepsake nor as a receptacle for the tears of grief, and certainly not because it is "beginning to ... to ... mean something" (27), but because as a "stancher" it serves the practical function of a provisional bandage.

After the Second World War, Beckett immediately returned to France, where he worked as a quarter-master in the Irish Red Cross Hospital at St Lô, a Normandy town devastated by the Allies during the D-Day invasion. These experiences, from August to December 1945, not only exposed him to the catastrophic destruction of the war, but also to the brutally pragmatic ethics of triage and the promiscuous hedonism of the reconstruction (Knowlson 345-51). In a never-broadcast report written for Irish radio, Beckett claimed that what the Irish volunteers gained from the French, and perhaps vice versa, was an occasional glimpse

> of that smile at the human condition as little to be extinguished by bombs as to be broadened by the elixirs of Burroughes and Welcome,—the smile deriding, among other things, the having and the not having, the giving and the taking, sickness and health. (Beckett 1995b, 277)

It was just the kind of situation in which Beckett may have found himself forced to announce: "There's no more pain-killer." And yet, his report is preoccupied with the practical business of clearing the debris and finding provisional applications, "in this universe become provisional" (278), for the unaccountable remainders of the war. It is this refusal of melancholy, and a thoroughly humanistic acceptance of the work of mourning, that is what Beckett claims to have found in France in 1945: "a vision and sense of a time-honoured conception of humanity in ruins, and perhaps even an inkling of the terms in which our condition is to be thought again" (278).

Russell Smith, Australian National University

Notes

[1] Of course, critics were quick to interpret the "forlorn particular" of Hamm's handkerchief as a reference to the Sudarium, or holy kerchief, the cloth with which, according to legend, St Veronica wiped the face of Christ on the way to Calvary, and upon which his features were miraculously impressed. But Hamm is no dying Christ and the handkerchief is no holy relic. Indeed, as with the teasing name of Godot, Beckett sprinkles Biblical references throughout *Endgame* with deliberate perversity, aiming to provoke and thereby frustrate symbolic interpretations (see Bersani and

Dutoit, 28). As Beckett wrote in his first piece of literary criticism: "The danger is in the neatness of identifications" (Beckett 1983, 19). The difficulty of producing a coherent reading from *Endgame*'s many Biblical allusions is demonstrated in Mary Bryden's "The Sacrificial Victim of Beckett's *Endgame*" (1990). See also Stanley Cavell's analysis of Noah's Ark references in "Ending the Waiting Game: A Reading of Samuel Beckett's *Endgame*" (2002).

[2] One of the (often repressed) contexts of "trauma studies" is the well-documented explosion in the course of the 1980s in the number of cases of "recovered memories" of childhood sexual assault revealed in therapy. As discussed by John Frow, the truth-status of these repressed memories, which were often readily accepted by therapists, courts, and sometimes even the alleged perpetrators, only gradually came to be questioned "because of a pattern in which recovered memories more and more often came to refer to abuse within satanic cults, to the ritual mutilation and murder of children, to cannibalism and the breeding of babies for sacrifice, to abduction by aliens, and to past-life abuse" (231-232). Frow discusses how a particular therapeutic apparatus contributed to the production of "recovered memories" which drew "as much from the culture as from the archives of individual memories" (238).

[3] Cf James Berger: "[In] revelations of this sort—'We had to destroy the village in order to save it'—enlightenment is indistinguishable from barbarism" (8).

[4] For instance, in one passage Adorno claims of the final tableau, "No spectator, and no philosopher, would be capable of saying for sure whether or not the play is starting all over again" (1991, 269), even though earlier he had noted "the deaths of the two old people move [the play] forward to that exit from life whose possibility constitutes the dramatic tension" (267).

[5] It is also possible to read Hamm's first mention of a dog, at the beginning of the play, as in fact referring to Clov:

> HAMM: Can there be misery—*(he yawns)*—loftier than mine? No doubt.
> Formerly. But now? *(Pause.)* My father? *(Pause.)* My mother?
> *(Pause.)* My ... dog? (12)

Daniel Katz notes how, in *Molloy*, the dog Teddy plays the role of Lousse's surrogate son, a role taken over by Molloy after he accidentally kills the dog. Katz associates this passage with an incident from Beckett's life when in 1926 he ran over and killed his mother's Kerry Blue bitch in the family driveway, an incident that apparently plunged Beckett into a period of "excessive mourning" (249-250).

[6] It is important to note here that LaCapra criticises Zizek himself for conflating historical loss and structural absence in his Lacanian reading of historical catastrophes as merely so many undifferentiated instances of a kind of trans-historical traumatic real. Thus Zizek claims:

> All the different attempts to attach this phenomenon [concentration camps] to a concrete image ('Holocaust,' 'Gulag'...), to reduce it to a product of a concrete social order (Fascism, Stalinism...)—what are they if not so many attempts to elude the fact that we are dealing here with the 'real' of our civilisation which returns as the same traumatic kernel in all social systems? (1989, 50)

LaCapra comments: "Here, in an extreme and extremely dubious theoretical gesture, concentration camps are brought alongside castration anxiety as mere manifestations or instantiations of the Lacanian 'real' or 'traumatic kernel'" (1999, 727).

[7] In *Writing History, Writing Trauma*, LaCapra discusses Beckett's writing as exemplary of a practice that has perhaps been especially pronounced since the Shoah but may also be found earlier, notably in testimonial art: experimental, gripping, and risky symbolic emulation of trauma in that might be called traumatised or post-traumatic writing. [...] One crucial form it takes—notably in figures such as Blanchot, Kafka, Celan, and Beckett—is what might perhaps be seen as a writing of terrorised disempowerment as close as possible to the experience of traumatised victims without presuming to be identical to it. (106-107)

Bibliography

Adorno, Theodor W. 'An Essay on Cultural Criticism and Society' in *Prisms* translated by Samuel and Shierry Weber. Cambridge, Mass.: MIT Press, 1981. (17-34)

—. 'Trying to Understand *Endgame*' in *Notes to Literature, Vol.1* translated by Shierry Weber Nicholson. New York: Columbia University Press, 1991. (241-275)

Agamben, Giorgio. *Stanzas: Word and Phantasm in Western Culture* translated by Ronald L. Martinez. Minneapolis: University of Minnesota Press, 1993.

Ball, Karyn. "Introduction: Trauma and its Institutional Destinies" in *Cultural Critique* 46 (2000): 1-44.

Beckett, Samuel. *Endgame*. London: Faber, 1976.

—. 'Dante . . . Bruno . Vico . . Joyce' in *Disjecta: Miscellaneous Writings and a Dramatic Fragment* ed. Ruby Cohn. London: Calder, 1983. (19-33)

—. *Texts for Nothing* in *The Complete Short Prose, 1929-1989* ed. S.E. Gontarski. New York: Grove, 1995a. (100-154)

—. 'The Capital of the Ruins' in *The Complete Short Prose, 1929-1989* ed. S. E. Gontarski. New York: Grove, 1995b. (275-278)

Berger, James. *After the End: Representations of Post-Apocalypse*. Minneapolis: University of Minnesota Press, 1999.

Bersani, Leo and Ulysse Dutoit. *Arts of Impoverishment: Beckett, Rothko, Resnais*. Cambridge, Mass.: Harvard University Press, 1993.

Boulter, Jonathan. "Does Mourning Require a Subject? Samuel Beckett's *Texts for Nothing*" in *Modern Fiction Studies* 50.2 (2004): 332-50.

Bryden, Mary. "The Sacrificial Victim of Beckett's *Endgame*" in *Literature and Theology* 4.2 (1990): 219-225.

Caruth, Cathy. *Unclaimed Experience: Trauma, Narrative, and History*. Baltimore: The Johns Hopkins University Press, 1996.

Cavell, Stanley. 'Ending the Waiting Game: A Reading of Samuel Beckett's *Endgame*' in *Must We Mean What We Say?* Updated edition. Cambridge: Cambridge University Press, 2002. (115-162)

Derrida, Jacques. *Writing and Difference* translated by Alan Bass. Chicago: University of Chicago Press, 1978.

Freud, Sigmund. 'Beyond the Pleasure Principle' in *On Metapsychology: The Theory of Psychoanalysis* (Penguin Freud Library, Volume 11). London: Penguin, 1991a. (269-338)

—. 'Mourning and Melancholia' in *On Metapsychology: The Theory of Psychoanalysis* (Penguin Freud Library, Volume 11). London: Penguin, 1991b. (245-268)

Frow, John. '*Toute la mémoire du monde*: Repetition and Forgetting' in *Time and Commodity Culture: Essays in Cultural Theory and Postmodernity*. Oxford: Clarendon, 1997. (218-246)

Katz, Daniel. "Principles of Pleasure in *Molloy* and 'First Love'" in *Modern Fiction Studies* 49.2 (2003): 246-60.

Knowlson, James. *Damned to Fame: The Life of Samuel Beckett*. London: Bloomsbury, 1996.

LaCapra, Dominick. "Trauma, Absence, Loss" in *Critical Inquiry* 25 (1999): 696-727. (Reprinted in LaCapra 2001, 43-85.)

—. *Writing History, Writing Trauma*. Baltimore: The Johns Hopkins University Press, 2001.

OED Online. Oxford: Oxford University Press, 2005. Online at: http://www.oed.com/ (consulted 04.08.2005).

Zizek, Slavoj. *The Sublime Object of Ideology*, London: Verso, 1989.

—. "Melancholy and the Act" in *Critical Inquiry* 26 (2000): 657-681.

Bare interiors, chicken wire cages and subway stations—re-thinking Beckett's response to the ART *Endgame* in light of earlier productions

Natka Bianchini

A few years before his death in 1989, Beckett amended the contract that licenses his plays in performance to include a clause forbidding any deviation from the script or stage directions. This clause was added largely in reaction to a very familiar and public debacle over a 1984 production of *Endgame* at the American Repertory Theater (ART) in Cambridge, Massachusetts, directed by JoAnne Akalaitis, that made several changes to the text. Chief among them was the relocating of the setting from its specified bare interior to a debris-strewn subway station. Beckett heard of the changes and sought to bring an injunction against the production to halt its performances—a move that attracted the attention of national media at the time and of theater scholars ever since. The public perception of this event is characterized by mistakes and misunderstandings, many of which portray Beckett as a recalcitrant playwright, and his intervention in the ART production as representative of his standard response to any artists attempting to deviate from his texts (Gussow C:14).[1] When viewing this event within the larger framework of his response to earlier productions of *Endgame*, however, this label seems hastily applied.

Prior to the 1984 *Endgame*, there were two important American productions to which Beckett responded in significant ways: Alan Schneider's 1958 American première, and Andre Gregory's radical reinterpretation fifteen years later. Unlike his reaction to the ART production, when Gregory's production made changes to the set, costumes and text (changes that were arguably more substantial than those in Akalaitis' production) Beckett did not intervene, despite the urging of both Schneider and of Barney Rosset, his American publisher. The main reason he cited for not intervening was that he felt it was not within his rights as a playwright to try to control the production.

I believe there is a chain of causality that links these three productions: Beckett's reaction to Schneider's production directly informed and inspired his response to Gregory, which, in turn, affected his response to Akalaitis. I will trace this chain through letters Beckett exchanged with Schneider and Rosset, and in other primary source material. These links will provide a wider context for understanding Beckett's response in 1984, which will be further aided by my reconstruction of the ART events, bringing to bear new evidence and interviews with some of the participants. Through this synthesis, I will bring some clarity to the factors surrounding the ART events, and I will dispel the generalization that Beckett was always rigid when it came to his work in performance.

It is virtually impossible to discuss any American production of a Beckett play without mentioning Alan Schneider. After a rocky start (the American première of *Waiting for Godot* that Schneider directed at the Coconut Grove Playhouse in Miami, Florida, was a fiasco[2]) he became one of Beckett's closest friends and his foremost American interpreter. Their collaboration spanned three decades: before his death in 1984, Schneider directed every play Beckett wrote, most of them American premières, five of them world premières. With some directors Beckett was wary, but with Schneider his trust was implicit.

Their relationship began in the fall of 1955, when Schneider traveled to Paris as part of pre-production research on *Godot*, a practice he repeated in the fall of 1957 before commencing *Endgame* rehearsals. The two would meet daily to discuss the play, Schneider asking dozens of questions and Beckett patiently trying to provide answers. Several times they went together to see the French première of *Endgame* (*Fin de Partie*) directed by Roger Blin,[3] which was in the last weeks of its run when Schneider arrived. He left the visit feeling that he understood *Endgame* "a hundred times more clearly" than before. At their parting, Beckett wished him well and imparted his blessing: "Do it the way you like, Alan, do it ahny way you like!" in his familiar Irish accent (Schneider 250), a comment that reveals how comfortable Beckett was trusting Schneider with his work. After having demonstrated such fidelity to Beckett's text with *Godot*, Schneider had gained his complete trust.

Back in America, Schneider began work on *Endgame* in earnest. He continued his consultation with Beckett through letters in much the same way he had in person. He wrote frequently with questions for Beckett to answer about the play. His first letter was full of details about designers and potential casts. He concluded the multi-page letter with a list of a dozen questions about the script, ranging from the more mundane need to find an American equivalent for the British "Spratt's Medium" to the more sublime difference between Beckett's use of "ending" and "dying."[4]

By early January 1958, rehearsals were well underway in New York. Schneider's approach to working with actors was to try to elicit performances that were as close as possible to what Beckett intended. I asked Alvin Epstein, who played Clov, what he remembered about Schneider's approach to blocking, and he said:

> I think what we did was to try and stick as closely to Beckett's stage directions as possible. That meant when Beckett said a stiff, staggering walk, we tried to do my version of a stiff, staggering walk. I think that was part of Alan's basic approach, to take Beckett at his word.[5]

He remembered having a sense immediately of how close Schneider and Beckett were during the rehearsal period: "He was in touch with Beckett all the time. A lot of what he wanted to do had to do with those conversations with Beckett. My sense was Beckett was approving of Alan's ideas, saying yes to everything."

Schneider enlisted designer David Hays to design the set for the production. Hays initially went in the wrong direction, trying to complicate and clutter the stage while Schneider repeatedly insisted on simplicity. He eventually succeeded in convincing Hays to use the Cherry Lane's back brick wall as the back of the bare interior and to simply paint the appearance of windows onto the brick, rather than create an artificial back wall (Schneider 251-252). Beckett approved of the set and was pleased with the production photos once he saw them.

Endgame opened on 28 January at the Cherry Lane Theater, produced by Noel Behn and Rooftop Productions, with the following cast: Alvin Epstein as Clov, Lester Rawlins as Hamm, P.J. Kelly as Nagg and Nydia Westman as Nell.[6] Opening night reviews were decidedly mixed, but the two most important ones, Brooks Atkinson of *The New York Times* and Walter Kerr of the *New York Herald-Tribune,* were both essentially positive. Atkinson noted that Schneider had understood the play and had given it a thoughtful rendition on stage. He also mentioned Schneider's fidelity to Beckett's text, remarking: "Whether or not his theme is acceptable or rational, his director, Alan Schneider, has had the grace to take him at his own evaluation and stage his play seriously."

The lesser reviews are a mixed bag, ranging from one that calls Schneider a "hero" (Bolton) to one that slams the production for being "hopelessly abstruse" and "carelessly conceived" (McClain). Nonetheless, Schneider was pleased enough that he phoned Beckett at dawn in Paris to tell him the good news (Schneider 257). Beckett and Schneider's next series of letters deconstructed the production: Schneider wrote with news of all the various reviews, and both men agreed that the whole event was quite a success. *Endgame* ended up running for three months and over one hundred performances. It was, in Schneider's estimation, one of the highlights of the off-Broadway season (257).

Having absolved himself of the *Godot* misadventure with the success of *Endgame*, Schneider had now permanently attached his name to Beckett's. In an interview he summed up what seems to have been his primary legacy: "In all the Beckett plays I get credit for following Beckett's intentions. Rightly or wrongly, I consider that to be my responsibility; if the intention is specifically stated, I try to follow it as specifically as it's stated" (Schechner 77). With Beckett, the intention is always precisely stated. The meaning behind the intention may be vague, but there is little question that Beckett writes his scripts in a deliberate way that tells the reader exactly what the stage is supposed to look like, how the actors are supposed to move and sound. For the first American production, Schneider had given New York audiences as faithful a rendition of *Endgame* as could be produced, something that would not be repeated by Andre Gregory fifteen years later.

Gregory's avant-garde theater company of the 1970s, the Manhattan Project, was looking for a follow-up to their first success, *Alice in Wonderland*, a production that toured internationally and won the company an Obie award. A *New York Times* profile of the group in 1971 discussed their interest in canonical texts; they initially explored

Dante's *Inferno, Sir Gawain and the Green Knight, Bleak House* and Marlowe's *Doctor Faustus*. As Gregory said: "We tried to live up to our reputation as a company dedicated to the destruction of English classics" (Gussow 1971). Although the company did not leave behind a manifesto or mission statement, Gregory's comment is a revealing glimpse into the group's ethos. As their very name evokes, they were a group that was trying to explode a text, deconstruct it, take it apart.

The group settled on *Endgame*, presumably because they considered it a modern classic—in 1971 the text was only fifteen years old, far too young to be considered classic in a temporal sense. I asked Gregory whether or not he takes the age or 'status' of a text into consideration when he begins work on it; he said no. He considers a play to be a "skeleton for a production, [something that] is not fully achieved until that production." Gregory here places the primacy of interpretation upon the director and his fellow actors; they should interpret the text as they see fit, not as the playwright intended. His philosophy is that a director can "create things the playwright never imagined" and that the work "belongs to the universe," not to the playwright.[7]

Just as with their first production, the company workshopped *Endgame* for many months, interspersing their rehearsals with various types of performances. On 7 February 1973, after eighteen months of work, the play 'premièred' in a theater space converted from a New York University attic. New York critics and audiences were surprised when confronted with the unconventional choices of Gregory and his designer, Jerry Rojo.

The audience was seated in four cubicles, each section separated from the other, and from the stage, by chicken wire. Gregory explained to me that the audience was seated on two levels inside these steel-wire boxes, and that the actors were also in boxes. I asked him the reason for this concept and he replied that he did not know since his work always comes from the unconscious. He guessed that the set was probably inspired by the tiger cages used in Vietnam during the war, but that was only a hypothesis. Instead of the customary ashbins, Nell was inside a GE refrigerator box and Nagg was inside a laundry hamper (Kalb 1989, 78). Clearly there was no attempt to recreate the bare interior that Beckett calls for in the script. Since the set was not created with a specific concept in mind, its main effect was to be evocative and different to what the audience would expect.

Equally unsettling to the audience's expectations were the numerous additions that Gregory brought to the text (although he made no subtractions from the script). One review noted that the production was two and a half hours long (Gottfried 14). (Performance logs from the ART production—which performed the text essentially unchanged—note that the performance ran well under two hours.[8]) The lines were embellished throughout the performance with a series of noises. Walter Kerr described them as "cock-crows, halloos, clucks, brrs, burbles, bugle sounds, imitations of automobiles and rockets, screeches, machine-gun rat-a-tat-tats, interpolated 'yucks' to express disgust, and innumerable repetitions of that sound that is made by bringing tongue and teeth together while blowing out the cheeks" (D:20). Besides these verbal tics, Gregory added a number of American songs, including bits of "Stars and Stripes Forever," "My Merry Oldsmobile," and "Give My Regards to Broadway." The choice of songs clearly Americanize the play, perhaps because it was viewed as too remote or 'European,' although Gregory insisted to me that he added the songs only because he thought they would be funny.

The reviews from the February performances were varied. Some found Gregory's work revolting, others saw it as refreshing; few reviews were middling in opinion. Schneider's faithful production had set the tone in America, and this was the first major American production since his première fifteen years earlier to really deviate from that norm. Here was a director willing to fly in the face of Schneider's standard. *The New York Times* ran two reviews on the production: a rave by Clive Barnes on February 9 and a pan by Walter Kerr on February 11. Barnes betrayed his bias in the opening line of his article, stating that he loved Gregory's work, and praised the production for being innovative. Kerr, on the other hand, lamented what Gregory had done to the play. He went into great detail describing the extra-textual additions, which he believed destroyed Beckett's rhythms. Gregory's production, to Kerr, was reckless in approach; his changes did "nothing to improve the play" (D:20). The reviews stand as confirmation that Gregory's approach to *Endgame* was to impose his directorial interpretation by deconstructing the text, because they all read as a reaction for or against Gregory's alterations.

As he customarily had done with many significant Beckett productions in New York, Schneider served as Beckett's watchman. Two years before *Endgame* opened, Schneider heard about Gregory's plans and mentioned it in a letter to Beckett of 3 May 1971:

> Andre Gregory group, which has had great acclaim for workshop [sic] of *Alice in Wonderland* is, I've been told, working on *Endgame* for the fall. They're interesting and very Grotowski group [sic], but inclined to use text for own purposes. But with their standing in theatrical community, hard to refuse them permission though not sure you'd be happy with results. (Harmon 253)

This letter shows how protective Schneider was, even early on, and it also demonstrates how prominent Gregory's group was at that time—too prominent, in Schneider's estimation, to try to prevent their work from proceeding.

When the show did open, Schneider went to see it early in its run, accompanied by Rosset. Beckett did not see the production himself as he rarely traveled to the United States.[9] He wrote to Schneider on 27 January 1973 that he heard Schneider and Rosset had seen the production and that it was "quite scandalously bad by all accounts" (BSC2). On 13 February Schneider replied to Beckett in a lengthy letter detailing the production for him. In his opening remarks, Schneider talked about how "shocked" he and Rosset were "to see [such a] self-indulgent travesty, determined to be 'different' for the sake of being different." Schneider approached Gregory about the production after he saw it; he wrote in the letter Gregory's defense: "he said this was the way he saw the play; he was free-ing it from a rigid adherence to your directions [...] he is trying to follow in Peter Brook's footsteps as experimenter and guru" (BSC1). Immediately in his letter Schneider sets up the paradigm that I have been discussing: Gregory saw the production as being under the stranglehold of Beckett's direction (in both senses of the word, his stage directions and his direction of the play). His was a choice of either honoring that or doing away with it altogether.[10] Schneider continued with a discussion about how some New York critics felt that Schneider had "mesmerized Beckett into some sort of permanent possession of his works." It is clear that these critics had been personally attacking Schneider and rooting for other directors to claim Beckett for themselves. Schneider reported that the critic Martin Gottfried had been particularly vindictive towards him.

However, even Gottfried's opposition to Schneider could not prevent him from writing a scathing review of the production, entitled "*'Endgame'*: A Travesty." In it, Gottfried maintained that the disservice Gregory did to the play was all the more regrettable because "it is desperately important to break Alan Schneider's hammerjack [sic] on staging Beckett and this will only strengthen it" (Harmon 303).[11] Other critics besides Gottfried got involved in taking sides in what increasingly seems like a Schneider-versus-Gregory battle. As Schneider continued in the same letter, he even speculated that Gregory influenced Clive Barnes at *The New York Times* to write a "defensive" and "inaccurate" review of the play.

Upon receiving accounts of the production, Beckett had to make a choice. Schneider and Rosset both wanted to know if he wished them to intervene on his behalf. Beckett wrote to Rosset from Ussy on 13 February 1973:

> Judging from these and from what I gathered on the phone this production seems quite inacceptable. [sic] And yet, I simply do not feel justified at this distance, with nothing more to go on, not having myself seen a performance, in asking that steps be taken to have it stopped. [...]
>
> Even in the hypothesis of a personal request from me to Gregory have we not to consider the amount of work, however misguided that has gone into this production and the situation of the actors?
>
> This kind of massacre and abuse of directorial function is happening the whole time all over the place. I have simply been spared it in N.Y. thanks to Alan.
>
> The best I can suggest is that we ensure a strictly limited series of performances at NYU at the conclusion of which the rights revert to us and this production lapses. Anymore drastic procedure seems to be unadvisable.[12]

Rosset and Schneider had both been gunning for a legal intervention, but Beckett's response from Paris was no. His reaction, though obviously distressed that someone has done this to his work, is rational and considerate. The reasons he cited—that he did not personally see the production and that the actors had put a lot of effort into the production—were enough to him to prevent him from getting involved.

For at least some period of time in the seventies, Beckett refused to get involved in halting any licensed productions on aesthetic grounds. His preferred approach was to review the initial licensing request and deny rights to a production that proposed substantial deviations from his script. Once licensed, Beckett felt it inappropriate to monitor the production further and preferred to distance himself from productions he was not directly overseeing, particularly since he found most artistic changes grievous. As Deirdre Bair noted in her biography, Beckett once wrote to Rosset: "he would not interfere with productions of his plays on aesthetic grounds even if he had the right to do so, because once started, there would be no end" (Bair 634). Since Bair's biography was completed in 1977, it is obvious that Beckett changed course on this policy in the last decade of his life. What strikes me as significant, however, is that Beckett felt that once he got involved in stopping productions, "there would be no end," a comment that now sounds prophetic.

Gregory's production was allowed to continue its New York run. Beckett's course of action was to allow the cast to finish out its run and then see that the contract not be renewed for the production to travel elsewhere. He also wrote in this letter on 20 February 1973: "My work is not holy writ but this production sounds truly revolting and damaging to the play" (BSC2). Beckett's reactions to this production cast him in a positive light, one at odds with the familiar stereotypes against him as inflexible. Rather, he was generous and permissive.

The matter, however, was not closed in February 1973. Gregory, as he had done several years earlier with *Alice*, had planned on taking his *Endgame* to Europe following its New York performances. At the same time that his rights to the play were cancelled, he was in France trying to obtain permission to bring his production to the Bordeaux Theater Festival, which was under the auspices of Madeleine Renaud in Paris. Schneider and Beckett continued to correspond about the matter throughout the year. On 11 July Schneider wrote: "News here is that Gregory has been trying like mad to reach you to get permission for French tour" (BSC1). Beckett replied on 17 July that there had been no sign of Gregory, "thank God" (BSC2). However, Beckett did not directly prevent Renaud from accepting Gregory's production into her festival. As he wrote in a letter to Rosset earlier in the same week (11 July):

> The only sign of Gregory here so far came through Madeleine Renaud to whom he proposed his ENDGAME for a theater festival in which she has a say. She consulted me and I told her what I had heard about the production, leaving her free to accept or decline as she pleased. She declined.

> No application for permission has been made here so far either to
> the Societé des Auteurs, Lindon or myself and I hope none will be. Frankly
> I don't know what the answers should be. I only know I'll regret it in either
> case. (BSC2; The Estate of Samuel Beckett)

What is surprising about this letter is not that Beckett intervened with Renaud (as one would expect), but that he left the matter in her hands. Even more unexpected is that he expressed doubt and remorse about the entire situation. Again his responses defy the prevailing image of him. Even after intervening in New York, Beckett was still not sure that he had the prerogative to have done so. As wrong and misguided as he felt Gregory had been, Beckett was still reluctant to insist that he deserved final say over someone else's artistic creation.

Gregory never did perform *Endgame* in France; as Bair notes, Beckett's influence was such that even without his explicitly preventing it, no one would accept his production for performance. I asked Gregory what he remembered of these occurrences, but his own memory of the events, now thirty years later, is vague. He did recall that it was Schneider who had first told Beckett of the production. As he put it, Schneider called the production "obscene" and asked Beckett to stop it. Gregory also told me that he wrote to Beckett directly, sending him and his wife tickets to the production so he could judge for himself whether or not it should be closed. Beckett never came and the production was never stopped, he told me. When prompted, Gregory did remember that the Beckett estate (as he referred to it) made it difficult for the group to travel to Europe, although he did not offer, and perhaps does not remember, further details.

This production was a seminal moment for Beckett: his first real introduction to a problem that would plague him for the rest of his life and with increasing frequency—the radicalization of his text in performance. Gregory's transgressions and Beckett's response now serve as prologue to the events of December 1984 in Cambridge, Massachusetts.

In a press brochure publicizing the American Repertory Theater's upcoming sixth season, the notice for *Endgame* read: "we are delighted to present Beckett's most timely play directed by one of his foremost American interpreters, JoAnne Akalaitis, with a specially commissioned score by the internationally celebrated composer, Phillip Glass."[13] It is interesting to note that the brochure labels

Akalaitis as one of Beckett's "foremost American interpreters" when she had only officially directed one Beckett play (an adaptation of his radio piece, *Cascando*), and Beckett had not approved of it. Perhaps the ART marketing arm was trying to sell her as part of a larger group, Mabou Mines. Robert Orchard, executive director of the ART, mentioned in an interview why Akalaitis was hired: "She was a founding member of Mabou Mines, which had done a lot of work with Beckett; it's not that this was unfamiliar territory for her so we thought that she would bring a kind of fresh vision to the piece."[14]

The ART had made its reputation on the basis of its bold directing and lavish design, often bringing in guest directors outside the mainstream. Orchard reinforced this in describing why Akalaitis was chosen for the project:

> We knew that she would bring an interpretive perspective on it that would be interesting and we wanted her to provide us with that. We knew what we were getting into. JoAnne Akalaitis is not a four-square, suburban director; she's a very provocative figure in the theater world, and I mean that in the most positive sense. So, we expected we'd get a glimpse of this play in a way that perhaps hadn't been done before and would give us [...] another perspective on it, another point of view.

What is interesting if not surprising about Orchard's statement is that it confirms that the ART was interested from the beginning in mounting a significant challenge to the play's traditional interpretation. Akalaitis, in an interview, concurred with Orchard's statement: "After a play has been done a long time, it really is the job of directors and designers to figure out how to wake it up. We were not there to buy the Samuel French edition of the play. We were there to react to the script."[15]

Akalaitis has said of her own directing philosophy that it is the director's responsibility to be politically aware, without being overtly propagandistic. In an interview given shortly before she came to the ART, she said: "I do feel that theater artists have a special responsibility at least to try to put work into some kind of political or social context" (Kalb 1984, 9). She rode the subway with her designer, Douglas Stein, for inspiration. The final set was comprised partly of found objects; they even frequented the Boston transit junkyard to scavenge pieces of it.[16] The end result, by most accounts, was a striking image. One reviewer described it thus:

> A wrecked subway car rests on its rusted shocks. Glaring light bulbs dangle
> from an unseen height. Seven oil drums are off to one side. The pitted
> cement floor is awash. Fixed ladders lead up steep walls. A plastic sheet
> hides a mound of debris center stage. (Kelly D:68)

Clearly the ruins on the set suggested a nuclear explosion, fire or some
other similar calamity. Akalaitis confirmed for me that the setting was
intentionally post-nuclear. In fact the imposition of this concept onto
the production stands as the boldest directorial decision she made with
the show.

Other aspects of the design picked up on the theme of urban
devastation. The costumes, again encompassing many found items,
were designed to make the characters look disheveled and homeless.
Akalaitis wanted them to look like real people, just as she wanted the
set to look like a real place. She described sitting in a New York City
restaurant and looking out at the passersby:

> My god, look at how all these people are dressed! This is how we want the
> people in *Endgame* to look [...] It just seemed quite wonderful to me that
> Hamm and Clov are real people, and not European, French actors from
> 1955. They belong in 1985. (Kalb 1989, 171)

In this remark, Akalaitis directly references the *Endgame* première of
Blin in Paris and reveals a desire to break free from the Blin-
Schneider mold by which so many directors clearly felt constrained.
She wanted to offer her audiences something fresh and contemporary,
yet something that was still true to the spirit and essence of the play.

Early in December 1984, Rosset got word about the ART
production and telephoned Beckett straight away, leaving the
following message:

> An inform that Brustein [then Artistic Director (and co-founder) of the
> ART] with Boston Rep Company [sic] plans producing *Endgame* as taken
> place [sic] in subway station and costuming Hamm and Clov as black
> Rastafarian and narcotics dealer. If this is true what do you wish me to do?
> Await word. Love, Barney. (BRP-BColl13)

So much of what follows this phone call is based on
misunderstanding, and this first message sets the tone. Rosset is
clearly misconstruing the ART design, or at the very least
exaggerating it, and this is even more bewildering since he had not

himself seen the production. Who his informant was is unclear, but it was clearly not a neutral party.

Beckett responded immediately with the insistence that Rosset try to stop the production, which was scheduled to open Wednesday, 12 December. On the previous Thursday, Orchard received a phone call from Samuel French inquiring about the alleged changes. He was surprised, since one of the objections was the Glass score, which had been mentioned in a letter to Samuel French back in May and had just been reported in a 22 October *New York Times* article profiling the production.[17] This was the first sign of trouble that the ART was aware of, less than a week before opening.

The following day, Friday, 7 December, there was a flurry of activity. Rosset called Orchard and asked him to stop the production. A *New York Times* reporter called Brustein about a telegraph from Rosset asking him to stop the production, although Brustein had not yet even seen any such telegram. The telegram read: "Samuel Beckett refuses permission for production of *Endgame* with any changes in scenery, costume or sound not described in text."[18] Meanwhile, a second telegram was sent to either Orchard or Brustein, this one from Samuel French with the demand: "cease and desist with your production of *Endgame*."[19]

Brustein, clearly frustrated with the indirect attack coming through the *Times* reporter, fired back an angry telegram to Rosset:

> I do not normally respond to messages which are delivered to the press before I've received them, but I feel compelled to remind you that our production of *Endgame* has been authorized by Samuel French, I firmly believe that it is faithful to the text and spirit of the play. I am further startled that anyone, particularly a publisher with your experience of censorship, would attempt to interfere with our interpretation of the play or inhibit its performance. We hope that Mr. Beckett and you will take the opportunity in the coming months to actually see the production.[20]

Endgame was now in preview performances, and Brustein and Orchard were still bewildered as to how this attack could come before anyone objecting had even seen the production. Over the weekend, in an attempt to avoid any further legal snares, the ART furnished complimentary tickets to Fred Jordan of Grove Press and Jack Garfein, who was then producing his own New York production of *Endgame*, who were sent to evaluate the production on Rosset and Beckett's behalf.[21] Garfein was repeatedly criticized for conflict of

interest, and many felt that he could not possibly have offered Rosset
or Beckett an unbiased account of the ART's production.

On Monday, 10 December, Brustein was called again by a
reporter, this time Jeff McLaughlin of *The Boston Globe*. Rosset had
contacted him with a letter denouncing the production, which he then
proceeded to read to Brustein over the phone to get his reaction. The
letter had not yet been mailed to Brustein, but clearly both sides were
now fully manipulating the press to fan the flames of the controversy.
The particularly vicious letter from Rosset was published in abridged
format in McLaughlin's article on Wednesday, 12 December. The
entire letter, dated 10 December, eventually made its way to Brustein
and contained the following complaints, first about the changed
setting:

> We are given parameters of its world [*Endgame*], its movement, its actors
> and its scenery. Everything is set in place for total concentration [...]
> absolutely mapped out by its author (whom you say you "revere") to be a
> spare, integrated whole, and you tore it apart to embellish it with your own
> ideas.

Next the letter criticizes the casting: "two of the actors are
purposefully black." The letter also mentions the objection to Glass's
score. Finally, it concludes with a scathing denouncement of the
production, labeling it insensitive and "resulting in bowdlerization and
puerile over-simplification" (BRP-BColl13). This was possibly the
first time Brustein had all of the objections together: that of the set,
casting and use of music. The letter was written by Rosset, but it is
clear both from things Beckett said subsequently, and from letters he
wrote, that Rosset was speaking for him. Obviously, given the tone of
the letter, the conflict would not be settled without legal intervention.

Among the most puzzling of Beckett's complaints was his
objection to the casting. His opponents in the aftermath certainly used
it as a means to portray him as racist, and people were sufficiently
offended to the point that the Actors Equity Union released a
statement publicly denouncing him for it. However, this is an unfair
label; back in 1957 Beckett was thrilled when an all-black cast of
Waiting for Godot made it to Broadway, and was deeply saddened
when it closed after a few performances, a commercial failure
(Knowlson 389). Furthermore, for decades during apartheid in South
Africa, Beckett refused to grant licenses for his work to be performed

in any theaters that permitted racial segregation (Knowlson 561). His objection to this production was, he claimed, because the mixed-race cast introduced the idea of miscegenation, which he felt added a complicated overtone that he did not intend. However, this feels to me like a paltry justification. It has always seemed that the interracial casting complaint was added in a desperate and irrational manner to try and bolster the charges against the production. Its placement among the other objections never really fit and seemed misguided from the beginning.

By Tuesday, 11 December, only one day before the opening night, lawyers for each side got involved and further telegrams were exchanged. Rosset called McLaughlin, who was by now being used as a pawn between the two parties, and explained that he talked to Beckett, who was very upset, saying: "I might add that this was the angriest I had ever heard Beckett in the more than thirty years I have known him" (BRP-BColl13). That day, Martin Garbus, lawyer for Grove Press and Beckett, sent a telegram to Orchard notifying him of official legal intervention and ordering him to stop the production:

> Samuel Beckett has directed us to stop your production of *Endgame*. Your play is not Beckett's. It distorts the meaning of the play. After having had your production described to him, Samuel Beckett says "this has nothing to do with my play. You cannot do this. It should be stopped." Accordingly, we insist that you do not go ahead with the present production. If you fail to advise us that you are stopping your present production, we shall be compelled to immediately take legal action, including claims for copyright violation, Lanham Act violations and other violations of law. (BRP-BColl13)

At this time Garbus was preparing an order to show cause for a preliminary injunction and a temporary restraining order based on three charges: 1. copyright infringement,[22] 2. claim under the Lanham act,[23] and 3. claim for breach of contract.[24]

On 11 December, Garbus and ART counsel James Sharaf talked all evening and into the early morning to reach a settlement. The parties were able to solve the dispute without going to trial.[25] The play opened without any court proceedings, and the ART agreed to publish a program insert with statements from Rosset and Beckett denouncing the production, as well as a statement from Brustein defending it. The program insert, which was stapled to the already-printed program, included a photocopy of the first page of the Grove

Press edition of *Endgame*, with Beckett's stage directions. This page details the setting (bare interior, grey light, etc.) as well as the long paragraph of pantomime instructions for Clov. Next to the copied stage directions was this statement by Beckett:

> Any production of *Endgame* which ignores my stage directions is completely unacceptable to me. My play requires an empty room and two small windows. The American Repertory Theater production which dismisses my directions is a complete parody of the play as conceived by me. Anybody who cares for the work couldn't fail to be disgusted by this.[26]

Below this was Rosset's Grove Press statement, of which I will include only an excerpt:

> In Beckett's plays the set, the movements of the actors, the silences specified in the text, the lighting and the costumes are as important as the words spoken by the actors. In the author's judgment—and ours—this production makes a travesty of his conception. A living author of Beckett's stature should have the right to protect himself from what he perceives to be a gross distortion of his work. We deplore the refusal of the American Repertory Theater to accede to Beckett's wishes to remove his name from this production, indicate in some way that this staging is merely an adaptation, or stop it entirely.

Clearly Rosset and Beckett felt that the change of setting was so significant it was paramount to an adaptation of the text. Orchard disagreed. When asked about this point, he contended that the ART never seriously considered agreeing to call the production an adaptation; they felt they were "doing the play."[27]

Brustein's longer response in the program mentioned several past productions of *Endgame* that deviated from the stage directions with no reciprocal response from Beckett's agents. These included both the Gregory production and a 1983 Belgium production that set the play in a warehouse flooded with 8,000 square feet of water. (Brustein was probably unaware at that time of Beckett's private response to Gregory's work and of the fact that Beckett had intervened, insofar as the production was not allowed to travel beyond its initial NYU run. What Brustein was referring to in that case was the fact that there was no public protest from Beckett, Rosset or French.) Brustein's response ended with the following:

> Like all great works of theatrical art, the play is open to many approaches, and each new production uncorks new meanings. To threaten any deviations

from a purist rendering of this or any other play—to insist on strict adherence to each parenthesis of the published text—not only robs collaborating artists of their interpretive freedom but threatens to turn the theater into a waxworks. Mr. Beckett's agents do no service either to theatrical art or to the great artist they represent by pursing such rigorous controls.[28]

Once this compromise was reached, the play went on to enjoy an uneventful run; audiences responded well to the performances and the controversy began to fade into the background. The agreement the two parties came to had less to do with artistic matters and more to do with the reluctance of both Grove Press and the ART to pay for a trial which would have been both costly and prolonged (Kalb 1989, 79).

Akalaitis, for her part, remained largely silent during the controversy. She was not involved in any of the legal proceedings and did not make public statements at the time. As Orchard recalls, there was nothing she could do in the situation; the production was already up and running (in preview performances) and there was no way it could be substantially changed. She has since given two public interviews on the subject but has otherwise avoided discussing it. A recently published book by Deborah Savietz that examines her entire directing career does not even mention the incident. When I asked Akalaitis why she was noticeably absent from the controversy, she mentioned that the theater was the producer, not she, and therefore it was not her place to get involved in the dispute. Interestingly, she remarked that she would not have been against a trial. She told me: "I didn't think that a trial would be a bad thing at all. I think it could have been interesting, and brought things to light. But it was not for me to decide."[29]

In the aftermath of these events, partly as a result of growing frustration over the past decade since Gregory's production, Beckett increased his control over his work. A letter from Garbus to Samuel French less than two weeks after the ART *Endgame* opened included instructions to add the following clause to all Beckett productions:

There shall be no additions, omissions, or alterations of any kind or nature in the manuscript or presentation of the play as indicated in the acting edition supplied hereunder: without limiting the foregoing: all stage directions indicated therein shall be followed without any such additions, omissions or alterations. No music, special effects or other supplements shall be added to the presentation of the play without prior written consent.[30]

This remains true today, as all contracts handled through the Beckett estate still contain this rider to standard-issue Samuel French contracts.

Beckett also wrote to Rosset on 22 December to thank him for his efforts throughout the ordeal:

> Your admirable letter to Brustein moved me greatly.
> Thanks from the heart for your heroic action in defense of my work.
> Thanks also to Fred for his horrific account of that Endcircus.
> Love to you all and again my deep gratitude. (BRP-BColl14; The Estate of Samuel Beckett)

The events of 1984 are remembered today in the theater world as both bizarre and something of an aberration. Orchard called it a "chilling" experience that shocked many artists over what had historically been considered the "interpretive rights of directors and institutions." He emphasized how irrational the whole response was, and his own speculations are that Beckett was sorely misled and misinformed as to the nature of the ART production. (For example, he thinks Beckett may have been told that the play was made into a musical, which it was not, or that subway trains were running in and out of the set throughout the performance.) What were the reasons for this irrational response?

1984 had been a difficult year for Beckett personally. He suffered the loss of his two most trusted directors just months apart: Roger Blin in January and Schneider in May. Schneider's life was abruptly cut short when he was struck and killed by a motorcyclist while crossing the road in London. Articles filled major newspapers, memorializing Schneider. A *Washington Post* tribute that focused on his relationship with Beckett quoted Schneider as having said: "Sam is the only man outside my immediate family that I really love" (qtd in Richards B:1). Just over three months earlier, Roger Blin had passed away; Beckett attended his funeral in Paris. Although Beckett was not as close to Blin as he was to Schneider, he still had a lot of fondness for the man who was the first person ever to bring his plays to life (Knowlson 611). Now Beckett, himself seventy-eight and in declining health, had lost both of the most significant directors of his work—one of them a very close friend.

Each loss had been devastating for Beckett personally and that spilled over into his professional dealings. Given how tirelessly Schneider worked to protect Beckett's plays in America, he must have felt particularly vulnerable now that Schneider was gone. I can only imagine that, had he lived, it would have been Schneider who came to Boston to see the ART production in previews and who would have negotiated how Beckett responded, as he had done with Gregory in 1973. As it was, the ART dedicated this production to Schneider, something that Beckett took only as an insult. Two years after the event, Jonathan Kalb spoke with him about it:

> His thoughts presently moved on to the idea of directors preferring to work with dead authors. 'But I'm not dead yet,' he said. 'Not quite. I'm a dying author, certainly.' I then asked him why it was less important to respect an author's text after he's dead, and he answered, 'Well, just because then you can't hurt his feelings.' (Kalb 1989, 78-79)

This was a telling statement from a man who thought of *Endgame* as the favorite of his plays—or the "play he disliked the least" (McMillan and Fehsenfeld 163). When he dedicated it to Roger Blin, it was with this inscription: "For you, if you really want it, but only if you really want it. Because it really has meaning, the others are only everyday" (Bair 479). Considering Beckett's fondness for this work, and his pain over Schneider's death, it is easy to understand his very personal response to the ART's production.

Beckett had clearly come to increasingly feel, since the early seventies, that directors felt entitled to disregard his writing, his intent and even his feelings, to do with a script what they pleased.[31] *Endgame* in particular seems to have been used for a number of highly conceptual productions, having been staged in a playpen, a boxing ring, and inside a model "skull" (Bair 468),[32] in addition to the chicken-wire cage and ruined subway station of the two productions detailed here. He said in 1986: "I detest this modern school of directing. To these directors the text is just a pretext for their own ingenuity" (Kalb 1989, 71). However, it is clear from both the unusual circumstances surrounding the ART production for Beckett, and from his response to Gregory's production, that his reaction in 1984 was not representative of his usual approach when dealing with directors. The image of him as recalcitrant playwright is one formed mostly on the basis of the last five years of his life and cannot fairly be considered representative of his thirty-five year career as a professional playwright and artist.

Natka Bianchini, Tufts University

Notes

[1] Gussow implied that Beckett had always interceded when he felt his work was being violated.

[2] Mis-marketed as the "laugh *sensation* of two continents," the American première of *Waiting for Godot* is one of the biggest opening-night flops in recent theater history. Intended as a pre-Broadway try-out, the production baffled Miami audiences and critics alike and closed after a few weeks. The producer, Michael Myerberg, later assembled a mostly new cast and a new director for the Broadway première some four months later. The problems with the production seemed to center on clashes between Bert Lahr, who was playing Estragon, and Schneider.

[3] Blin directed the world première of *Waiting for Godot* (*En attendant Godot*) in Paris and was among Beckett's closest European directors and collaborators.

[4] Schneider to Beckett, 8 November 1957, Beckett/Schneider Correspondence, Box 1, Burns Library Special Collections, Boston College. Subsequent items from the correspondence will be noted in the text as: (BSC2) for items in the Beckett/Schneider Correspondence, Box 2; (BSC3) for items in Box 3.

[5] Personal interview with the author, December 10, 2003.

[6] *Endgame* Playbill, 1958, *Endgame* File, Harvard Theater Collection, Harvard University.

[7] Personal interview with the author, January 31, 2004. Subsequent quotations from Gregory are taken from this interview.

[8] ART Promptbook, 1984, American Repertory Theater Papers, Harvard Theater Collection, Harvard University (hereafter ARTP).

[9] His only trip was in the summer of 1964 when he oversaw Schneider's direction of his short cinema piece, *Film*, with Buster Keaton.

[10] Beckett first directed *Endgame* in Germany in 1967 and left detailed records of his work on that production. It was his first experience directing his own work.

[11] I first saw Gottfried's review at the Billy Rose Theater Collection, but it was here that Harmon connects the review to Schneider's mentioning of Gottfried in his letter.

[12] Beckett to Rosset, 13 February 1973, Barney Rosset Papers, Beckett Collection, Box 3, Burns Library Special Collections, Boston College. The Estate of Samuel Beckett. Subsequent items from the correspondence will be noted in the text as: (BRP-BColl3) for items in the Barney Rosset Papers, Beckett Collection, Box 3; (BRP-BColl13) for items in Box 13; (BRP-BColl14) for items in Box 14.

[13] ART Season Brochure, 1984-1985 (ARTP).

[14] Personal interview with the author, December 9, 2003. Subsequent quotations from Orchard are taken from this interview.

[15] Personal interview with the author, January 25, 2004. Subsequent quotations from Akalaitis are taken from this interview unless otherwise stated.

[16] The ART News, Volume 5, November 1984 (BRP-BColl14).

[17] ART Internal Memorandum to Advisory Board, 14 December 1984 (ARTP).

[18] Western Union Telegram Rosset to Brustein, 7 December 1984 (ARTP).

[19] Telegram Samuel French to Brustein and/or Orchard, 7 December, 1984 (BRP-BColl13).

[20] Western Union Mailgram Brustein to Rosset, 7 December 1984 (ARTP).

[21] ART Internal Memorandum to Advisory Board, 14 December 1984 (ARTP).

[22] Garbus argued that by changing the setting and adding music, the ART had violated Beckett's copyright as sole proprietor of his work, under the 1856 copyright law.

[23] The federal Lanham Act has to do with "false designations of origin" and protects playwrights and authors from misrepresentation of their work resulting from changes, additions or deletions.

[24] Garbus, "Playwright vs. Director" (BRP-BColl13). To summarize Garbus' claim regarding breach of contract, the ART had not paid a $500 advance to Samuel French one week prior to opening night, a stipulation of their contract. Orchard explained in our interview that, while Samuel French contracts do contain the $500 advance clause, it is not something they enforce with large repertory theaters such as the ART and that the ART has never, on any production before or since, paid the advance.

[25] ART Internal Memorandum to Advisory Board, 14 December 1984 (ARTP).

[26] *Endgame* Program, ART,1984 (ARTP). The Estate of Samuel Beckett.

[27] Personal interview with the author, December 9, 2003.

[28] *Endgame* Program, ART, 1984 (ARTP).

[29] Personal interview with the author, January 25, 2004.

[30] Garbus to M. Abbott Van Nostrand, Samuel French, Inc., 21 December 1984 (BRP-BColl14).

[31] In a letter to Beckett on 31 July 1973, Schneider mentioned plans for a production of an all-female *Godot* to which Beckett refused permission. "Seems as though everyone here is always looking for a 'gimmick' instead of sticking to the text of something," Schneider wrote, underscoring how prevalent Gregory-type productions were in New York at the time (BSC1).

[32] Bair does not refer to the place and date of these productions.

Bibliography

American Repertory Theater Papers, 1984-1985, Harvard Theater Collection, Harvard University.

Atkinson, Brooks. 'The Theater: Beckett's *Endgame*' in *The New York Times* (29 January 1958). 1957-1958 New York Stage Reviews, Billy Rose Theater Collection, Lincoln Center.

Bair, Deirdre. *Samuel Beckett, A Biography*. New York: Harcourt Brace Jovanovich, 1978.

Barnes, Clive. 'The Theater: *"Endgame"* Innovative Andre Gregory's Work Staged in Setting of a University Attic' in *The New York Times* (8 February 1973). *Endgame* Clippings File, Harvard Theater Collection, Harvard University.

Bolton, Whitney. '*Endgame* Crawls with Symbolism' in *The New York Morning Telegraph* (30 January 1958). 1957-1958 New York Stage Reviews, Billy Rose Theater Collection, Lincoln Center.

Endgame, ART Program, 1984, American Repertory Theater Papers. Harvard Theater Collection, Harvard University.

Endgame, ART Promptbook, 1984. American Repertory Theater Papers. Harvard Theater Collection, Harvard University.

Endgame, Cherry Lane Theater Playbill, 1958. Harvard Theater Collection, Harvard University.

Gussow, Mel. 'Enter Fearless Director, Pursued by Playwright' in *The New York Times* (3 January, 1985): Sec. C:14

—. 'Gregory Play Group Seeking New Areas' in *The New York Times* (4 May 1971). Manhattan Project Clippings File, Billy Rose Theater Collection, Lincoln Center.

Gottfried, Martin. '*Endgame*, A Travesty' in *Women's Wear Daily* (9 February 1973). 1972- 1973 New York Stage Reviews, Billy Rose Theater Collection, Lincoln Center.

Harmon, Maurice, ed. *No Author Better Served: The Correspondence of Samuel Beckett and Alan Schneider*. Cambridge, MA: Harvard University Press, 1998.

Kalb, Jonathan. *Beckett in Performance*. Cambridge: Cambridge University Press, 1989.

—. 'JoAnne Akalaitis, an Interview' in *Theater* 15 (1984): 6-13.

Kelly, Kevin. '*Endgame* Takes its Course' in *The Boston Globe* (13 December 1984): Sec. D:68. *Endgame* Clippings File, Harvard Theater Collection, Harvard University.

Kerr, Walter. 'Oh Beckett, Poor Beckett' in *The New York Times* (11 February 1973): Sec. D:20. 1972-1973 New York Stage Reviews, Billy Rose Theater Collection, Lincoln Center.

Knowlson, James. *Damned to Fame, The Life of Samuel Beckett*. New York: Simon and Schuster, 1996.

McClain, John. 'Beckett Fails in *"Endgame"*' in *The New York Journal* (29 January 1958). 1957-1958 New York Stage Reviews, Billy Rose Theater Collection, Lincoln Center.

McMillan, Dougald and Martha Fehsenfeld. *Beckett in the Theater: The Author as Practical Playwright and Director.* London: John Calder, 1988.

Richards, David. 'Staging the Inner life, Director Alan Schneider and His Theater of Humanity' in *The Washington Post* (4 May 1984): Sec. B:1. Alan Schneider Clippings File, Harvard Theater Collection, Harvard University.

The Samuel Beckett Collection. Burns Library Special Collections, Boston College. (Beckett/Schneider Correspondence; Barney Rosset Papers)

Savietz, Deborah. *An Event In Space, JoAnne Akalaitis in Rehearsal.* Hanover, NH: Smith and Kraus, 2000.

Schechner, Richard. 'Reality is Not Enough. An Interview with Alan Schneider' in Rebecca Schneider and Gabrielle Cody eds. *Re-Direction, A Theoretical and Practical Guide.* London: Routledge, 2002. (73-83)

Schneider, Alan. *Entrances: An American Director's Journey.* New York: Proscenium, 1987.

Trans-cultural *Endgame/s*

Antonia Rodríguez-Gago

When directing *Endgame* in Berlin in 1967, Beckett said: " I don't claim my interpretation is the only correct one [...] it's possible to do the play quite differently, different music, movements, different rhythm; the kitchen can be differently located and so on," adding later that "each director will contribute his own music."[1] The cultural and theatrical modifications introduced in three Spanish productions of *Endgame* (*Final de Partida*) demonstrate the process of theatrical adaptation across cultures. Three Spanish stage directors—Julio Castronuovo (1980), Miguel Narros (1984) and Rodolfo Cortizo (2001)—have "contributed their own music" to the play. The directors have left their mark on staging, acting, setting, costumes and rhythm, while at the same time trying to grasp the basic dramatic situation of the original. They produce three different and interesting trans-cultural *Endgame/s*. The process of trans-culturalization performs the role played by culture in perceiving, translating and constructing reality. These three Spanish productions of *Endgame*, while sharing the theatrical characteristics of their own time and culture, still tried to be faithful to the aesthetics of the original play, hoping to achieve some of its effects, emotions and dramatic impact.

It is a well-known fact that, throughout history,

> the time-sharing of texts has been an important aspect of intercultural theater and, for a brief moment, each at a time, translators and other theater practitioners have occupied foreign texts as tenants. Some texts may have been expected to look as if nobody was visiting them or, even if somebody called, as if texts have been left untouched. Others have been allowed or even encouraged to bear the marks of the lodgers. (Aaltonen 9)

Although Aaltonen here is speaking of textual translation, her idea of translators occupying texts as lodgers, changing the aspect of the apartment they occupy according to their own style and taste, is useful when discussing theatrical adaptations of foreign plays. If dramatic translation always implies changes and all kinds of adaptations, this is more so when producing foreign plays. For theater is a multidisciplinary and collaborative art which includes many people with different techniques from different fields. Thus the changes effected by directors-lodgers "visiting" a given play will multiply. When staging a foreign play, directors have to deal with a different tradition and culture, different experiences and theatrical techniques, not to mention the different theatrical politics of the receiving country. Foreign drama is introduced into the repertoire of a given country for various reasons: the prestige of the plays, the taste of a given director, or the appeal of a certain author to contemporary audiences. Foreign plays are often used in production, not so much to present different issues contained in the original production, but more often to discuss domestic issues at a particular time. Stage productions often function as mirrors of the culture of a given period in a given country, and relate to the historical, cultural, experiential and even political situation of this country. Theater adaptations of foreign plays are always cultural hybrids, but the same could be said of plays produced in the original language at different times. Therefore one could argue that we have as many *Endgames* as there are theatrical productions of this play, for staging is always bound to include temporal and cultural changes—even when Beckett has done his best to clear the stage of any specific spatio-temporal details.

The most important changes effected in foreign productions of plays are not merely linguistic, that is, related to drama translation, but are related to the process of adapting paralinguistic, visual, kinetic and proxemic elements. Chief among these are acting and directing styles and techniques, which can vary sharply from country to country. "On a theater stage, culture affects every element of production" (Aaltonen 11), for as Eugenio Barba has remarked, "theater is made up of traditions, conventions, institutions and habits that have permanence in time" (qtd in Pavis 4). One always expects changes in different theater productions at different times. However these changes are more revealing in foreign productions, even when a given director tries to be as respectful as possible to the original work and tries to act as an interpreter of the author's intentions. Taking into account that since the 1960s and 1970s stage directors have acted more as co-authors of the plays they direct than as interpreters, directorial marks are quite evident in most productions and these marks are examples of how intercultural theater works.

A critical question here—given that time, cultural differences and theatrical conventions of a particular country always affect theatrical production—is at what point will one strong production of *Endgame*, with many intercultural changes and directorial interferences, seriously damage the original conception of the play? Cultural and directorial interference particularly affect Beckett's plays, whose *mise-en-scène* is carefully created in the texts themselves, and is meticulously detailed by Beckett as director in his *Theatrical Notebooks*. It is well known that in Beckett's theater "it is the shape that matters" and that form and content are inextricably related. Therefore all the paralinguistic elements—setting, movement, gesture, stillness, sound, silence, light and darkness—form the pattern of his plays, and are as essential to the play's meaning, sometimes even more so, than the words themselves. Theatrical elements related to the rhythm and to the visual aspects of production—echoes and repetitions of gestures and sounds—are essential to Beckett's dramatic style. Theater directors who choose to ignore or substantially change these paralinguistic elements risk failure, though of course they should be free to do so. Beckett himself, as director, introduced changes in his own productions: there is not really only one way of doing Beckett "as Beckett wanted," a much repeated line among theater critics. Who knows what Beckett wanted? Directorial freedom is vital, even when misconceived.

Before analyzing the directorial marks left by three Spanish directors in their productions of *Endgame,* I would like to clarify the vague term "trans-cultural." Trans-cultural theater not only refers to going "beyond the particular cultures on behalf of a universality of the human condition" (Aaltonen 13), but more specifically refers to *the journey* which takes place between two different cultures, and the variety of changes involved during this process. During this journey one moves from one particular culture to another, before locating (wherever this might be possible) the latent common values probably shared by the original and the target cultures. There is something in *Endgame* which makes it excellent trans-cultural theater in the sense Aaltonen uses this term, but especially, as Julie Campbell argues, in the sense of subverting a familiar culture, or familiar ideas about this culture. "The play," Campbell says, "works against the consensus and the reassurance that can result from the recourse to shared cultural associations" (128). It is in this sense that *Endgame* can be called trans-cultural, for its poetic and visually stunning central image—of people trapped in an extreme situation—seems to bear universal echoes beyond the particular original culture. In this play, Beckett was perhaps searching for what "connects people beyond and beneath ethnological and individual differences" (Pavis 6)[2] and gives an image of men/women as prisoners of time and space: "the Proustian vision" he repeats again and again in all his plays. Three Spanish directors of *Endgame* have travelled from the play's original culture to their own culture, integrating in their journey the artistic, cultural and even political discourses of their time.

Ever since the first performance of *Waiting for Godot* (*Esperando a Godot*) in 1955, Spanish stage directors have considered Beckett a great theater innovator and a "hard realist." His plays have often been taken as oblique comments on contemporary Spanish reality and related to "the political climate of the moment when they were produced" (Rodríguez-Gago 141).[3] Early critics' response to Beckett's plays show how his theater was received in Spain and how widely their various interpretations contrasted. Conservative critics rejected the plays for political, or moral, rather than for aesthetic reasons. The kind of critical attack or praise of a given play can offer a glimpse of the production in question. One conservative critic, for instance, described the première of *Esperando a Godot* as a kind of "Bolero de Ravel" of the theater, full of unnecessary details of repulsive crude realism (174). It would seem as if Spanish audiences of the time had to be warned, or protected, against this kind of "repulsive, crude realism," although the musical comparison is quite to the point. Only two years later a more perceptive critic praised *Godot* for its poetry and its "profound realism."

When the first number of the influential theater magazine *Primer Acto* appeared in 1957 it included a translation of *Waiting for Godot,* together with one of the best early articles on this play, 'Siete notas sobre *Esperando a Godot*,' written by the dramatist Alfonso Sastre. In this article, Sastre considers the play a modern tragicomedy and emphasizes the play's "profound realism," differentiating Beckett's kind of realism from Ibsen's naturalism.

For Sastre *Waiting for Godot* shows "not a photographic but a radiographic representation of reality" (qtd in Cohn 101-106). This early article had a considerable influence on the reception of subsequent productions of Beckett's plays in Spain, especially during the dark years of the fascist regime in the 1960s and 1970s when Beckett's theater was only admired by a minority of dramatists and critics. It was rejected openly by the majority of official critics on the main charges of "bad taste and atheism" from which Spanish audiences of the time had to be protected. A few more examples will illustrate the strong socio-religious and political bias of drama criticism at this time.

If *Waiting for Godot* was to be received by the official critics with mocking irony, the première of *Final de partida*—produced in Madrid on 1 June 1958 by Josefina Sánchez Pedreño's group "Dido Pequeño Teatro"—was initially received with open hostility. Most reviews were negative. Alfredo Marquerie, a well known conservative critic of the newspaper *ABC*, attacked the author's construction of character and the negative message of the play, saying that "its characters are nothing, less than nothing [...] projects, sketches, outlines of creatures who have not developed from their embryonic state" and that "the play was destructive and repulsive." "Official" reviews of *Krapp's Last Tape* were even worse. Again Marquerie wrote: "This play is a joke in a very bad taste, to provoke disgust and nausea is one of the aims of the so called 'theater of shock,' people who think this can be called art are really wrong." He did not attack Beckett alone, but Ionesco, Genet, Adamov and many other non-realistic dramatists of the time for similar reasons. Writing about the same play, Gómez Picazo emphasizes the religious bias: "it is an atheistic and immoral play [...] with no value whatsoever in our world, which still believes in higher values. The actor Italo Ricardi, God forgive him!" It is worth taking into account that the "higher values" mentioned here were those of the fascist regime in government at the time. There were a few exceptions of more perceptive theatrical criticism. García Pavón, a dramatist and critic, wrote about the same production of *Krapp's Last Tape*: "It is impossible to stage more economically and with such dramatic intensity, the tragedy of a man who suddenly sees frustration pouring upon him." Enrique Llovet wrote: "what is fantastic about this play is Beckett's determination to place us inside a man [...] he wants to shake up the established order and he achieves it" (qtd in

Rodríguez-Gago 146).

    This passionate criticism, both for and against, changed a little when Beckett was awarded the Nobel Prize in 1969, but the effect of "canonizing" Beckett also affected Spanish theater directors who, in the 1970s, approached his plays with a certain "seriousness," solemnity and reverence. As Lefevere pointed out, "writers and their work are translated differently when they are considered 'classics,' when their work is recognized as 'cultural capital,' and when they are not" (Bassnett and Lefevere 109). The same could be said of theater productions. During the 1970s some Spanish directors cut most of the comedy from Beckett's plays and stressed their darker aspects: by unnecessarily elongating their playing time, an atmosphere of "seriousness," heaviness and boredom was conferred on these productions, which worked against the plays themselves. This is not the case with the three Spanish directors of *Final de partida* discussed in this essay.

Trans-cultural *Endgame/s*

The three productions of *Final de partida* at issue were aesthetically quite different from each other, while at the same time they shared certain features, such as acting styles. Although the three stage directors professed to admire Beckett's theater and tried to stage the play closely following his stage directions, each one of them had a different vision of the play, a different directing style, and therefore had left his own individual directorial mark on his staging of the play. However, a common feature of these three productions is their emphasis on patterns of dominance and submission in *Endgame*, relating them to Spanish culture or, more specifically, to events of the time when the play was produced. The two productions of the 1980s relate the play more to current Spanish cultural and political discourses, while the most recent production of 2001 focuses more on the particular: the problems of human relationships trapped in an extreme situation. Formally, these three productions managed, after Beckett, to create a powerful and poetic central stage image by the most economical means. I discuss these productions chronologically, in order to show how a play, as dramatic material, changes in time while at the same time it remains basically the same play.

1. Julio Castronuovo's 1980 *Final de partida*: "loneliness and "nuclear terror"

My discussion of Castronuovo's 1980 production of *Final de partida* is inspired by many conversations with the director,[4] by the reports of the actors, and by reading the play's reviews. Unfortunately I cannot give a direct report of this production for I was unable to see it. Castronuovo confesses that this is his favorite Beckett play. He has directed it on four occasions with only slight changes, accommodating his ideas about the play to the specific theater where it was staged and to the different actors he was working with in each of his productions. His conception of the play, he tells me, has not significantly changed since 1961 when he directed the première of *Final de partida* in Buenos Aires. "It was a great experience," he says, "though the theater was closed, only a week after the première, for I refused to eliminate the expression, 'el hijo de puta' (bastard), addressed to God, from the play." It may be possible to get away with this line in French, but not in Spanish. In the late 1950s and early 1960s *Endgame* was a problem with the censors, and not only in England.[5]

Julio Castronuovo, Argentinian by birth, moved to Spain in 1967 and since then he has been teaching and directing in Spain and Portugal. In 1980 he was asked to direct *Final de Partida* by the well-known theater group "Teatro Estable Adefesio" of Logroño. Ricardo Romanos played Hamm, Agustin Oteiza, Clov, and Damian Rodríguez and Pilar Santamaría were Nagg and Nell respectively. Castronuovo still believes that the central theme of the play is "the complete loneliness of four human beings forced to live together, trapped in a sort of bunker after, perhaps, an atomic explosion. The world is dead and they who should be dead are, mysteriously, still alive." He adds, "in this play three generations are isolated and their relationships deteriorate, little by little, creating a situation of growing tension and violence [...] one *feels* the oppression of human beings over human beings." To emphasize the director's ideas, the stage designer, Cesar Ocho, built a kind of metallic closed structure which looked like the interior of a submarine, or a nuclear refuge, with two very high and small rectangular windows. A door to the right led to Clov's kitchen. Two huge tin dustbins dominated the set, along with a big, unfamiliar looking armchair on casters, with two unusual long poles on its back. This hard, cold and claustrophobic space was very suited to *Endgame,* as was its predominant color: gray.

Acting was non-realistic. Contrasting moments of inaction and silence were followed by exaggerated gestures and loud voices. This was, no doubt, a directorial choice to show the tension implied in the characters' relationships and it also very effectively increased the dramatic tension of the play. Being a mime actor himself, Castronuovo always devotes great attention to finding the specific movements and gestures best suited to each specific role. Thus in this production of *Final de partida* he achieved what he calls "robot-like movements for Clov, with strong changes of rhythm." In the opening mime, for instance, Clov ascended the steps sometimes very slowly and then descended very quickly, or vice versa. Hamm's gestures were also very stylized: "sometimes he moved his arms very slowly and at others with exaggerated symbolic gestures, especially when he is (or pretends to be) furious with Nagg or Clov." Castronuovo says, for instance, that Hamm used very ample gestures and a loud voice when he says: "Get out of here and love one another! Lick your neighbor as yourself!" This would be followed by, softly and ironically, "[w]hen it wasn't bread they wanted it was crumpets" (44).[6] These contrasting movements and voices established a visual parallelism between Clov's and Hamm's acting and help to create echoes between the verbal and the visual patterns. Characteristic of Castronuovo's emphasis on gesture was Nagg's telling his story about "the world and the pair of trousers." His exaggerated gestures made "the story much funnier because they underlined the verbal comedy." Audiences liked Nagg's "little act" very much, although one could argue that he was too alive and too visible for his role, if one takes into account Beckett's advice about Nagg and Nell's limited physical appearance—only their heads and hands were to be visible. However Castronuovo allowed the actors to be more "alive" and to exaggerate their gestures, and this kind of "burlesque" acting seemed to have worked very well in this production, by all accounts.

The themes of mutual dependence and enforced imprisonment were very much stressed in this production, where the characters were seen as the only humans to remain after a "nuclear explosion." In the program note this idea of *nuclear terror* is emphasized, together with other similar impending terrors of the moment: "Under the empire of nuclear, multinational, microelectronic terror [...] of hunger, of lack of energy, of

Jomeinisms and apocalyptic redeemers around the corner [...] to stage Beckett seemed to us the necessary step to start this hopeful 1980." It is interesting to see now, after the horrible Madrid massacre of 11 March, 2004, how these words still relate to our present of apocalyptic, cruel and violent redeemers inflicting so much suffering on fellow human beings.

The stage space created for Castronuovo's production evoked not only a nuclear refuge, but also a prison cell, helped visually by Clov's costume: his striped black and white t-shirt and dirty black trousers gave him, according to the director, "a convict look." Castronuovo's additions in this particular production of *Final de partida* were intended to evoke simultaneously domestic and also more universal situations. Apart from the theatricality added to the actors' gestures and movements, Castronuovo gave strong emphasis to sound, thus creating his own music. As I have already pointed out, the set was made out of metal: all objects made a strong and unpleasant sound when hitting the ground. This had a very disturbing effect on the audience. For instance, the theatrical surprise of Nagg and Nell's first appearance—popping out of their dustbins—was emphasized by the fact that the lids of their house-like receptacles fell on the ground, making a very loud clang. A deliberate contrast was established between moments of silence and stillness, and moments of sounds and noises, and also between the different tones of voice of the different characters. All of these visual and aural effects contributed to the surprising and discontinuous rhythm of this production of *Endgame*.

Reviews of this 1980 *Final de partida* were all very favorable. The staging, acting and directing was described, repeatedly, as "brilliant," "intelligent," and "imaginative." Although one cannot always trust theater critics who have not seen many productions of the play under review, or who have preconceived ideas about the author or the director or the play, in the case of this production their enthusiasm seems to have been justified. The following remarks from a local critic who signed himself as Doctor B, help to summarize the type of enthusiastic response given to this particular production. This critic starts praising the group, Adefesio, for its "splendid production of Beckett's play," then the actors for their "perfect performance and perfect diction" and, finally, the director of the play for his faithfulness "to Beckett without renouncing his own creativity and imagination [...] Castronuovo was there, but Beckett also." It is evident that this director created his own music and left strong personal and cultural marks in his staging of *Endgame*—especially in the creation of the central image and in the rhythm, sound and acting techniques—but he did so without destroying the great poetic and emotional impact of the play.

2. Miguel Narros 1984 *Final de partida:* "the end of a dictator"

I can report directly on Miguel Narros' *Final de partida*: I attended rehearsals, helped the actors re-translating a few lines and saw the play several times. On 4 January 1984, the company "Teatro del Arte" staged the play in the 'Sala Cadarso,' a fringe theater of Madrid. This production was directed by one of Spain's best and most popular theater directors, and was regarded by many critics as an authentic première o f *Final de partida*. This production evolved around what Narros saw as the central idea of the play, "the end of a dictator"—it should be remembered here that the end of Spain's dictatorship had occurred only a few years before, in 1975. Narros' staging also stressed the play's "nec tecum nec sine te" situation: the mutual dependence between the two main characters and the latent hatred and violence that such a situation engenders. To show this Narros had two excellent actors in the main roles: Francisco Vidal as Clov, and Manolo de Blas as Hamm, both physically very well suited to their roles. Vidal is small, thin actor and de Blas is tall and corpulent.

There were many directorial marks in this production, reflected mainly in setting, acting, lighting and stage properties. Juan Gutiérrez and Andrea D'Odorico created the stage space—a wonderful bare gray room.[7] They incorporated some extra elements to those suggested by Beckett's stage directions, the most visible being a large closed door upstage center. Another added prop was a conical lamp hanging up center-stage, projecting a circular pale luminosity on the central playing area which included Hamm's chair and also Nagg and Nell's large metal dustbins, placed downstage left. Stage right, close to Clov's kitchen door and establishing a sort of visual parallelism with the two dustbins, a huge ladder could be seen. It was initially covered by a white cloth like the rest of the stage elements, adding an extra mystery to the setting. There were also some other domestic contributions to Beckett's props. Clov's possessions at the end of the play, when he is ready to go, were increased to include a backpack and an oar that appeared to be tied to his suitcase.

Lighting was excellent in creating a decaying atmosphere. The predominant color was gray, with luminous touches of pale gray center stage provided by the extra lamp. An extra lighting effect was added at the end of the play, creating a great theatrical moment of suspense. When Clov is ready to depart, he opens the large backstage door—closed during the whole performance but now strongly illuminated—only to find another closed door behind it. This action suggests, perhaps, that there is an endless number of closed doors, and the audience is made to feel, visually, that there is no way out for Clov. At the same time, the fact that another door exists suggests the possibility of an opening to the outside world, and thus it maintains the play's open ending. The audience assumes that should Clov ever gather the necessary strength to depart, he may open the final door and thus abandon Hamm. So the final image of the play remains ambiguous: the final blackout intervenes before the spectators know if Clov, who remains standing by an open door with a closed door behind it, will find the necessary strength to open that door. The suspense remains, though caused by different theatrical means. One could certainly argue that these extra elements are totally unnecessary in the play, that in the staging of a Beckett play "less is always more" and so all extra additions work against the production. However in this production these few extra elements added by the play's director were dramatically very effective and did not mar the visual economy essential in staging *Endgame*.

Another directorial mark was evident in the play's rhythm. Miguel Narros directed *Final de partida* at a relentlessly slow pace. Its performance lasted about two hours, with the opening mime stretched to last ten minutes. By unnaturally prolonging Clov's painful and funny business going up and down the step-ladder and moving from one window to the other, Narros deliberately irritated the spectators who were waiting for some kind of action or dialogue to take place, and who were faced with constant repetitions of the same inanities. The director had an explanation for this: Narros said that in *Final de partida* "time turns around itself with endless monotony and it is measured only by Clov's trailing footsteps [...] which reach us with a discontinuous rhythm, the only living beat in this dead space" (10). Stressing the mutual dependence of the two protagonists and the tension it produces,

the director offered a political reading. He compared this
oppressive relationship and the violence it generates to the one
felt by people living in countries under fascist regimes, who wait
daily for the death of the dictator in order to be released from an
unbearable situation where a lack of liberties, torture and violence
prevail. The desired death seems to be delayed endlessly and, like
Clov, the people endure all kinds of cruelties and humiliations.
Domestic Spanish politics and experiences filtered Narros' words
about his staging of *Endgame*. Narros' creation of Hamm was also
related to Spanish culture: he is not only a dictator, but also a kind
of cruel divinity upon whom people are dependent. Religion is
often used by fascist regimes to control the populace, as was
especially the case in Spain. In relation to this idea, Narros wanted
Manuel de Blas—the actor playing Hamm—to adopt a very
majestic and hieratic attitude, like "a kind of Pantocrator."[8] His
powerful physical presence was perfect in suggesting such an image
of absolute power.

Miguel Narros is a great director of actors. In this
production controlling de Blas's excessive movements and gestures
was a problem, so much so that, in order to prevent his Hamm
from falling off his chair, the director decided in some rehearsals to
have the actor tied to it. After this forceful checking of extra
movements, de Blas's acting was superb. His imposing physical
presence and his extraordinary range of voice were very powerful.
He mastered Hamm's frequent changes of tone and rhythm
wonderfully, although at times he spoke too loudly. His delivery of
Hamm's chronicle, for instance, was quite impressive. I will never
forget the power of the following words delivered straight to the
audience: "But what in God's name do you imagine? That the earth
will awake in Spring? That the rivers and seas will run with fish
again? That there's manna in heaven still for imbeciles like you?"
(37) This was trans-cultural theater at its best, as anyone could
perceive the power and universality of Hamm's attack on human
delusions.

Francisco Vidal also played an excellent Clov, conveying
the right note of contained desperation through the tone of his
voice, with his constant doubts and hesitations before obeying
Hamm, and also by his rigid, painful walk. One could feel his fury
and anger facing Hamm's orders and constant humiliations. He was
especially moving in his "They said to me [...] I say to myself
[...]" speech, delivered with contained rage. Enrique Menéndez and

Paca Ojea were perfect in the roles of Nagg and Nell, with their white, old, but childish-looking faces covered with white plaster, which at times fell, visibly, when they were talking. This produced a comic but also pathetic effect, for they almost seemed to be talking corpses. At the same time, their evocation of sentimental memories deluded themselves, and the audience, into thinking they were still very much alive, in spite of their being treated as organic waste thrown into their respective dustbins. My only criticism was that they were too visible and their voices, especially Nagg's, too strong. Nell was not, as Beckett wanted, "a whisper of life. Just a whisper of life" (qtd in Knowlson 668). However, both actors achieved the right mixture of pathetic/poetic comedy in their dialogues. Nagg's gestures were at times excessive, but Nell's performance was more contained and poetic.

In spite of my few reservations, this was a very good production of *Endgame*. Spanish theater critics saluted this *Final de partida* as excellent and as a true première, which, for them, made more sense in 1984 than in 1958, when the play was first produced in Spain. If Beckett's plays were received initially with open hostility or with excessive reverence, now almost all critics concur in highlighting the power of Beckett's characteristically poignant humor: "now audiences laugh and laugh at that which is unhappy." In 1984 Spanish theater critics also appreciated the author's courage to present extreme situations of human impotence embodied in such powerful stage metaphors. They considered Beckett a great dramatic poet and some of them established analogies and connections between this play and Spain's recent fascist political past, especially when talking about the oppressive dominance-submission relationship between Hamm and Clov. More personal interpretations, however, were also made. One perceptive critic, the poet Juan Mollá, confessed to have been "deeply moved and disturbed by this extraordinary play," where "one is made to feel, dramatically, the last moments of a game, or of a life, reaching thus a kind of mystical experience." He praised director and actors for their "wonderful work." Almost all the reviews repeated the idea that we understand Beckett's theater much better now than in the 1950s and 1960s. Our generation has absorbed the menace of a possible nuclear war and hecatomb, and thus we can easily imagine such empty and devastated landscapes, and such extreme and painful situations as his plays present.[9] The trans-cultural quality of this production is evident in most of the

critics' statements quoted above. Most of them see the domestic
Spanish connection but also point out the universality of the
central image of the play and of the dominance-submission
relationships. When discussing the play, Narros evokes the echoes
of and connections to his own cultural and political moment. His
production successfully transcended these connections: it did not
reduce Beckett's great theatrical metaphor simply to illuminate the
events and culture of his own country at a particular time.

3. Rodolfo Cortizo's 2001 *Final de partida*: "traces of pain, traces of laughter"

Rodolfo Cortizo's 2001 staging of the play—with two women
actresses impersonating the central roles but acting as if they were
men—is perhaps the most "trans-cultural" of the three
productions discussed here. For it contained few echoes, allusions,
or references to current discourses and events. Even Cortizo's
decision to cast women in the central roles was not taken for
gender or political reasons but merely for technical and economic
ones. His theater group, "La Pajarita de Papel," includes more
women than men actors, and they do not have enough money to
hire actors from outside the group. Therefore they decided to cast
one excellent actress, Concha Roales-Nieto, as Hamm, and a young
actress, Sayo Almeida, as Clov. Carlos Romero and Eva Varela
played the roles of Nagg and Nell respectively. Ms Varela was also
responsible for the adaptation of a very poor translation, and she
did a good job with a difficult text. Theatrical adaptations that seek
to make published texts aurally effective are the rule in Spanish
productions of foreign plays, generally due to bad translations of
these plays. Unfortunately this is the case with most of Beckett's
plays. Cortizo informed me that once he had his cast they spent a
lot of time together working on the text and on all aspects of this
production. Particular attention was given to the creation of the
setting, costumes and to finding the stage properties most suited to
his production. This creative process was quite complicated, for
they had to make or manipulate some of the props. For instance,
they made Hamm's chair and changed the look and colour of other
props they had bought cheaply in Madrid's antique shops, all in
order to make them look more strange, old and unfamiliar.

 Rodolfo Cortizo confessed that he had not read Beckett's
Endgame Notebook or other criticism on the play before he had a

clear idea about how he wanted to stage it: "I did not want to be influenced by any interpretations of the play." Most of the criticism on *Endgame* that he and the actors read after they had already been working on this production, was, Cortizo says, "stupid and useless." He had conveniently forgotten the names of the critics when I pressed him on this point. This director sees the dramatic situation of *Final de Partida* as "cruelly tragicomic." He staged this play to show "the problems of a compulsory living together. Men and women waste their lives in impossible situations while making fools of themselves." He added: "this is a play about lost opportunities. Three generations of human beings waste their lives waiting for an impossible end. In a grotesque way, Beckett also shows how human beings are aware, even in extreme situations, of the *luck* of being alive." Cortizo sees Hamm, Clov, Nagg and Nell as "personifications of fundamental human attitudes, like the characters of Calderon's *Autos Sacramentales*, or like the Virtues and Vices of Medieval Morality Plays."[10] In this production, the director stated that "nothing was improvised, the actors worked a lot to establish a physical relationship with their props and costumes. There was endless trying-on of costumes especially in order to make the two women actresses embody their male roles." Movements and gestures did not provide any problem, for, according to Cortizo, they are "given by the dramatic text." In staging *Final de partida,* Cortizo was most impressed by what he calls "the aggressiveness of Beckett's moments of waiting" and he explains this by stating that "silences and pauses, together with the stage image, create the rhythm of the play, and pauses and silences are action in Beckett's plays." This is true of Beckett's theater where the characters seem to be on stage to kill time and to fight silence with their words and actions, even when these words are less and less audible, and their actions become more and more limited. Deterioration, decay and entropy are the great maladies affecting all Beckett's characters.

The shape of the theater also influenced this production, which was shown in two small fringe theaters in Madrid, "La fabrica de pan" and "Lagrada." Setting and stage properties had to be adjusted to fit their small stages, although, according to its director, these changes did not affect his production. From the point of view of staging, one of the most distinguishing marks of this 2001 production of *Final de partida* was the ocher color given to the barren stage landscape. Setting, characters and props all shared this earthy color, as if all belonged to the same kind of organic matter. Walls and floor were gray, but they were also infected, as it were, by the yellowish light, skilfully created by Nacho Ortiz. Nagg and Nell's metal dustbins, also painted ocher, were surrounded by sand of the same color. The yellowish stage lights helped to give a touch of beige to the dirty white characters' costumes. Cortizo commented that he opted for an old white shirt for Hamm because he believed a dressing-gown "was too homely for such a situation." Clov also wore a dirty white shirt and black trousers. Nagg wore a striped beige and black pyjama, intended as "an echo of the kind of attire used in concentration camps"—the only historical comment the director made about this production. Nell wore a beautiful laced beige nightgown. All the props were tainted in light ocher, especially Hamm's blanket, thus establishing visual echoes with the color of his chair and that of his "old stancher." Another directorial mark in this production was the situation and shape of the two dustbins. They were placed downstage left, touching the wall, instead of parallel to the audience. Nagg's dustbin was bigger than Nell's, as if the containers have to be adjusted to the characters' body shapes. The lids of the dustbins were left open behind the characters' heads, forming a kind of halo. I found this effect particularly interesting, although the director claimed it was not intended. The acting was generally good, especially Roales-Nieto's Hamm: her changes of rhythm and tone of voice were quite impressive and one soon forgot she was a woman playing a male role (although she never tried to pretend she was a man). Carlos Romero and Eva Varela, as Nagg and Nell respectively, emphasised the comic aspects of their roles, exaggerating at times gesture and voice. At other times their faces were Buster Keaton-like, blank, quite frozen, and these contrasts characterised their grotesque style of acting. A very memorable image was achieved when they repeatedly tried and failed to kiss: their pathetic gestures were perfectly suited to the moment. The weakest part was Almeida's Clov. It was not so much a question of bad acting, but she was too young for the part. Despite this, her work on gesture and movement was quite good.

Unlike the two productions discussed above, this fringe group did not receive long press reviews, but only general comments in local theater magazines, most of which were favourable. They had, though, very enthusiastic audiences of mostly young people who had never seen the play before and were

very impressed by its cruel stark imagery and also by the acting.
The fact that audiences were physically very close to the
actors—the two theaters where this production was staged are very
small—contributed to its greater impact.

A final program note entitled "traces of pain, traces of
laughter" serves to summarise Cortizo's approach to *Final de
partida,* and also to Beckett's theater. "What is wonderful about
Endgame," he says,

> is its objectivity. The greatness of Beckett is his power to create a stage
> image, a stage relationship, a stage machinery which originates in his
> most intense inner experiences. His characters and images are born on
> stage, in an inspired moment, in front of our eyes with a perfect and
> absolute entity. They are symbols without being symbolic.

This essay has dealt with some of the problems that arise
when a play crosses the borders of language, of culture and of time,
illustrated by three Spanish productions of *Endgame.* The "trans-
cultural" quality of this play is shared by these productions, in spite
of their domestic intra-cultural acting styles and theatrical
techniques, and in spite of the necessary intercultural exchanges
between the original and the target culture. It is quite evident that
the historical and political remarks relating these productions to a
specific time and place were made by directors, critics, actors, or
were written in program notes in order to clarify the play's
relevance and meaning to their audiences, yet these remarks were
not present in the actual productions. Sirkku Aaltonen says that
trans-cultural directors "seem to be concerned with traditions only
in order to grasp more effectively what they have in common and
what is not reducible to a specific culture" (13). This is the case, I
believe, of the three Spanish directors considered in this essay.

The three *Final de partida/s* serve to clarify the
problematic process of trans-culturalization when dealing with
Beckett's plays. Theatrical exchanges between two cultures are
inevitable and will always bear the traces of their cultures. John
Calder once commented that "if the proliferation of adaptations
and alterations of Beckett's plays persist, [...] in twenty-five or
thirty years, Beckett will be known only as a writer of great novels,
and people will look back and wonder what the fuss about his plays
was all about" (qtd in Linda Ben-Zvi xii). In the light of the
productions discussed here, and many other productions of
Beckett's plays I have seen in different countries, I do not share

Calder's pessimism. I believe that Beckett's plays, which are steeped in many cultures, have a trans-cultural quality and will survive and endure all kinds of stage changes and adaptations—even when these are based on bad translations and are staged by directors who don't know much about Beckett and pretend to be the authors of the plays they direct. Beckett, as director, admitted that "neither text nor production are final or invariable." They depend on the directors and the actors of a given production at a given time. He also admitted, while directing *Endgame*, that "it is possible to do the play quite differently, different music, movements, different rhythm" (*Endgame* Notebook xviii). These remarks not only reveal Beckett's understanding of theater production, which he learned directing his own plays, but also his flexibility regarding textual and staging changes. The only thing he considered essential in directing *Endgame* was to achieve *a specific pattern* through the repetition of gestures, movements, sounds, pauses and silences, words being only "dramatic ammunition"; apart from this each director will contribute his/her own music. These ideas on staging make Beckett a trans-cultural director, for his plays have shown how people connect beyond and beneath ethnological, cultural and individual differences.

Antonia Rodríguez-Gago, Universidad Autónoma de Madrid

Notes

[1] These words answered Michel Haerdter's question as to whether Beckett had come "to give Berlin the authentic version" of *Endgame*. Beckett replied " No," along with the lines quoted above. See S. E. Gontarski ed. *The Theatrical Notebooks of Samuel Beckett: Endgame* (London: Faber & Faber, 1992): xviii. Further quotations to this book will appear as "*Endgame* Notebook" followed by the page number.

[2] Pavis's words here refer to Peter Brook, not to Beckett.

[3] My general comments on early productions of Beckett's plays in Spain are from my paper 'Beckett in Spain: Theater and Politics,' originally written in English and published in Italian in a special number of *Drammaturgia* devoted to Beckett and edited by Anna Maria Cascetta and S. E. Gontarski.

[4] I am very grateful to Julio Castronuovo for sharing his memories of directing *Final de partida* and other Beckett's plays on several occasions and in different countries. I have interviewed Castronuovo several times, the last time on 17 March 2004.

[5] In 1958 the Lord Chamberlain refused to grant *Endgame* a license and George

Devine thought it was for cultural reasons. "It's because it is in English," Devine told Ann Jellicoe, "you can get away with much more in French [...] think what you could get away with in Japanese" (Knowlson 449).
[6] All quotations from *Endgame* are from the 1958 Faber & Faber edition of the play.
[7] I am very grateful to the stage designer of this production, Andrea D'Odorico, for his comments on the creation of setting and costumes. I have talked with D'Odorico about Beckett's theater several times, the last on 14 April 2001.
[8] I am very grateful to Miguel Narros for all his comments on this production. All quotations without specific reference were recorded in rehearsals or in subsequent conversations with Miguel Narros.
[9] I have quoted or paraphrased the following critics: Juán Mollá, José Monleón, and Eduardo Haro-Tecglen.
[10] I am very grateful to Rodolfo Cortizo, whom I interviewed 29 March 2004, for sharing his memories and experiences of working in this production of *Endgame*. If not otherwise stated, all quotes from Cortizo are from this interview. Translations from Spanish are mine.

Bibliography

Aaltonen, Sirkku. *Time Sharing on Stage: Drama Translation in Theater and Society*. Clevedon (UK), Buffalo, Toronto, Sydney: Multilingual Matters, 2000.

Alvaro, Francisco ed. *El Espectador y la Crítica: The Theater in Spain in 1958*. Valladolid: Ediciones del Autor, 1960.

Bassnett, Susan and André Lefevere. *Constructing Cultures: Essays on Literary Translation*. Clevedon, Philadelphia, Toronto, Sydney, Johannesburg: Multilingual Matters, 1998.

Beckett, Samuel. *Endgame*. London: Faber & Faber, 1958.

Ben-Zvi, Linda, ed. *Drawing on Beckett: Portraits, Performances and Cultural Contexts*. Tel Aviv: Assaph, 2004.

Campbell, Julie. '"There is no More...": Cultural Memory in *Endgame*' in Linda Ben-Zvi (2004): 127-140.

Cohn, Ruby. *A Casebook on* Waiting for Godot. London: Macmillan, 1967.

El Doctor B (pseudonym). '"Adefesio" interpretó de forma expléndida a Beckett,' review of *Final de partida* in *La Gaceta del Norte* (20 January 1980): 21.

Gontarki, Stanley, ed. *The Notebooks of Samuel Beckett*: Endgame. London: Faber & Faber, 1992.

Haro-Tecglen, Eduardo. 'Risas para Beckett' in *El País* (6 January 1984): 28.

Knowlson, James. *Damned to Fame: The Life of Samuel Beckett.* London: Bloomsbury, 1996.

Marquerie, Alfredo. Review of *Final de partida* in *ABC* (3 June 1958). Reprinted in Alvaro (1960): 174.

Mollá, Juán. 'Viaje al fondo del problema' in *El Ciervo* (January 1984): 41-42.

Monleón, José. 'Un poco más cerca' in *Diario 16* (21 January 1984): 11.

Narros, Miguel. 'Notas sobre *Final de partida*' in *Diario 16* (5 February 1984): 10.

Pavis, Patrice, ed. *The Intercultural Performer Reader.* London and New York: Routledge, 1996.

Rodríguez-Gago, Antonia. 'Le Messinscene di Beckett in Spagna: Teatro e Politica,' in Anna Maria Cascetta and Stan Gontarski, eds. *Beckett in Scena: Interpretazioni Memorabile nel Mondo* (Drammaturgia 9). Roma: Salerno Editrice, 2002. (141-169)

Masking and the Social Construct of the Body in Beckett's *Endgame*

Mary F. Catanzaro

Central to *Endgame* is the theme of coupling and partnership—and its seeming impossibility—where we see the full spectrum of broken promises that undermines agreement and accord. In the physical impediments and emotional ruptures of the couple there is a virtual metaphysics of discord. From the outset, the couple manifests itself within the inner structure and scaffolding of a master-servant relationship. In this framework, power struggles signify physical and emotional dependency where bodily handicaps, pain, and even torture are prominent. The master-servant relationship involves dramatic and fetishistic manipulation of objects, speech patterns, and role-playing.

The master-servant relationship in *E n d g a m e* is phenomenological in essence. This can be understood as meaning a relationship between dual axes, rather than conflicting personalities. Power and primordial loyalty are paramount to Hamm and Clov, and their interactions are played out in verbal battles, where one exercises an almost feudal lordship over the other at alternate moments in the play. The planar aspect of Clov's subservience locates him at a pure surface level off which Hamm deflects an obsessive energy. Thus, while Clov absorbs Hamm's outbursts with exceptional tact, this is not to suggest that Hamm does not resent his tyranny being undermined by the other's studied grace. In a household where distinct verbal identities are a crucial issue, the spoken words are as convoluted and contradictory as the physical gestures themselves. In order that his own utterances dominate, Hamm views himself as the virtuoso in verbally manipulating those around him.

Hamm's voice, however, is hallucinatory—it is one that always betrays present-tense reality. For him, living time is translated to "fictional" time. The result is denial on several counts. For one,

Hamm sets up a battle between signification and its denial, and this is perhaps the reason that he slips so easily into mythic interpretations regarding the past, his lineage and his relationship with Clov. Alternately opportunistic and compassionate, bombastic and fragile, undisciplined and focused—it is a binary personality code that applies vividly to Hamm. In the play, the power inequities between the two men therefore suggest a deep skepticism toward symmetrical coupling. *Endgame* therefore suggests to us the question: is partnership in the long run impossible, or, if it is to be sustained, must there be sufficient distance between subject and object? It would appear that Beckett sees enduring relationships as highly suspect.

That *Endgame* involves paired men rather than a man and a woman poses no problem to the notion of coupling in this play. Rather, Beckett draws from a long tradition of eccentric men paired together, dating as far back as Aristophanes' *The Birds*, Cervantes' *Don Quixote*, Sterne's *Tristram Shandy* and Flaubert's *Bouvard and Pecuchet*. Hamm and Clov also join the ranks of various male duos of modern literature and film, among them P. G. Wodehouse's Wooster and Jeeves, Arthur Conan Doyle's Sherlock Holmes and Dr. Watson, as well as the Lone Ranger and Tonto, Ralph Kramden and Ed Norton and Batman and Robin. These ambiguous figures have long been the subjects of academic efforts to extract the hidden meanings of their mutual attachment and repulsion.

Endgame also shows a particular concern for the tensions and pleasures of collaboration. Prefiguring the tradition of Starsky and Hutch, Hamm and Clov are an original maverick pair. Other heirs might include Crockett and Tubbs in "Miami Vice," where Clov (as Don Johnson) overshadows the more tormented suavity of Hamm. Alternately, Hamm and Clov could be viewed as precursors to the mismatched pair in Elaine May's 1976 film, "Mikey and Nicky," where Mikey's walkout on his friend is revealed to have so many complex roots (as is Clov's exodus), that the departure comes to seem inevitable and even necessary—a working definition of modern tragedy. Although Hamm and Clov's partnership might suggest a diabolical variation on the modern buddy conceit, the fact that theirs matures while they are both psychologically and physically codependent gives their relationship its jarring, fascinating complexity. Their strained interchanges—grim riffs on the kind of idle palaver that occupies a traditional dysfunctional married couple—gather nuances and recapitulate the equally ill-fated overtones of rivalry, aggression and awkward sympathy between the two.

The problems that Beckett inevitably encountered in seeking a way to define the awkward nature of relations between men are in evidence here—though not always so necessarily and so clearly defined as in *Waiting For Godot*, because here Beckett concentrates on so many conflicting issues. When we hear the particularly pointed, woundingly moving example of Hamm's opening lines—"Can there be misery—*(he yawns)*—loftier than mine?"[1]—we hear a man coping with the forces of two realities, the nature of which we will only gradually learn as the drama unfolds: his master/slave issue and his parent/shame issue. From the outset, we might be led into thinking that Beckett is making a portrait of the philosopher who questions the meaning of life. But what Beckett might be exploring is the nature of cruelty and sadism. What if he wants to show the anger and dark passions lying beneath so-called normal households? Who among us has not felt rage and distrust of the power that we think our parents or mate represent?

The bully in the family is an aspect of flawed family relations that bears scrutiny in *Endgame*. Often in families there is a child who cleverly figures out the means to get what he or she wants: by intimidating parents or other family members through tantrums and surly black moods. Also, the use of one's intelligence is a way to make parents and siblings, even friends, cower. In this way, the hierarchy of the entire family is disassembled. Seen in this light, *Endgame* is a ruthless devolution of power as well as it is a sharing of power. Although we see an active relationship at work between Hamm and Clov, it is an impaired one. *Endgame* is a work about regret on a different axis. It is as relentless and bleak as clinical depression but as Beckett wants the play staged it turns towards farce, upon which many critics have already commented. In a way, *Endgame* could be described as a meditation on the human appetite for destruction or as an eschatological journey that, as with the one in Dante's *Divine Comedy*, begins in hell. As the play shifts into the purgatory known as the present, the dialogue thereafter varies consistently in image and tone, developing into a kind of musical code that exposes the fragile nature of two men's partnership.

What Hamm and Clov are to each other does not quite have a name: not friends, obviously, but not entirely enemies either. If they present themselves to the audience as acquaintances in a business partnership of valet and gentleman linked by a passing transaction, they somehow end up understanding each other better than anyone else does. Are they soul mates? Sublimated lovers? Improbable colleagues? How about sadist and masochist locked in a phenomenological embrace?

Endgame's appeal, strangely, comes from its cold-heartedness. Its monocular focus of keeping a dysfunctional relationship in motion has a lurid blend of egalitarianism and disturbed purity. Over the whole play hangs an air of menaced irresponsibility. Moreover, there is something decidedly unconventional about Hamm's sexuality. Some of his behavior can be described as what Graham Robb, in his recently published *Strangers: Homosexual Love in the Nineteenth Century*, has called "coded gay" (97).[2] One of the more arcane markers of homosexual inclinations, according to Robb, included beating servants.

Yet sex is not the issue in this play—though it comes to mix in the fierce dominance of one man over another and the weak one's willingness to remain in the relationship as long as possible, however humbled he may be. Hamm, a brilliant *auteur*, a man of possibly aristocratic family roots, now lives in reduced circumstances as a result of some vaguely "untoward events" that have left him disabled. He is enamored of high tragedy, declamations, flashy dress and eccentric accoutrements. Characterized by anger and denial, and often returning to the steady state of needful companionship, Hamm is alternately Homeric and sadistic in his explosions. Hamm and Clov are not overtly gay, thus their sexual orientation hardly matters. Their primary codependency lies mainly in the fact that Clov can't sit and Hamm can't walk.

Here we enter the gray area of the significance of Hamm's paralysis. The viewer is immediately struck by the presence of a flamboyant personality, attractive in its seductive brilliance and awed by the power and cruelty he exerts over family and servant. Barely suppressed paranoia—in particular a fear of being stranded or trapped—is Hamm's silent, ever present, *other* companion. Is there a trace of sexual cruelty here, a lashing out in anger over his impotence? In Hamm these emotions are defined in the metaphor of the mask.

Professionally acerbic and philosophically fatigued, Hamm is never without his mask. A common device used by various artists, the mask serves as a social metaphor in the play. We all wear social masks, to be sure; they assign us identities and obscure our true natures. In this way we become a combination of our public and private faces. The bloody handkerchief covering Hamm's face and his dark glasses project the image of a hero, a wounded warrior or a martyr—the blood representing scars earned on the mythic battlefield. Even his toque looks like a kind of crown; and the rug over his knees and wheelchair in which he sits throughout the play curiously resemble a mantle and a throne. In fact, Hamm takes full advantage of this image to further his primary ambition. Above all, he nurtures his disability in order to gain the upper hand over his caregiver and his parents. Just as important, his oratory disguises his dread of having his outsider status blown open.

Endgame gets to the essence of charisma and influential power, which is that there is always an erotic undercurrent to which both men and women are susceptible. Hamm's ironic anger, seething with inarticulate rage and locked-down demons, is clearly seductive, yet he's also a man seemingly in charge of his public image. Like a practiced CEO, he runs an efficiently crafted dictatorship over his reduced fiefdom of parents and valet. Above all, Hamm is a force, his slightly hysterical energy recalling an Oriental-Romantic tradition of impassioned gestures and exotic emotions. A dandy in his dressing gown and dark glasses, he exudes the air of the campy, mature bohemian, the urban gypsy, seductive and aware of it. *Endgame* is, above all, a study in nasty professionalism, an idea that registers not only in its meticulously composed blocks of dialogue but also in the psychological grounding of the narrative line.

It is the play's willingness to engage the harsher realities of family dynamics with the stage's bizarre surroundings that makes *Endgame* so memorable. Beckett has contrived that the main room be a rather congenitally cold climate—an anti-Eden where the "perfect" couple can bicker and decay. When Hamm whistles for Clov at the beginning of the play, he greets his servant with contempt: "You pollute the air!" (3). In this manner, the set and the ensuing dialogues give the viewer an entrée into the characters' inner lives, lavishing special attention also on the fraught relationship between parents and child. From the outset, Hamm schemes to marginalize Nagg and Nell—exhorting them to extinction, and concentrating in particular on shaming his father's sexual potency with cruel mantras: "Accursed progenitor!" (9), "Accursed fornicator!" (10). As if those humiliations were not enough, the mere presence of mother and father occasions derisive sarcasm: "The old folks at home! No decency left!" (9). Nagg and Nell's stoic freakishness is engaging partly because their conversational style and personal conduct are so quaintly fastidious. Even though they appear so briefly as to seem mere shadows, their voices act as a chorus that foreshadows the *other* drama—that between their son and his caregiver. This kind of family tension sets the match to long simmering resentments among all parties.

Beckett juxtaposes these melodramatic aspects with jolts of comedy that light up the landscape, but the laughs are unsettling because the play is built on a fault line of dysfunction to begin with. The stinging brilliance of Beckett's skill and discipline with Hamm and Clov's dialogue seems to grow out of a haunted brand of obsessive-compulsive disorder; one, actually, that matches his characters' disorders. The verbal battles between them, regardless of their gender, are really battles against the ordinariness of partnership. The mechanical trips to the window, the routine spins around the room, and the daily sight of aged parents—this gives anomie to the relationship. Hamm requires Clov, a stand-in for the baffled viewer, to listen to his stories, and since a figure like Hamm can't exist outside of stories, he is far worse than lost without Clov.

There is a peculiar sort of hell that Beckett revisits in much of his work. Its landscapes, not unlike those portrayed in the work of Ingmar Bergman, are bleak interiors. The set of *Endgame* consists of the family home: the front room, the kitchen beyond, and the so-called bedroom of ashbins at front left where the parents dwell. But here mother and father are servants. The son cannot sleep, the nearness of his parents' quarters are too unnerving. The suggestion of sexual innuendo and Oedipal rage is not off the mark. When his father taps at his mother's bin, she responds, "What is it, my pet? *(Pause.)* Time for love?" to which Nagg suggests they kiss (14). Not surprisingly, their paralyzed son can only *dream* of sexual potency. "If I could sleep I might make love" (18), he muses. Fully grasping the futility of ever seeing family harmony, Nell summarizes the domestic situation succinctly: "Nothing is funnier than unhappiness" (18).

In the Victorian era and in the early twentieth century, unexplained paralysis was thought to be a product of hysteria, sometimes stemming from repressed anger or frigid sexuality. Notwithstanding the source, the paralytic typically exerts a major control over family members. For parents, it causes guilt. For caregivers the burden can be overwhelming. Arguments and power struggles arise. In particular, any withholding of sexual favors from a partner is often interpreted as passive-aggressive tactics. In Hamm's household, there seems never a way out of this searing bind. Or is there a hypnotic allure to the paralytic?

Hamm's ability to fascinate and bewitch, together with his heightened sense of prestige, are clues that begin to crack open the enigma of his volatile personality. His alternately solicitous and extortionate behavior toward Clov may suggest ambivalent erotic desires he harbors towards him. Whatever ghost manifests itself in Hamm, it reveals an insatiable appetite to wield power over those he deems beneath him. Because he thinks of himself as utterly *outré*, he delights in assuming the air of a man possessed, a special person engulfed by tragedy, the linchpin in some evolving thriller. That Hamm may be all these things at once is what gives this greatly discomforting play its torque. Hamm, who keeps up a running conversation with himself while berating others, may be suffering from something other than everyday narcissism. He often acts as though he were a furloughed prisoner gratefully returned to the cell of his wheelchair. The question of whether he was forced into this position by the loss of a loved one, much less the loss of love from the parents before him, gives the play the aspect of a psychological mystery, one that takes a disquieting turn later on in the play when Clov pushes him around the room in his chair to the back wall. That exercise turns into a sado-masochistic event, one that seems to stimulate them both.

All the play's unanswered questions about this curious man—the twinned spectacle of his angry outbursts and naked vulnerability, the melancholy chatter about a missing, perhaps phantom child, the lack of an intact family that truly loves and accepts him—swirl, filling the cramped room like a toxic vapor. In an instant, Hamm permutes from a figure of tentative compassion to a subject of full-blown suspicion. It's a startling turn, made all the more unsettling because Beckett isn't just playing with our sympathies: he is playing with our assumptions about what happens when a man takes an interest in his valet or even a missing child. Hamm never breaks the skin of his mask to reveal the underlying turmoil, much less the roots, of his paralysis. That helps keep the tension going, but it also keeps his mystery intact and makes a strong case for even the most ostensibly unsympathetic and wretched among us. The irony of the drama is that while Beckett's approach verges on melodrama, he grants his troubled, difficult character the full measure of his humanity.

For Hamm, the melodrama is about a sense of being perceived as an outsider, rather like the experience of looking in the mirror and not being shocked at seeing someone you don't quite recognize. Hence his need for masks. Throughout the play, Hamm's masks are not so much images as after-images that seem to have burned through one scrim-like layer of his personality to reveal another. There is a paradox to Hamm's behavior that even in his most casual and natural conversational modes he seems to startle himself. Hence, since it is his custom is to speak in paradoxes and witty jokes, this ingenuousness is all the more a surprise. Given Hamm's dark view on life, it is only predictable that when his icy charm toward Clov grows ever more threatening, his affect grows equally detached and methodically cruel.

Like many low-wage workers, Clov is accustomed to the politics of opposition, to resisting whatever Hamm suggests and to harboring feelings of *ressentiment*. Frederic Jameson explains Nietzsche's concept of *ressentiment* as an emotion that "marks the Other as reactive and attributes the vengeance taken by the weak over the strong to the former's envy" (131).[3] This discordant atmosphere might explain Hamm's *Schadenfreude* as an attempt to put to rest a sordid or impoverished past of his own, one that Clov seems to intuit. "If I could kill him I'd be happy" (27), he mumbles. In this spirit, Clov is a perverse truth teller, a kind of classic Mephistophelean character who deflates his superiors. In his shrewdly self-conscious obliqueness, Clov consents to play the game. Yet he does not altogether escape a collision with self-performance. Clov's deliberately emblematic performances in this way parlay themselves into a powerful diagnosis of the societal body.

The dynamics between Nagg and Nell and their child Hamm are as equally conflicted as their son's with his caregiver. Knowing the old theme that it takes two to tango, Hamm feeds into his parents' sense of isolation and their clichéd interchanges. His behavior toward them indicates that he deplores his ancestry—no doubt belied by his father's cockney accent—thus he aligns himself with a mythic royal past. Holding both mother and father in custody in filthy ashbins ensures their continual dependence on him. To boot, Hamm seems to relish prying into their marital past. Did they bring Hamm into the world because they desired a child, or was he the result of mechanical sexual interchange? "Scoundrel! Why did you engender me?" he asks his father. "I didn't know" (49), Nagg shrugs. This interplay between father and son also touches on a master-slave dynamic inherent in the parents' interactions. After the father's drawn-out story of the Englishman and the tailor, a story freighted with hilarious homosexual overtones, Hamm grows annoyed and screams, "Have you not finished?" and orders Clov to "Clear away this muck! Chuck it in the sea!" (23). These exchanges are gruesome reminders of the wounds that ill-loved, neglected children carry around well into middle age. Nagg and Nell clearly have not been forgiven, perhaps because they apparently still do not understand or care to learn what they did wrong.

Precisely because Hamm has not forgiven his parents, his toy dog stands in as a surrogate and occupies a special position in the play. In a drama filled with unforgettable characters, it is worth underlining the contribution of the toy dog, which in two or three scenes creates an indelible portrait of Hamm's sense of inadequate parental love and the absence, as well, of a reciprocal adult relationship with another person. Deleuze and Guatarri parse the layered meanings of animals in a section of their monumental work, *A Thousand Plateaus*:

> We must distinguish three kinds of animals. First, individuated animals, family pets, sentimental, Oedipal animals each with its own petty history, 'my' cat, 'my' dog. These animals invite us to regress, draw us into a narcissistic contemplation, and they are the only kind of animal psychoanalysis understands, the better to discover a daddy, a mommy, a little brother behind them.[4]

Hamm's toy dog is a not a mere fireside companion, in which he invests feelings of warmth and loyalty. There is also the power component involved in the training of one's dog. In addition, there is the sly and covert sense of being beautiful for your pet if, as is sometimes the case, you view your pet as an ersatz partner. In fondling his toy dog, Hamm quickly notices that he cannot discern the creature's sex. "You've forgotten the sex," he points out. Clov replies with an epigrammatic pun, "But he isn't finished. The sex goes on at the end" (40). Then, when the three-legged toy dog will not conform to Hamm's fumbled attempts to make it stand upright, loyally by his side, he grows impatient. Beckett uses sexual gamesmanship in this verbal duel about the dog to explore and satirize the complexities and duplicities of the two men. Hamm and Clov obviously are playacting parts to each other, yet the dialogue subtly negotiates the arena of sexual conquest, gender roles, and the exchanges of power inherent in their erotically repressed, coded relationship.

Beckett retrieves from repression certain psychodynamics of masculinity that Freud perhaps left unexplained, particularly the agitation that one can produce in the other's body. When, after Clov has locked down the aged parents in their bins for the night, Hamm declares, "My anger subsides, I'd like to pee," Clov thereupon responds, *"(with alacrity):* I'll go and get the catheter" (24). Not only is this exchange illustrative of Hamm's frustrated dominance over Clov, but it also could be interpreted as an erotic signal. Since the request involves a catheter, Hamm's order might be his not-so-subtle cue to initiate in Clov a flurry of excitement in the events that will follow. True, Hamm genuinely enjoys Clov's readiness, but his so-called kindness is often prefaced with innocuous remarks intended to seduce. In his novel, *The Joke,* Milan Kundera encapsulates this notion: "the vanity of power manifests itself not only in cruelty but also (though less often) in gentleness" (89). Everybody, it seems, from Dickens to the psychoanalyst Melanie Klein, has at some point rightly observed that benevolence is not far from greed.

Hans-Georg Gadamer's concept of play as a mode of being further exemplifies how the dramatic structure of *Endgame* involves play-acting with sexual components as a subtext. In his *Truth and Method*, he explains: "We can certainly distinguish between play and the behavior of the player. By play I mean its (special) relation to what is serious." In playing, "all those purposive relations that determine active and caring existence have not simply disappeared, but are curiously suspended" (102).

Hamm certainly "plays" in the philosopher's sense. Gadamer observes:

> when children enjoy dressing up [...] they are not trying to hide themselves, pretending to be something else in order to be discovered and recognized behind it; but, on the contrary, they intend a representation of such a kind that only what is represented exists. The child wants at any cost to avoid being discovered behind his disguise. (113)

Hamm's play has no end. His dress-up *IS* his presentation. As Gadamer simply puts it: "Self-presentation is the true nature of play" (116). Hamm's dress-up and masking therefore represent his engagement with Clov, not to win as in a sport but simply to *be*. In addition, the to and fro of their talk evokes what is understood as the play between gears or the play of forces. But there are risks involved in the play of forces. Even the play of a mechanical fan entails the risk of it "not working." Despite the risks, Hamm and Clov's pursuit of the creative process of play brings excitement into the picture.

Hamm delights also in playing the role of a "crossover artist," having traveled the route from the abused and sensitive boy to arrogant, vain Method actor.[5] He tries on King Lear's emotions, as it were, in order to expose his own wounds from the latent memory of his childhood. With the King's arrogance he can denounce the affection of persons he deems his "children"—Clov and his parents. To be sure, *Endgame* speaks of our collective delight in laughing at other people's disabilities and the mistreatment of our elders. It is a touchstone drama, not only on the strength of Hamm's grievous errors and baroque misgivings but also on the emotional centrality and legibility of his servant. Clov could have been something of a caricature[6] but with his unspoken routines and formal gestures running in parallel with Hamm's high-flown drama, the play becomes a pantomime of the social construct of the body, one not confined to artificial "anecdotes."

Hamm's florid mannerisms are just as revealing and entertaining: his effete mode of folding his handkerchief and pressing it into the breast pocket of his dressing-gown is a time-capsule view of a once sought-after opulent life, eccentric and replete with moth-eaten Turkish rugs, worn out, tasteless furniture, and specimens, too, of the tastes of the would-be rich as evolved in houses where furniture was moved, but almost never discarded. His parents' nightcaps resemble the fossil evidence of a class laid down in sedimentary layers across eras that might be termed proto-Moderne. Organically weird, Hamm's dresses himself and his parents in exactly the way he socializes, preferring the company of servants to aristocrats. Undoubtedly, Beckett's costuming for the play is another reliable source of voyeuristic pleasure and social information.

With his high camp version of the paralytic, Hamm breaks taboos against denigrating the disabled, made acceptably chic by his decadent affectations. His personal display has something to do with sexuality, to be sure. In drawing attention to himself repeatedly, what he does best is to produce an uncomfortable but memorable image of the highly charged outré, the extravagant and outrageous Wildean

Romantic. The viewer senses, too, that Hamm's stiff comportment bears witness to a body marshaled to quell unconscious erotic tendencies. When, perhaps after a brilliant career he stumbles, he finds the solace of the mask the only medium through which life can be made bearable. A man now merely capable yet still charismatic, Hamm is the ghost of his former self. His flighty behavior, fantastic apparel and exaggerated gestures shade in the dark edges of feeling like he's living as a man apart—a status that might otherwise force him to admit that he is nothing but a caricature of the wounded romantic. The result is a sense of separateness that enables both Hamm and Clov to share an affinity for culture and esthetics, and to distance themselves from the mundane circumstances in their midst.

At any rate, it is Beckett's biting humor that aligns his work with the surreal domestic comedies of John Guare, Christopher Durang and John Patrick Shanley.[7] Hamm chooses to think of himself positively as having achieved a strange sort of victory—through the courtly, cagey manners of an outsider—always gauging a response, planning a parry. He doesn't really disagree with Clov's essential presence or retorts; he simply restates the point as though it were someone's *else's* opinion until it resembles his own. His display of flamboyance, affection and humor sometimes causes him to relapse into gay Edwardian comedy as in his wily comment to Clov: "Don't we laugh?" (11). We can almost see his lips purse.

On the page, the text itself lacks the high camp quality that creeps into the spoken word. When the play was written, camp was a relatively new concept, but the behavior has existed for centuries. An example can be seen in William Congreve's *Love for Love* when Sir Sampson berates Jeremy, his beloved servant: "How were you engendered, muckworm?" Jeremy returns the dagger, "I am, by my father, the son of a chairman; my mother sold oysters in winter and cucumbers in summer; and I came up stairs in the world, for I was born in a cellar" (244). Clearly, playing the game of one-upmanship has a long literary history.

Endgame exposes the two sides to every turn of phrase. The homoerotic suggestions not only spark the conversation between man and servant; the domestic suspicions that define Hamm's relationship with his father also drive the play along. His tormented relationship with his parents becomes the metaphorical template for his physically and emotionally maimed body and psyche. As the father character,

Pop, in Shanley's play, *Beggars in the House of Plenty* (1991), puts it: "You look for love to stop the starving thing in you that I put there, but nothing will stop the starving thing. I'll never approve of you" (qtd in Witchel 34). Hamm appears never to have changed from his own upbringing and foists the same dysfunctionality on his valet. Persons with problems with parental approval often choose somebody who is going to continue giving them the same problem to wrestle with. In fact, one character's complaint is often echoed verbatim later in the play by another character. Earlier, Nell complains to her husband, "Why this farce, day after day?" (14). Halfway through the play Clov repeats the same: "Why this farce, day after day?" to which Hamm responds, ho-hum, "Routine. One never knows" (32). Sometimes Hamm's inability to keep the games going full-tilt reveals a lack of confidence, thus his need for masks.

The theme of the mask warrants further consideration with regard to seeing and non-seeing. In *The Joke*, Kundera's main character, Ludvik, comments on an unattractive aspect of his personality: "I had always staggered under the weight of my masks."[8] In Beckett's play, masking and the construct of the body have to do with the indeterminate relationship between appearance and reality and it is this quality that makes Hamm's masking inscrutable. Seated in his chair throughout the play, Hamm is posed rather like a statue. Behind dark glasses he seems to stare into the distance, not seeing anything in particular. His face resembles one of those ancient busts with blank spots for eyes. Deleuze and Guattari have written that "the face is not a universal [...] the face is by nature an entirely specific idea, which did not preclude its acquiring and exercising the most general of functions: the function of biunivocalization, or binarization" (176). They elaborate on the binary aspect of the face: "The empty eye or black hole absorbs or rejects, like a half-doddering despot who can still give a signal of acquiescence or refusal" (177).[9] Placed in his chair by Beckett as a conceptualized composition, Hamm exudes gravity, enigma, formal beauty—and exceptionalness, as if time itself had stopped to look at the face of the person sitting. His face assumes an aura of isolated originality and is, we are being told, what it means to be Other.

Susan Sontag has said that "[e]veryone has felt (at least in fantasy) the erotic glamour of physical cruelty and an erotic lure in things that are vile and repulsive" (57). As the play moves forward, the

audience begins to sense that Hamm's paralysis seems to mean more
than the obvious; and after it has learned that both parents have no legs
at all but only stumps which sink in filthy sawdust, we feel the
awkward embarrassment at witnessing questionable scenes not meant
to be seen. Later on in the play Hamm and Clov, like an old married
couple ossified in their ways *exactly* like his parents, speak in a manner
that exposes the two sides of their erotic misgivings:

> Hamm:
> Kiss me.
> *(pause.)* Will you not kiss me?
> Clov:
> No.
> Hamm:
> On the forehead.
> Clov:
> I won't kiss you anywhere.
> *(pause.)*
> Hamm: *(holding out his hand):*
> Give me your hand at least.
> *(pause.)*
> Will you not give me your hand?
> Clov:
> I won't touch you.
> Hamm:
> Give me the dog.
> *(Clov looks round for the dog.)* (67)

In this interchange, the viewer witnesses a blunting of the erotic
edginess usually attendant in Hamm and Clov's sweet-talk. For if Clov
will not kiss Hamm, let alone touch him, there is always the dog to
which he can transfer affection. What else do these words evoke, other
than an invitation to the audience to vicariously experience Clov's
rejection of his mate Hamm?[10]

   Peggy Phelan has written persuasively on the function of
seeing, and not seeing, in the work of Beckett. She argues that Beckett
dramatizes the rhythm of looking as one that "oscillates between
seeing and blindness, between figuration and abstraction, between the
void at the center of sight and the contour of the slender ridge that
brooks it" (1280). The optical, psychological force of our being able to
see the unsighted Hamm is what in part allows us to see the drama of
his un-seeing sight. Strangely, Hamm's opaque gaze is one that is
inescapably erotic. His soliloquies are much more than the summation

of his ruminations about the lure of the pleasures of clouded vision. The unsighted gaze asks what fantasy is buried deep in the history of his past.

Beckett made this fantasy patently clear in a scene earlier in the play, but it is one whose meaning critics never seem to be able to agree on. A crucial erotic moment occurs when Hamm orders Clov to take him for a "ride" around the room and to stop at the back wall. This episode makes clear that Hamm experiences sexual, even pornographic, sensations when he is being moved around in his chair. Though blind, he instinctively knows where the chair is to be positioned with regard to the wall. Knowing in advance not to inflict harm on each other, Hamm and Clov substitute the slam against the wall for a shared event, one that focuses on a strange kind of erotic climax. This moment occurs rather early in the play and sets a pictorial tone for the verbal nuances and dissonances that constitute much of the dialogue throughout the play. The episode at the back wall, far from being a fresh air constitutional, is a played out, shared sado-masochistic moment. It is a particularly poignant moment for the paralyzed Hamm, as it is his chance to physically challenge the unknown Other on the opposite side. When Clov reaches the wall, Hamm cries out:

> Stop!
> *(Clov stops chair close to back wall. Hamm lays his hand against wall.)*
> Old wall!
> *(Pause.)*
> Beyond is the ... other hell.
> *(Pause. Violently.)*
> Closer! Closer! Up against!
> Clov:
> Take away your hand.
> *(Hamm withdraws his hand. Clov rams chair against wall.)*
> There! (25-26)

Whatever one thinks of him, Hamm is remarkable for his clarity of mind. With his dry, secular, spartan spirit, he is an odd stickler for a certain kind of erotic precision. When he touches the wall and caresses it lovingly, as one would a lover, we can see how accustomed Hamm is to tactile foreplay and hence appreciate how vitally crucial the gesture is to this scene. Like the to and fro motion of their speech, the chair's violent thrust is an illustration of the accelerating rhythm of replication inherent in sexuality. The vibrations resulting from the slam against the wall increase in direct proportion to the visible intensification of Clov's obedient submission.

One result of this enigmatic structure is that it allows Beckett to expose us to "the disconcerting fact that [...] we can sometimes begin to see what makes our usual not seeing such a vital failure."[11] Hamm endures the tedium of waiting for time to pass in order to repeat this masochistic ritual the next day, hopefully in exactly the same way as the previous day—but not before he enjoys the spectacle of being seen by his partner, and of course by the viewer. The payoff for Hamm is that his blindness permits him to refine his erotic movements voyeuristically in the mode of play, for, as Gadamer explains, the "implication is that play implies a spectator" (116). Beckett says through a voice in *Fizzles*: "I'll let myself be seen before I'm done" (qtd in Phelan 1285). Phelan observes: "Seeing was always already a way of saying for Beckett, and so too was saying a way of seeing" (1285). This binocularity showed how much he understood that speaking creates a visual image.[12]

Hamm's scotophilia—his love of visual dimness—illustrates how attached he is to the blind spots in his emotional visual field. In terms of Freudian sexuality, the use of scotophilia in *Endgame* further explains Hamm's exhibitionism and sexual cruelty. In his *Three Essays On the Theory of Sexuality,* Freud describes a connection between sexual development in the child and the development of the instinct of scotophilia and cruelty: "Children who distinguish themselves by special cruelty towards animals and playmates usually give rise to a just suspicion of an intense and precocious sexual activity arising from erotogenic zones" (qtd in Bersani 36). Freud situates this drive somewhere in the zone between sadism and masochism. Verbal disputes, intellectual strain, wrestling with playmates, among others, can take the form of cruelty. There is no doubt that Clov utilizes the toy dog to behave in a cruel manner toward Hamm. Although Clov himself sewed the dog together for Hamm, toy or no toy, the dog stands for exactly what it represents: a real animal. Earlier, Clov voiced a concern to Hamm that he says he will never understand: "Why I always obey you" (76). Hamm then asks for the dog:

Hamm:
 Give me the dog.
Clov: (*looking*):

Quiet!
Hamm:
   Give me the dog!
   (Clov . . . looks for the dog, sees it, picks it up, hastens toward Hamm
   and strikes him violently on the head with the dog.)
Clov:
   There's your dog for you!
   (The dog falls to the ground. Pause.)
Hamm:
   He hit me! (76-77)

If examined carefully, the fact that Hamm and Clov switch roles in this scene shows just how the suffering of others—as distinct from why we wish to exercise power over others—can arouse individuals. Freud defines sadism in "Instincts and Their Vicissitudes" as a masochistic identification with the suffering object. There, Bersani explains that the suffering of others provides a key to our understanding how "sadomasochistic sexuality would be a kind of melodramatic version of the constitution of sexuality itself" (41). Bersani argues that masochism operates as a sort of solution to the dysfunctional sex itself. To find a fix for it, masochism then becomes "repeated as a dysfunctional choice" (41). Perhaps because of his physical limitations in the first place, Hamm enjoys an even more intense suffering by allowing Clov to be the sadist and strike him, first against the wall and then with his precious toy. Clov, however, needed to remind Hamm in the first place, "He's not a real dog ..." (56). Even Freud himself could not quite comprehend fully the role that sadism plays in erotic life. He pondered the issue anew when he wrote *Beyond the Pleasure Principle* at sixty-four years of age (1920). He writes: "But how can the sadistic instinct, whose aim it is to injure the object, be derived from Eros, the preserver of life? [...] Wherever the original sadism has undergone no mitigation or intermixture, we find the familiar ambivalence of love and hate in erotic life" (48).

Although Hamm cannot literally see, he has the vision of a voyeur. Freud writes in the first essay in *Three Essays*: "In scotophilia and exhibitionism the eye corresponds to an erotogenic zone in sexuality involving cruelty" (qtd in Bersani 39). In *Endgame* the scotophilic eye takes up where words leave off. In this regard, the visual, erotic aspects of *Endgame* also can be examined in terms of film noir effects. Beckett obviously grasped the degree to which film noir is synonymous with visual fantasy and a primal longing for the forbidden, and he understood how passions bordering on obsessions drive these. As we know, a successful film noir is an act of seduction in which the story, dialogue and imagery lead us to imagine a shadow world of temptation and corruption. Traditionally, a toxic femme fatale who lures the main character into disaster is as ruthless as she is charming.

Here the femme fatale is the psychologically predatory Hamm. Feral and lupine in his gestures and manner of speaking, Hamm is an expert in delivering different versions of the same story subjected to modification, first as past fact, then as the present retooled in his imagination. Yet for all his malicious wit, he seems to recognize that his essential need is for some kind of special space and a heightened relationship with another. There are delicate aspects to his speech, along with the steely charm of his actor's unabashed effeminacy, but all this changes when he realizes that Clov intends to leave for good. Before Hamm throws everything away at the play's end some (but not all) of the relevant aspects of their master/servant bondage are more daringly exposed, evident in one of their last exchanges. Clov has made it utterly clear that he is leaving. In a final verbal flourish, Hamm tries to extract a quotidian of forced love from him. Like a couple breaking up unwillingly, Hamm keeps the pressure up. "Before you go" he pleads, "say something." Clov retorts with the terse answer, "There is nothing to say" (79).

Who is in bondage to whom? The reader might ask. What accident, torture, or romantic game has caused Hamm to be so entirely at the mercy of his servant? Because Clov is rather sexually ambiguous on the most fundamental level, this fact does not in any way detract from the domestic nature of their relationship, either in their conversational mode or the roles that each plays. The attraction and repulsion exerted by the two lend the play all the heat and tension any unusual domestic arrangement might need. Hamm is above all the dramatic chameleon shuffling between three faces: ruthless tyrant, charming raconteur, and glamorous seducer. All of these suggest the play's willingness to incorporate elements of comedy even as it contemplates the human instinct to embroider reality in order to make a situation reveal more conclusive, if less strictly factual, information about troubled partnerships. *Endgame* thrives on various levels of irony and the dissection of illusion and fact. This theme is illustrated by Karl Marx in the opening sentences from his *Eighteenth Brumaire of Louis Napoleon*: "Hegel remarks somewhere that all great world-historical facts and personages occur, so to speak, twice. He forgot to add: the first time as tragedy, the second time as farce."

Roland Barthes had an answer to this enigma. In *S/Z*, he explores the proairetic code—that is, stereotypical physical and psychological archetypes, such as walking, turning away, envying, and so on. What Barthes means by the proairetic code is that our trivial, repeated daily acts reveal aspects of our personalities that can be interpreted as a kind of code. He calls this category that of the "already-done" or "already-written" (Barthes 1974, 203-204). As Jameson explains: "these gestural archetypes are in reality nothing but clichés *before the fall*" (80). In *Endgame*, repeated behavior is ubiquitous, such as Clov's endlessly threatening to "making an exit," and Hamm's counter-threat to withhold love, food and shelter should the former actually occur. The result is the familiar transforming itself into the unfamiliar, although in a "familiar" way. Thus, when a simple motion of walking out of a room becomes less familiar, it turns into "a struggle, a contest of every instant, a situation of strategic embattlement in which one can make the right or the wrong move" (Jameson 46). But a superior opponent can always outwit a weaker one, as Clov's final exit proves. *Endgame* offers an almost Shakespearean appreciation of human complexity, paradoxically centered on two characters who are anything but self-aware.

Endgame is a 24-hour study of combat habitat. I do not think Beckett is necessarily pointing a bleak finger at the universe; instead, he may be proffering his view of close relationships: although there are ties that bind, they are difficult to maintain. *Endgame* focuses on just that—trying to reach an endgame—but here there is no negotiated capitulation. Is Clov an enabler? A placater? Is the appeasement legitimate or corrupt? The art of a successful negotiation is to find an endgame, literally, in which it gets down to a single issue—in this case, "Who is in charge" versus "who is subservient"—and then to capitulate. To get what you want from others you must appeal first of all to the self-interests of others, not to their mercy. No one will come and work for you asking for gratitude or mercy. Perhaps Clov's departure is a kind of relief for Hamm because it is easier to endure a terrible outcome than to imagine it, to wait for it endlessly.

After Clov's exit, Hamm calls the departing shot: "Deuce. *(Pause. He takes off his glasses.)* Wipe. *(He takes out his handkerchief*

and, without unfolding it, wipes his glasses.) … We're coming. A few
more squirms like that and I'll call" (82-3). Here, Hamm's bearing
switches from restlessness to depletion: Beckett's familiar themes of
the mind and the body, and of couples who cannot find the right
rhythm. That may be the fundamental paradox of the play. The
interplay between the two men is a game that reinvents not only the
notion of roles but also the master-slave dynamic inherent in their
"coded" sex play, as it changes from simple bickering to playful erotic
games. Lastly, Hamm throws away his dog and whistle, and softly
calls for Clov:

> Clov!
> *(Long pause.)*
> No? Good.
> *(He takes out the handkerchief.)*
> Since that's the way we're playing it …
> *(he unfolds handkerchief)*
> … let's play it that way … (84)

Hamm repeats his initial physical position at the end of the play. He
takes up his mask and covers his face with it. There is no doubt that
Beckett addresses head-on the problems of men in troubled
partnerships. *Endgame* resolutely refuses transcendence: the play's
affect is entirely under control because it never tries to mean more than
it says. The ending tableau of violence becomes a human inquisition
into dreams, reality, guilt, augury and terror.

Beckett collapses the proairetic into a new kind of aesthetic
agent, one just like Hamm himself who makes stories out of stories.
Dreams, doubles, masks—so many of the elements that appear again
and again in Beckett's drama and fiction—are symbols of the psyche
turned inward. It is because he knows that there is finally no difference
between murderer and victim, chaser and fugitive, performer and
audience. They are one and the same. This view can be frightening,
since the line between monism and solipsism is thin and porous, more
to do with emotion than with mind per se. This kind of collapse of
individual identity is also paradoxical, requiring a grotesque self-
obsession combined with an almost total effacement of self and
personality. Tics and obsessions aside, what defines Hamm is the odd,
ineluctable sense he projects that no one and everyone is responsible
for his plight. This view encompasses distortions of the body, sexual

cartooning of situation, the gothic, camp, burlesque—all forms of an expressionism that bursts convention, with its implicit strain of dark comedy, one that has been around forever. As John Ruskin once put it: "the grotesque is, in almost all case, composed of two elements, one ludicrous, the other fearful" (qtd in Cotter B27).

The grotesque is everywhere—even in the *contempus mundi* of satire. One of the unexpected depths of *Endgame* is the grappling with erotic satire itself, the way it demeans and wounds, as well as enlightens and amuses. Graham Fraser has observed in a salient scene in the play where Hamm insinuates that Clov's intermittent trips to his kitchen satisfy his servant's erotic needs: "What do you see on your wall? Mene? Mene? Naked bodies?" (40). The slyly subversive voice of Beckett can be heard underneath Hamm's lines; they are as interesting for their insights into how drama takes shape as they are is for their ostensible talking points on gay interchanges.

Despite his moodiness and scurrilous innuendo, there is a fierce, quicksilver intelligence at work in Hamm. His wheelchair and the parental ashbins imply vulnerability and impotence, without question. In *Camera Lucida* Barthes wrote about the *punctum* of a photograph, the singular point of a picture that sears into your brain. He refers to the *punctum* as the "element which rises from the scene, shoots out of it like an arrow, and pierces me. A Latin word exists to designate this wound, this prick ..." (26). I think Hamm's chair, bloody handkerchief and dark glasses comprise a compendium of puncta, provoking an almost physical reaction in the viewer. Adorned with theses objects, Hamm becomes the consummate picture of tired ennui. As social statements of the body, they allow him to live in our imagination with the obvious discomfort of his physical condition and the authenticity of his weariness.

With *Endgame*, Beckett has written a darkly scintillating play, a work that gestures at tragedy or grand opera without trying to summon it. The social construct of the body that issues from all axes offer a profound glimpse of how social ills—ranging from indifference to others, to domestic violence and so on—are exacerbated, provoked, and sometimes even produced by our deepest psychological needs and vulnerabilities, forces of which we are largely unaware. Beckett's penchant for the surreal mixture of strange objects and odd couples allows him to exploit the human fear of being abandoned and to turn this existential fear back on itself into cultural commentary. The verbal wrestling matches among all parties as well as Hamm's dread of exposure are Beckett's way of physicalizing, *and* masking, his own signature ambivalence.

Mary F. Catanzaro, Milawukee, Wisconsin

Notes

[1] Samuel Beckett, *Endgame* (New York: Grove, 1958), 1. Further references will be from this edition, and will be incorporated into the text with page numbers.

[2] Robb notes other behaviors and personalities who join the literary ranks of gay intellectuals. Poe's sleuth, Auguste Dupin (254) glances forward in time to J. Edgar Hoover, with suggestions on the behavior of Melville's Redburn (259). Behaviors between male couples included closing windows and pulling curtains (257), thus the significance of the curtained windows in *Endgame*. Clothes were worn tight-fitting (90), adding homoerotic significance to Nagg's story of the Englishman and the tailor. Assuming the tailor's voice speaking to the customer, Nagg regales his audience: "'a neat seat can be very ticklish [...] a snug crotch is always a teaser [...] at a pinch, a smart fly is a stiff proposition'" (22). Hamm and Clov meet other criteria for gay behavior. As Robb points out, sex is viewed as an intellectual adventure (92); shame is exhibited concerning the sexual orientation of family members, as well as self-shaming (106); and gays are perceived as members of an intelligent "existential avant-garde" (254).

[3] Jameson has analyzed Nietzsche's concept to explain the resentment of the have-nots for the haves. The resentment is not limited to material wealth. He writes: "since the culture critique has been conceived as the diagnosis of pernicious attitudes and toxic ideas, the agents of cultural decay are specified in advance and can be no other than the very guardians of culture, the intellectuals themselves, by definition disgruntled and embittered, failed artists and would-be unsuccessful politicians—in short, the very archetype of *ressentiment* at its purest" (131-32).

[4] In their giant work, *A Thousand Plateaus: Capitalism and Schizophrenia*, Gilles Deleuze and Felix Guattari, elaborate: "Finally, there are demonic animals [...] that form [...] a tale [...] There is always the possibility that any given animal, a louse, a cheetah, or an elephant will be treated as a pet, my little beast" (241). Hamm's behavior with his toy dog acts out the deep structure embedded in his relationship with his parents.

[5] Gadamer speaks of the actor: "If we describe from the point of view of the actor what his acting is, then obviously it is not transformation but disguise" (111). Clearly, the actor's mode is Hamm's preference.

[6] See Lee Siegel, 'The Method Conspiracy: How a Russian-born Acting Technique Took Over America at the Height of the Cold War' in *The New York Times* Magazine (August 8, 2004): 17. It was Siegel who emphasized that affect-laden memories of the past can alter behavior in the present. An interesting comparison to Clov can be seen in Siegel's observance that the cartoon figure "Magoo first appeared in 1949, at the threshold of the cold war, a weak, bumbling, stumbling character, bullied and pushed

around by the more powerful figures around him. Yet he always managed to prevail in the end. After all, the words 'Ya magoo' meant 'I can.' In Russian, that is" (qtd in Siegel 17). Obviously, Clov refuses outright bullying and true verbal abuse from his partner.

[7] Witchel observes other conflicted pairs in Shanley's plays. *Danny and the Deep Blue Sea*, which opened November 10, 2004, at Second Stage Theater in New York, is a two-character play about lovers afraid of love.

[8] Kundera's character, Ludvik, wryly observes: "Nothing brings people together more quickly (though often spuriously and deceitfully) than shared melancholy: for one has to lay aside cultivated restraints, cultivated gestures and facial expressions [...] how I managed to do it [...] I who'd always fumbled behind my false faces, I do not know" (68).

[9] Deleuze and Guattari's exploration of the binarized face lends significance to Hamm's appearance. Underneath the bloodied handkerchief or his dark glasses, Hamm's face becomes an "abstract machine of faciality" behind which he controls others: "Even masks ensure the head's belonging to the body, rather than making it a face" (176).

[10] Leo Bersani argues in his *The Freudian Body* that throughout Freud's *Three Essays on the Theory of Sexuality* there runs a counterargument that states that "sexuality would not be originally an exchange of intensities between individuals, but rather a condition of broken negotiations with the world, a condition in which others merely set off the self-shattering mechanisms of masochistic *jouissance* [...] In order to account for the mystery of sadistic sexuality—that is, how we can be sexually aroused by the suffering of others, as distinct from the easier question of why we wish to exercise power over others—Freud is led to suggest that the spectacle of pain in others stimulates a mimetic representation which shatters the subject into sexual excitement" (41). For Hamm and Clov, sadomasochism is clearly a game ending in playful *jouissance*.

[11] Peggy Phelan is here discussing the dangerous blindness of the sightless Pozzo in *Waiting for Godot,* but we can see how Beckett figured this propensity in Hamm just as effectively.

[12] Beckett described how he himself came to understand that saying was a way of seeing: "For it is not at all about a sudden awareness, but a sudden visual grasp, a sudden shot of the eye. Just that" (1287). Phelan is quoting in her essay from Oppenheim (2000): 75.

Bibliography

Barthes, Roland. *Camera Lucida: Reflections on Photography* translated by Richard Howard. New York: Hill and Wang, 1981.

—. *S/Z* translated by Richard Miller. New York: Hill and Wang, 1974.

Beckett, Samuel. *Endgame*. New York: Grove, 1958.

Bersani. Leo. *The Freudian Body. Psychoanalysis and Art*. New York: Columbia University Press, 1986.

Congreve, William. *Love for Love. The Comedies of William Congreve* ed. Eric S. Rump. London: Penguin, 1985.

Cotter, Holland. 'Intersection of Big Egos: One Jolting the Art World, One Amassing a Collection' in *The New York Times* (30 July, 2004): Sec.B: 27, 31.

Deleuze, Gilles and Felix Guattari. *A Thousand Plateaus: Capitalism and Schizophrenia* translation and forward by Brian Massumi. Minneapolis: University of Minnesota Press, 1987.

Fraser, Graham. "The Pornographic Imagination in *All Strange Away*" in *Modern Fiction Studies* 41.3-4 (1995): 515-536.

Freud, Sigmund. *Beyond the Pleasure Principle* translated and edited by James Strachey. New York: Norton, 1961.

Gadamer, Hans-Georg. *Truth and Method*. Second, rev. ed. Translated by Joel Weinsheimer and Donald G. Marshall. New York: Continuum, 2000.

Jameson, Fredric. *Agons of Agression: Wyndham Lewis, the Modernist as Fascist*. Berkeley: University of California Press, 1979.

Kundera, Milan. *The Joke*. Def. version and revised by the author. New York: Perennial, 2001.

Marx, Karl. *The Eighteenth Brumaire of Louis Napoleon* translated by Saul K. Padover from the German Edition. Prepared by Engels (1869). Moscow: Progress Publishers, 1937. Also available online at Marx/Engels Internet Archive (www.Marxists.org) 1995, 1999.

Phelan, Peggy. "Lessons in Blindness From Samuel Beckett" in *Publications of the Modern Language Association of America* 119.5 (October 2004): 1279-1288.

Robb, Graham. *Strangers: Homosexual Love in the Nineteenth Century*. New York: W. W. Norton, 2003.

Siegel Lee. "The Method Conspiracy: How a Russian-born Acting Technique Took Over America at the Height of the Cold War" in *The New York Times Magazine* (1 August, 2004): 17.

Sontag, Susan. 'The Pornographic Imagination' in *Styles of Radical Will*. New York: Farrar, Straus and Giroux, 1967. (35-73)

Witchel, Alex. "The Confessions of John Patrick Shanley" in *The New York Times Magazine* (7 November, 2004): 30-35.

Hamm Stammered: Beckett, Deleuze, and the Atmospheric Stuttering of *Endgame*

Paul Shields

> Death and life *are* in the power of the tongue:
> and they that love it shall eat the fruit thereof.
> —Proverbs 18:21

> There's English for you.
> —Hamm, *Endgame*

> There are many ways [...] to stutter.
> —Gilles Deleuze, "He Stuttered"

In his provocative essay "'Outside of Here It's Death': Co-Dependency and the Ghosts of Decolonization in Beckett's *Endgame*," Nels C. Pearson examines the postcolonial undertones of Samuel Beckett's 1957 play. Pearson envisions the main character, Hamm, as a "metonym" (224) for a defunct British imperialism, and Clov, Hamm's forlorn attendant, as a remnant of the voiceless colonized. Throughout the play, Clov struggles for a language that will speak without reference to the assumptions or logic of colonialism, yet, according to Pearson, the slave's attempts to find such a way of speaking paradoxically re-imprison him in the fetters of the colonizer. Even when Clov tries to convey "autonomous perception and experience" (226), Pearson argues that he ends up stammering and, within his silences, only signifying, never actualizing, the "muted voice or voices beneath [his] words—a voice that cannot speak or communicate its desires in the language available to it" (226). Another way to read Clov's hesitating speech, however, is to understand it as one faltering voice among many. Indeed, Beckett's entire play is in a constant state of stuttering, quaking violently from the fragmented speech of all the characters, as well as from their stammering movements and shuddering milieu. Gilles Deleuze's essay "He Stuttered" helps to reveal an alternative postcolonial reading of the play, demonstrating how the atmospheric stuttering of *Endgame* emancipates, rather than impedes, the vanquished.[1] Ultimately, *Endgame* proves to be a world of equal-opportunity stuttering, a world in which faltering is the language of liberation.

Pearson begins his reading of *Endgame* with a caveat, asserting that the notorious ambiguity of Beckett's play, its adamant refusal to give up its secrets, complicates any political approach. Yet, Pearson remarks, "this is exactly the reason not to give up the project of trying to come to terms with the play's 'Irishness,' or, more specifically, with the relevance of the play's use of imperialist/colonial themes to both global and local (Irish) histories" (216). The author subsequently turns his attention to how *Endgame* speaks to the complex process of decolonization, and how Beckett's art perpetually sidesteps any neat or resolute commentaries concerning the master/slave dialectic. While he places Hamm on the throne as the has-been colonizer and leaves Clov to wander in the expanses of the has-been colonized, Pearson emphasizes that theirs is a distinctly, if paradoxically, co-dependent relationship. Pearson writes,

> What *Endgame* ostensibly dramatizes is not simply a master/slave relationship, but the lingering co-dependency between two leftover participants from an imperial/colonial (or at the very least ruler/subject) historical situation that no longer exists. The important thing is that Hamm and Clov maintain the respective roles of ruler and ruled, as well as the assumption that there is no alternative to these roles, long after the external causes or specific historical circumstances of those roles have deteriorated. (216-17)

Ghosts of the past, Hamm and Clov cannot give up their places in a defunct paradigm, according to Pearson. In the words of Stanley Cavell, the characters of *Endgame* are unable "*not* to mean what [they] are given to mean" (117). The blind Hamm, who sits in (or near) the center of his shelter-universe, gives orders to Clov, who remorsefully obeys. It is all they know on earth, and, to quote Hamm, there's no cure for that.

As his "Irish reading" of the play progresses, Pearson attempts to show (mostly through admitted speculation based on intimation) that Hamm is or once was British and that Clov is or once was Irish, as well as the son of a political prisoner at the former British military post of Cobh (223). In the context of an Irish reading, Pearson argues, the crux of *Endgame* concerns Clov's struggle to find or redefine himself in the phantasmagoric face of the exanimate British Empire. Hamm's stint as dictator and even as enlightened ex-Imperialist, however, ultimately prohibits the slave from personal discovery, as all of Clov's moves on the chessboard, to pick up on Pearson's and the play's central metaphor, are always already subject to the established rules of the games. Thus, even as Clov, at a pivotal point in the play, looks through his telescope and strives to assert his own vision of the world—"I see . . . a multitude . . . in transports . . . of joy" (29)[2]—he can only manage to use and misuse the language Hamm gives him. According to Pearson, Clov falters at every turn, fighting to find the right words but only re-instituting those of his ruler (226-27). Long after the fall of Empire, indeed the apocalyptic fall of the world, Clov and Hamm therefore remain in a political stalemate, as every move to get out of the trap only re-establishes the hierarchies and hegemonies that ensnared them in the first place:

> While the play is about the inability of Clov to find a voice of his own, it is also [...] a play about why expecting him to develop this alternative voice is in part what prevents him from doing so. It is a play in which the initial, unquestioned assumption that we must constantly raise our ladder of perception to the same high windows in search of alternatives becomes the very thing that negates all alternatives. (236)

Pearson's ultimate claim is that, as various postcolonial critics submit, the colonized cannot be free of the strictures of colonialism until the language and logic of the "discoverers" dismantles and falls away. As long as memory serves in Hamm's shelter-colony, so too will the linguistic binaries and hierarchies of colonialism, despite all attempts to circumvent them (229). The only solution is, according to Pearson's conclusion, not "to ask the question in the first place" (237) or to accept the fact "that freedom (whether it be artistic, psychological, or social and political) cannot be achieved as long as a specific colonizer/colonized paradigm is the foregrounded assumption" (237).[3]

Pearson's reading aligns itself with a number of essays that attempt to situate Beckett's play within the context of postcolonial criticism, viewing Hamm and Clov as oppositional forces in a colonial or postcolonial world.[4] Yet all of the characters, particularly Hamm, evidence problems with speech and articulation, as ellipses and dashes pervade the characters' dialogue and monologues. Deleuze's acute vision of minorities and oppression, as well as his theories about language and speech help to pave the way for a new political reading of the stuttering of Beckett's play in which Hamm and Clov both wear away a majoritarian system.

Deleuze's *Essays Critical and Clinical* deal largely with the oppression and salvation of minorities. Throughout, the staunch materialist aims to expose the means by which art can serve as a liberating experience for the voiceless. Many of the essays argue that literature, a term Deleuze never uses lightly, is a panacea for the "missing" people of colonized cultures. As Deleuze explains in his essay "Literature and Life," the writer—and "there are very few who can call themselves writers" (6)—

> is not a patient but rather a physician, a physician of himself and of the world. The world is the set of symptoms whose illness merges with man. Literature then appears as an enterprise of health: not that the writer would necessarily be in good health [...] but he possesses an irresistible and delicate health that stems from what he has seen and heard of things too big for him, too strong for him, suffocating things whose passage exhausts him, while nonetheless giving him the becomings that a dominant and substantial health would render impossible. (3)

For Deleuze, the achievement of "delicately healthy" writers is their ability to provide not merely a refuge but a voice for victimized peoples, who, because they lack an identity, are in a purgatorial state of not-yet-arriving, not-yet-living: "The ultimate aim of literature is to set free, in the delirium, this creation of a health or this invention of a people, that is, a possibility of life. To write for this people who are missing . . . ('for' means less 'in the place of' than 'for the benefit of')" (*Essays* 4). Deleuze goes on to explain that the location or invention of a missing people, a silenced and therefore invisible colonized culture, requires a careful manipulation of words, grammar, and syntax—a stuttering of language.

In "He Stuttered," Deleuze makes clear the difference between immature writers who merely tell readers that their characters stutter, who use "he stuttered" to indicate a speech impediment, and extraordinary writers whose artistic language itself stutters: "It is no longer the character who stutters in speech; it is the writer who becomes *a stutterer in language.* He makes the language as such stutter: an affective and intensive language, and no longer an affectation of the one who speaks" (*Essays* 107). The result of such an affectation is the forging of a foreign or "minor use" of a language that, in the mouths of ruling regimes, silences the voice of a missing colony. As Deleuze stresses throughout his essay, writers must find a way to estrange the majority from itself: "What they do [...] is invent a *minor use* of this major language within which they express themselves entirely; they *minorize* the language, much as in music, where the minor mode refers to dynamic combinations in perpetual disequilibrium" (*Essays* 109). Significantly, Deleuze's use of the word "language" in his essay implies not only speech but the myths and belief systems of a cultural majority. Artistic stuttering thus may include but also extends beyond an author's employment of characters who suffer speech impediments and refers to the way in which the entire language of a text (speech, bodies, environments) vibrates and fragments.

A number of writers manage to give voice to an otherwise unheard, otherwise unseen minority. Deleuze cites Kafka, Melville, Masoch, Artaud, e. e. cummings, and Beckett, among others, in his study of stuttering authors, revealing how their art serves as an oasis for the culturally oppressed. Such writers resort not to using a foreign tongue to escape the dominant voice of imperialists, but to taking the language of the majority and dividing it against itself. As Deleuze reveals over the course of his essay, "[t]here are many ways to grow from the middle, or to stutter" (*Essays* 111). The stuttering of Melville's or Kafka's fiction differs from that of cummings's poetry—"Every man his speciality," as Hamm says. Beckett is of great interest to Deleuze, not because of his abandonment of the language of Empire when writing in French, but because of his systematic corruption of it when writing in English.[5] Deleuze references the 1953 novel *Watt* and, in passing, the 1980s short prose text *Ill Seen Ill Said* to offer specific instances of Beckett's stuttering. Yet *Endgame* also exemplifies Deleuze's argument, demonstrating how both the speech and, more importantly, the language of Beckett's art "tremors from head to toe" (*Essays* 109).

All of the characters contribute to the play's tremoring. Clov's dialogues and monologues, to begin with, are filled with pauses, hesitations, and broken words. As Pearson observes, Clov speaks often in a slow, hesitating manner. His opening speech, for example, is a kind of stutter, an initial, albeit subtle, sign of his trouble with speech. Altering the precision of Christ's declaration from the cross, Clov repeats himself, trying to find the right expression: "Finished, it's finished, nearly finished" (1). As Katharine Worth comments, "'It is finished' loses its finality as Clov moves it toward the doubtful 'must be nearly finished'" (123). In conversation with Hamm, moreover, Clov demonstrates a hesitation to finish his sentences. His words come slowly, divided by the ever-present ellipses:

> HAMM: But you can walk?
> CLOV: I come . . . and go. (36)

At first glance, Clov's hesitations may seem to bolster the argument that the servant is slow of speech, further evidence that he is stifled by the only language he knows. After a word, a silence. Within every silence, a muted voice. Yet from a Deleuzian standpoint, the stuttering indicates not an inability to speak autonomously but, rather, the play's minorization of a majoritarian language. That is, the stammering itself helps to forge a new "minor" language that results from Beckett's manipulation of syntax and rhythm. Hamm, the master of the game in Pearson's reading, also plays a role in the process of minorization, as he trumps his longstanding crony with stammering of his own.

Hamm's opening lines are replete with interruptions of silence, yawns, pauses, and ellipses.[6] The blind invalid begins, vacillates, stammers, bifurcates words and phrases at their centers:

> HAMM: Me—(*he yawns*)—to play. (*He holds the handkerchief spread out before him.*) Old stancher! (*He takes off his glasses, wipes his eyes, his face, the glasses, puts them on again, folds the handkerchief and puts it back neatly in the breast-pocket of his dressing-gown. He clears his throat, joins the tips of his fingers.*)
> Can there be misery—(*he yawns*) loftier than mine? No doubt. Formerly. But now? (*Pause.*) My father? (*Pause.*) My mother? (*Pause.*) My . . . dog? (*Pause.*) Oh I am willing to believe they suffer as much as such creatures can suffer. But does that mean their sufferings equal mine? No doubt. (*Pause.*) No, all is a (*he yawns*) —bsolute [...] (2)[7]

The opening passage sets the tone for the entire play, in which Hamm defers formulating and finishing many of his sentences. His ensuing lines, for example, further reveal his playing with articulation:

"Enough, it's time it ended, in the shelter too. (*Pause.*) And yet I hesitate, I hesitate to . . . to end. Yes, there it is, it's time it ended and yet I hesitate to—(*he yawns*)—to end" (3).[8] Hamm here becomes one with the patterns of his speech. As the invalid hesitates to end, so too do his words, fighting vigorously against the coming period.

Hamm's stammering worsens as he begins his dialogue with Clov. When he inquires whether his companion is tired of their life in the shelter, he fails to find the right words to describe their strange existence. "Have you not had enough? [...] Of this . . . this . . . thing" (5), Hamm says with difficulty, revealing that he struggles in vain to give a specific account of his predicament. As the play progresses, Hamm continues to have trouble speaking and begins to give up on finishing many of his sentences. He resorts to mere repetition, beginning, trailing off, picking up again, and finally abandoning the effort. Shortly following what Pearson believes to be Clov's failed attempt to express an autonomous perception of the world, Hamm colludes with Clov to ruin language:

> HAMM. Nothing stirs. All is—
> CLOV. Zer—
> HAMM. (*violently*):
> Wait till you're spoken to!
> (*Normal voice.*)
> All is . . . all is . . . all is what?
> (*Violently.*)
> All is what?
> CLOV. What all is? In a word? Is that what you want to know? (29)

Pearson reads the exchange as evidence of Clov's subservience to Hamm's narrative of the world (228). According to Pearson, Hamm knows what "all is" but "dares Clov to come up with an alternative description of the outside world" (228), demonstrating that Hamm has the upper hand (the upper word) on Clov. Another way to read the passage, however, is to witness how both characters cause language to fragment, to hesitate, to stutter, to wait. Indeed, the passage reveals that both Hamm and Clov tear language apart, forcing each other's words to break prematurely. Clov cuts Hamm off in mid sentence, and Hamm cuts Clov off in mid word. Clov may defer to Hamm's demand to "Wait till you're spoken to!" but Hamm, too, impedes the smooth flow of speech.

Moments later, Hamm stumbles over one of the most famous
lines in the play, as he questions the changing value of his and Clov's
life together: "We're not beginning to . . . to . . . mean something?"
(32). Again, Hamm fails to speak without stuttering, faltering
temporarily before deciding where his sentence is leading him. He
continues to falter through his ensuing speech: "And without going so
far as that, we ourselves . . . (*with emotion*) . . . we ourselves . . . at
certain moments . . . (*Vehemently.*) To think perhaps it won't all have
been for nothing!" (33). Like Clov when trying to describe the
"multitude . . . in transports . . . of joy," Hamm struggles to find words
and finally gives up.

Some of Hamm's most stilted speech comes late in the drama.
In a moment of poignant reflection, for example, Hamm muses about
the future:

> HAMM: There I'll be, in the old shelter, alone against the silence and . . .
> (*he hesitates*) . . . the stillness. If I can hold my peace, and sit quiet, it will
> be all over with sound, and motion, all over and done with. (*Pause.*) I'll
> have called my father and I'll have called my . . . (*he hesitates*) . . . my son.
> And even twice, or three times, in case they shouldn't have heard me, the
> first time, or the second. (*Pause.*) I'll say to myself, He'll come back.
> (*Pause.*) And then? (*Pause.*) And then? (*Pause.*) He couldn't, he has gone
> too far. (*Pause.*) And then? (*Pause. Very agitated.*) All kinds of fantasies!
> That I'm being watched! A rat! Steps! Breath held and then . . . (*He
> breathes out.*) Then babble, babble, words, like the solitary child who turns
> himself into children, two, three, so as to be together, and whisper together,
> in the dark. (*Pause.*) Moment upon moment, pattering down, like the millet
> grains of . . . (*he hesitates*) . . . that old Greek, and all life long you wait for
> that to mount up to a life. (69-70)

Hamm's soliloquy is filled with pauses, hesitations, and echoes. When
he can't go on, he resorts to repetition, restating a phrase until the next
one presents itself. Hamm thus becomes a babbler—stuttering,
stumbling, stammering—even as he contemplates the day when he
will babble to himself in the dark.

Hamm's constant stuttering is enough at least to frustrate a
reading that understands him as the master of language and Clov as a
stammering subaltern. Indeed, Clov may be unable to speak
autonomously without hesitation, yet, as Hamm's dialogue reveals
time and again, the eyeless man in the center of the room makes more
of a mess of speech than Clov. Hamm's sentences, phrases, and words
tend to atrophy over the course of the drama. While one of the famous

lines in the play may reveal that Hamm introduces Clov to language—"I use the words you taught me" (44)—Hamm shows no singular ability to control it any better than his cohort. Thus when Hamm, like a mad director, exclaims "Articulate!" (80), he is talking as much to himself as to Clov.

Nagg and Nell, whom Pearson largely ignores in his postcolonial reading, contribute to the play's cracked dialogue. The decrepit husband and wife take turns cutting each other off, slicing sentences to pieces:

> NAGG: Do you remember—
> NELL: No.
> NAGG: When we crashed on our tandem and lost our shanks. (16)

Later:

> NELL: Nothing is funnier than unhappiness, I grant you that. But—
> NAGG: (*shocked*): Oh! (18)

Hamm adds to the fissuring of the old couple's speech, as Nagg haggles for two biscuits from his unyielding son:

> NAGG: Two.
> HAMM: One.
> NAGG: One for me and one for—
> HAMM: One! Silence! (50)

During the prayer scene, Hamm again truncates Nagg:

> NAGG: Our Father which art—
> HAMM: Silence! In silence! Where are your manners? (55)

Much like Hamm and Clov, Nagg and Nell evidence an inability to speak in smooth, glib patterns. Their language, to adapt Deleuze's vision of Walt Whitman's poetry, "sprouts dashes in order to create spatiotemporal intervals [....] It is an almost mad sentence, with its changes in direction, its bifurcations, its ruptures and leaps, its prolongations, its sproutings, its parentheses" (*Essays* 58). The broken dialogue of Nagg and Nell complements that of their fellow shelter-dwellers, reiterating the problems with vocalization that mark Beckett's entire drama.

Significantly, the egregious stuttering of the characters is not, by itself, enough to invent a revolutionary and liberating literature. The injured words and phrases of Hamm, Clov, Nagg, and Nell are speech acts (*paroles*) that take place in a greater system of language (*langue*)—that of the play as a whole.[9] The characters contribute to the materialization of a missing people, but they cannot bring about a full manifestation. According to Deleuze, a revolutionary writer employs "an atmospheric quality, a milieu that acts as the conductor of words—that brings together within itself the quiver, the murmur, the stutter, the tremolo, or the vibrato, and makes the indicated affect reverberate through the words" (*Essays* 108). Deleuze, in other words, calls for a merging of the form of expression with the form of content, of the words of the characters with the characters themselves, as well as with their surroundings. Various authors have the power to achieve such a feat:

> This, at least, is what happens in great writers like Melville, in whom the hum of the forests and caves, the silence of the house, and the presence of the guitar are evidence of Isabelle's murmurings, and her soft, "foreign intonations"; or Kafka, who confirms Gregor's squeaking through the trembling of his feet and the oscillations of his body; or even Masoch, who doubles the stammering of his characters with the heavy suspense of the Boudoir, the hum of the village, or the vibrations of the steppe. The affects [sic] of language here become the object of an indirect effectuation, and yet they remain close to those that are made directly, when there are no characters other than the words themselves. ("HS" 108)

Deleuze's *Watt* example is helpful in explaining how the merging occurs in Beckett. Deleuze points out that the author places the mumbling, bumbling protagonist of his 1953 novel in a world where all things mumble and bumble. Watt's bizarre locomotion, for instance, serves as an analogy to his equally bizarre way of speaking. Deleuze writes: "[T]his is how the transfer from the form of expression to a form of content is brought about. But we could equally well bring about the reverse transition by supposing that the characters speak like they walk or stumble, for speaking is no less a movement than walking" (*Essays* 111). *Watt*, then, is an exercise in both verbal and physical stuttering, or to employ a term Beckett uses to describe stuttering, an exercise in verbal and physical "battology."[10]

Texts other than *Watt* reveal Beckett's career-long battological experiment. The short stories of *More Pricks than Kicks*, for example, demonstrate the author's early experiments with artistic stuttering. While Beckett uses the expression "he stuttered" to describe some of Belacqua Shuah's speech, he also employs the protagonist's to and fro movements and surrounding environment to make the entire work of art stutter: "'Pardon me' stuttered Belacqua 'just a moment, will you be so kind.' He waddled out of the bar and into the street" (51). Belacqua's verbal stutter collides with his physical waddling, demonstrating Beckett's effort to make the language, not simply the speech, of his fiction begin to "scream, stutter, stammer, or murmur" (*Essays* 110).

The characters of *Endgame* persevere in a similar vibratory atmosphere, as Beckett, like Kafka or Masoch or Melville, doubles the stammering of his characters, causes the language of his play as a whole to "take flight[,] send[ing] it racing along a witch's line, ceaselessly placing it in a state of disequilibrium, making it bifurcate and vary in each of its terms, following an incessant modulation" (Deleuze, *Essays* 109). Like their speech patterns, the zone in which the characters move is everywhere unstable, everywhere trembling. As we put our ear to the hollow walls of Hamm's shelter, we hear constant banging, knocking, tapping, ringing, whistling—the rattle and hum of the missing.[11] We discern the staccato chuckling of Nagg, who "*breaks into a forced laugh, cuts it short, pokes his head toward Nell, launches his laugh again*" (23). We perceive murmurs—"*Unintelligble words*" (48)—that emanate from deep within the abyss of the bins. We detect the "*great groaning sigh*" (14) and "*humming*" (72) of the not-to-be-punished anymore. As we peer inside the windows, the stuttering scene arranges itself. We observe the "*Stiff, staggering walk*" (1) of Clov, the stammering bodies of the legless ashbin couple, the shuddering physique of Hamm, which begins to mimic the quivering of his voice: "[Y]ou give me the shivers!" (65), he tells Clov. We see the inarticulate picture, "*its face to wall*" (1), the unfinished three-legged Pomeranian, perfectly analogous to the half-complete sentences and words that reverberate throughout the play. The final tableau is perhaps most revealing, as Clov's physical hesitation, his stuttering to leave, puts no period at the end of the ungrammatical sentence that is Beckett's play. The concluding line, a stammer ("You . . . remain," says Hamm), trails off into darkness, as Clov's visual pause tacks on a perpetual ellipsis[12] to the constantly pausing, constantly hesitating speech of the characters.

A ninety-minute stutter, *Endgame* exemplifies Deleuze's (and Félix Guattari's) phraseology in *A Thousand Plateaus*: "Gestures and things, voices and sounds, are caught up in the same 'opera,' swept away by the same shifting effects of stammering, vibrato, tremolo, overspilling [....] The moment this conjunction occurs there is a common matter" (109).

(Beckett asserts famously that *Endgame* is a series of repetitions and echoes, and he suggests that the play has a musical quality. Significantly, however, Beckett also disclaims the *simultaneous* fusion of language and action. He told his Berlin cast, "Never let your changes of position and voice come together. First comes (a) the altered body stance; after it, following a slight pause, comes (b) the corresponding utterance" (*Theatrical* xix).[13])

The "common matter" levels the playing space, demonstrating an alliance of the characters rather than their division. They may argue and threaten one another, but they do so as part of a common opera of stutters in which Hamm is not the begetter of language but an extension of it, stammering along with the rest of the cast in an equally stammering milieu. Jeffers observes a similar conjunction of matter and words in *Krapp's Last Tape*, invoking Deleuze and Guattari's notion of the rhizome to describe how "Krapp enacts this very process on stage with spools, bananas, keys and words—all combine, disperse and rhizomatically connect and align heedless of a semiotic theory of coding" ("Krapp's Rhizome Identity" 65). A pseudo-quartet, Hamm-Clov-Nagg-Nell merges with its buzzing, ringing, whistling habitat, "carving a foreign language out of a major language," to invoke Deleuze's echo of Proust.[14] Such a reading is distantly similar to Amanda Cagle's postcolonial study of *Endgame*, which claims that Hamm and Clov are *co*-victims of imperialism, though Cagle views the play as an intimated struggle between British rule and impotent Irishmen.[15]

Endgame in its entirety thus emerges as the subaltern—exotic, anomalous, Other. Beckett's screaming, stuttering work of art is the ultimate opponent of colonialism, the worthy combatant of the majority, the evidence of a "mute and unknown minority that belongs only to [Beckett]" (*Essays* 109-10). To play on Deleuze's Bartleby example, Hamm-Clov-Nagg-Nell prefers not to—not to give itself over to the majority's treatment of language, not to honor the syntax, grammar, and smooth flow of a language that keeps minorities from living, from becoming.[16] In Deleuze's universe, Hamm and Clov are no longer stuck in the ditch, the "leftover" players in the what Pearson sees as a terminated but lingering chess match of imperialism but, rather, co-combatants on a stage-plane of consistency where transcendental differentiations have no place, where slippage is constant, where all language is in an unceasing state of becoming-minor, as Beckett's stuttering dramatic idiom "makes language grow from the middle, like grass; [...] makes language a rhizome instead of a tree" (Deleuze, *Essays* 111).

Daniel W. Smith asserts that as a majoritarian language becomes minor, so too do the myths of the colonizer. According to Smith, the value of a stuttering language in Deleuze's sense rests in its instantaneous deconstruction of the majority's cosmology. To adapt Smith, the language of *Endgame* functions as "a creative storytelling that is, as it were, the obverse side of the dominant myths and fictions, an act of resistance whose political impact is immediate and inescapable, and that creates a line of flight on which a minority discourse and a people can be constituted" (xlv).[17] To say that *Endgame* is replete with fragmented speech, repetition, and stuttering is to shine on the nothing new. To examine such language in light of Deleuze, however, reveals a novel perspective of the play's potential as a postcolonial text, a work that performs, in Smith's phraseology, as an "act of resistance."

Like many of Beckett's works, the *Endgame* machine "drills a hole"[18] in language, through which the oppressed may pass, come from the dead, come back to tell us all. The liberating power of *Endgame* rests in its formidable capacity as a "minor" drama, an "anti-authoritarian" work of art—to borrow Seán Golden's appraisal of *Finnegans Wake*—that, *in its entirety*, takes a stand against an oppressive syntax (441). Garin Dowd's astute observation about Beckett's *The Lost Ones* pertains extendedly to *Endgame*, as the play does not "*illustrate*" a philosophical or political principle but "*enacts*" one, is that thing itself (210).

A kind of foreign language, Beckett's drama is pro-active and forks the tongue of oppression, turning words inside out, voyaging not outside of but, as Deleuze stresses, to "*the outside* of language" ("HS" 112). The domain of language is, after all, where colonialism takes hold of its victim and, therefore, where a minor literature must "nibble away at [the] hegemony and create the possibility of new mythic functions, new cultural references, new vernacular languages with their own uses [...]" (xlvii). Pearson's essay asserts that *Endgame* finally offers few solutions to the problem of decolonization, as the characters are unable to get outside of "the black and white rules and oppositional strategies of the game" (237). Deleuze, however, believes that literature goes a long way in giving voice to minorities. For the French theorist, the writer's job is not to get outside of the game but to expose the vulnerabilities of majoritarian myths. Beckett's art represents a fissure in the foundation, revealing a writer who has the strength to force syntax to its crisis, who "gives rise to the musical and celestial Beyond of language as a whole" (*Essays* 72).

Paul Shields, Assumption College

Notes

I would like to thank Dustin Anderson, Stan Gontarski, Michael Rodriguez, Geoffrey Stacks, and Curt Willits for their inspiring comments and encouragement in the composition of this essay.

[1] A number of other critics situate Beckett's writings in a Deleuzian context. Uhlmann's now essential study *Beckett and Postructuralism* focuses on readings of Beckett's *Three Novels* in light of Deleuze and Guattari, Michel Foucault, and Jacques Derrida. Dowd has published several essays on Beckett and Deleuze. See his "On Four Kantian Formulas That Might Summarise the Beckettian Poetic," "The Abstract Literary Machine: Guattari, Deleuze, and Beckett's *The Lost Ones*," and "Mud as Plane of Immanence in *How It Is*." For a discussion of Beckett in the context of Deleuze's essay "L'Epuisé" ("The Exhausted"), see Bryden. Jeffers's book-length study *Uncharted Space: The End of Narrative* deals extensively with Deleuze and includes a chapter on Beckett's late theater. See also Jeffers's discussion of the rhizomatic nature of *Krapp's Last Tape* in her essay "'A place without an occupant': Krapp's Rhizome Identity." For a critique of Deleuze and Beckett's television plays, see Bogue.

[2] All references to *Endgame* are to the 1958 Grove Press edition. Importantly, Pearson and I both refer to the same edition of the play, but some of the lines to which we refer (including Clov's "I see . . . a multitude . . . in transports . . . of joy") are deleted from the Revised Text. Throughout the essay, I note which lines are deleted in the Revised Text.

  The reader should also here note that an essay on stuttering relies heavily on a clear understanding of when and how long the characters stutter, stammer, pause, are cut off, and fall silent. I therefore use brackets throughout the essay to indicate my own insertion of ellipses. All other ellipses, such as those that appear in Clov's line, are as they appear in the text.

[3] Notably, Pearson does consider the ways in which Clov gains (though finally loses) some ground on Hamm over the course of the play. For example, at one point Pearson mentions that Clov's pauses and silences "might be where the real alternatives to Hamm's view of the world ultimately lie" (224-25). Later, Pearson contemplates the possibility that Clov is undoing Hamm's authority by way of what Homi Bhabha calls "mimicry" (230). Significantly, Deleuze's theory of stuttering resembles the "mimicry" argument, though I argue that Hamm and Clov *both* play a part in thwarting a majoritarian language, whereas Pearson sees Hamm and Clov as oppositional forces in a language game.

[4] Declan Kiberd, Charles R. Lyons, and Seán Golden, all of whom Pearson discusses in his essay, address the political/postcolonial intricacies of Beckett's play. In *Inventing Ireland*, Kiberd writes: "[Hamm] appears the very epitome of a ruling class gone rancid [...] Clov speaks at times to Hamm with the ingratitude of a Caliban who knows that his master's language has been the medium in which his yearnings for expressive freedom have been improvised" (545). In his essay *"Fin de Partie/Endgame* as Political Drama," Lyons discusses the political complexities that surround language and identity in Beckett's work: "*Endgame* includes Clov's recognition that he can speak only within the language and structures of thought that he has been taught by his master, Hamm" (189). Incidentally, Lyons mentions, but never expands on, what he views as a connection between notions of *Endgame* as a monodrama and the "radical theories of *Anti-Oedipus*, in which Gilles Deleuze and Félix Guattari cite Beckettian texts to document the paradigm of the schizophrenic in which *'everything divides, but into itself'*" (195). Golden's Marxist approach to the play considers how "the proletarian, or colonial, or feminist writer [can] create art without using the forms and conventions handed down by bourgeois, imperial, or patriarchal systems without thereby perpetuating the hegemony and ideology of those systems" (433-34). Golden's allegorical reading of *Endgame* puts Hamm in the role of owner and Clov in the role of worker in a defunct but persistent bourgeois culture (444). Notably, Pearson, Kiberd, Lyons, and Golden all consider the characters in the drama as the final players of an archaic discourse/politics/ideology that simply refuses to die.

Amanda Cagle's essay, "Looking for Love on Samuel Beckett's Stage: Homoeroticism, Sterility and the Postcolonial Condition," is similar to all of the above interpretations, though Cagle views *both* Hamm and Clov as colonized, emasculated Irishmen. At the outset of her essay, Cagle writes, "[Beckett's] dramas identify Irish people, males in particular, as a people cut off from their pasts, cultures, and identities" (83).

[5] One of Deleuze's salient points is that a writer must not abandon the language of a majority but turn it against itself, inside out. Deleuze's theory diametrically opposes an idea Lyons posits in his essay (see n. 3). Lyons hypothesizes that Beckett moves to writing in French possibly to avoid the language of the colonizer, as well as the language of James Joyce (189). Golden's article (see n. 3), on the other hand, has much in common with Deleuze's ideas about stuttering authors. In the preface to his reading of *Endgame*, Golden argues that certain Irish writers, such as James Joyce and Beckett, do not necessarily abandon the English language but, rather, use a "disorienting" syntax in crafting their stories. Golden refers to *Finnegans Wake* as "anti-authoritarian" (441), suggesting that

The workings of its language are ambivalent and polysemous. Meanings of words and phrases are multiple, very often mutually and simultaneously contradictory. Meaning cannot be fixed. A generally English syntax and base vocabulary is subjected to disorientation. The text calls attention to itself, and confidence in language usage is shaken. (440)

Significantly, in one of his footnotes concerning Joyce's style, Golden alludes to John Cage's proclivity for a "nonsyntactical 'demilitarized' language" (qtd. in Golden 441 fn. 20), which is highly evocative of Deleuze's ideas about stuttering syntax in "He Stuttered."

Golden eventually turns his full attention to Beckett, asserting that he suffers from a "dis-ease" with inherited rules and conventions: "His attitude toward form, toward style and structure, seems to me to represent a radical reappraisal of received tradition, and his overt dissection of language and style and their forms a radical reappraisal of content" (442). Golden goes on to reveal how Clov's struggle to invent a style of his own in the language of his master allegorizes Beckett's struggle as an Irish writer (444-53).

[6] Pearson addresses the elliptical speech of Hamm on occasion (224, 231), but he is mainly concerned in his essay with the meaning of Clov's silences and pauses. At one point, Pearson mentions that the "numerous pauses and silences (in both characters' speech) do possess a certain agency" (224-25), though his focus quickly turns back to Clov's hesitating speech. Later, Pearson contends that when Hamm trails off at one point in his dialogue with Clov, it is not because he, too, has problems with articulation, but because he "has lost control of Clov" (231).

[7] For the Revised Text (see n. 2), Beckett deleted the yawns from these opening lines.

[8] Beckett deleted the yawn in this passage for the Revised Text (see n. 2).

[9] Notably, Golden prefaces his allegorical reading of *Endgame* with a lengthy discussion of what he views as various analogies between *langue* and *parole* and literature and writing: "Literature derives from tradition (or traditions), and perhaps the literary tradition assumes a systematic role akin to that of *langue*. Then each piece of writing becomes akin to *parole*, and a set of relations may be postulated between the author and his work considering the traditions the author works within similar to those postulated for language and speech" (429-30). Significantly, my usage of *langue* and *parole* is more straightforward, a trope to help express how the individual speech blunders of the characters are mini-stutters in a much more encompassing system of artistic stuttering.

[10] The term "battology" appears in *Watt* (165).

[11] In his notes to *Endgame* in *The Theatrical Notebooks of Samuel Beckett: Volume II: Endgame*, S. E. Gontarski reads the banging as part of the play's continuous allusion to the crucifixion of Christ: "Throughout the play, [...] all the banging, including Hamm's tapping on the wall, echoes this hammer-and-nail or crucifixion theme" (50).

[12] Jeffers (see n. 2) argues that *Krapp's Last Tape* is similarly without clear boundaries, "a text that does not follow a straight line of development, but spreads out in all directions. If *Waiting for Godot* seems cyclical, then *Krapp's Last Tape* seems to disperse in several directions at once, yet without a unifying central point that might orient us to the whole" ("Krapp's Rhizome Identity" 65).

[13] Gontarski offers a full account of the repetitions and echoes in his introduction to Beckett's *Theatrical Notebooks* (xix-xxi).

[14] Deleuze often refers to—and revises—Proust's remark: "Great books are written in a kind of foreign language." It serves as the epigraph for *Essays Critical and Clinical*.

[15] See Cagle (88-91). See n. 5.

[16] Deleuze views Melville's Bartleby as a character who invokes a linguistic formula ("I would prefer not to") to bring down the capitalist world of Wall Street. See his essay "Bartleby; Or, the Formula" in *Essays Critical and Clinical*.

[17] I am indebted to Smith for his insightful explications of some of Deleuze's salient points.

[18] I am here expanding on Deleuze's comment in his Preface to *Essays Critical and Clinical*: "Beckett spoke of 'drilling holes' in language in order to see or hear 'what was lurking behind'" (lv). Deleuze is apparently alluding to Beckett's 1937 letter to Axel Kaun, in which the Irish author explains his desire to voyage to the other side of language. See Beckett's *Disjecta: Miscellaneous Writings and a Dramatic Fragment* (170-71). In his essay on Beckett's television plays, Ronald Bogue (see n. 2) pursues Deleuze's interest in Beckett's efforts to bore holes through language.

Bibliography

Beckett, Samuel. *Disjecta*: *Miscellaneous Writings and a Dramatic Fragment* ed. Ruby Cohn. New York: Grove, 1984.

—. *Endgame: A Play in One Act followed by Act Without Words: A Mime for One Player* translated by Samuel Beckett. New York: Grove, 1958.

—. *Endgame*: Revised Text. Beckett, *Theatrical* 1-42.

—. *More Pricks Than Kicks*. New York: Grove, 1972.

—. *The Theatrical Notebooks of Samuel Beckett: Volume II:* Endgame ed. S.E. Gontarski. New York: Grove, 1992.

—. *Watt*. New York: Grove, 1953.

Bogue, Ronald. "Deleuze and the Invention of Images: From Beckett's Television Plays to Noh Drama" in *The Comparatist* 26 (2002): 37-52.

Bryden, Mary. "The Schizoid Space: Beckett, Deleuze, and *L'Epuisé*" in Sjef Houppermans ed. *Beckett & La Psychanalyse & Psychoanalysis, Samuel Beckett Today/Aujourd'hui 5*. Amsterdam and New York: Rodopi, 1996. (84-93)

Cagle, Amanda. "Looking for Love on Samuel Beckett's Stage: Homoeroticism, Sterility and the Postcolonial Condition" in *Atenea* 23 (2003): 83-94.

Cavell, Stanley. *Must We Mean What We Say?: A Book of Essays.*
New York: Charles Scribner's Sons, 1969.

Deleuze, Gilles. *Essays Critical and Clinical* translated by Daniel W.
Smith and Michael A. Greco. Minneapolis: University of
Minnesota Press, 1997.

Deleuze, Gilles and Félix Guattari. *A Thousand Plateaus: Capitalism
and Schizophrenia* translated and with a foreword by Brian
Massumi. Minneapolis: University of Minnesota Press, 1987.

Dowd, Garin. "The Abstract Literary Machine: Guattari, Deleuze, and
Beckett's *The Lost Ones*" in *Forum for Modern Language
Studies* 37.2 (2002): 204-17.

—. "Mud as Plane of Immanence in *How It Is*" in *Journal of Beckett
Studies* 8.2 (1999): 1-28.

—. "On Four Kantian Formulas That Might Summarise the Beckettian
Poetic" in Daniella Caselli et al., eds. *Other Becketts*.
Tallahassee: Journal of Beckett Studies Books, 2002. (53-68)

Golden, Seán. "Familiars in a Ruinstrewn Land: *Endgame* as Political
Allegory" in *Contemporary Literature* 22 (1981): 425-55.

Gontarski, S.E. Introduction. Beckett, *Theatrical* xiii-xxii.

Jeffers, Jennifer M. "'A place without an occupant': Krapp's Rhizome
Identity" in Jeffers, ed. *Samuel Beckett: A Casebook*. New
York: Garland, 1998. (63-79)

—. *Uncharted Space: The End of Narrative.* New York: Peter Lang,
2001.

Kiberd, Declan. *Inventing Ireland.* Cambridge: Harvard UP, 1996.

Lyons, Charles. "*Fin de Partie/Endgame* as Political Drama" in Paul
Hyland and Neil Sammels, eds. *Irish Writing: Exile and
Subversion.* New York: St. Martin's, 1991. (188-206)

Pearson, Nels C. "'Outside of Here It's Death': Co-Dependency and
the Ghosts of Decolonization in Beckett's *Endgame*" in *ELH*
68.1 (2001): 215-239.

Smith, Daniel W. Introduction. Deleuze xi-liii.

Uhlmann, Anthony. *Beckett and Postructuralism*. Cambridge:
Cambridge University Press, 1999.

Worth, Katharine. *Samuel Beckett's Theatre: Life Journeys*. Oxford:
Clarendon Press, 2001.

But Why Shakespeare? The Muted Role of Dickens in *Endgame*

Paul Stewart

1

"The facts – let us have facts, facts, plenty of facts," (32) cries the narrator of *Dream of Fair to Middling Women* echoing the words of Thomas Gradgrind in Dickens's *Hard Times* as he asserts that "we want nothing but Facts, sir; nothing but Facts!" (10)

Despite such allusions as this, the fact remains that the role of Dickens in the works of Beckett has been all but ignored. As far as I am aware, the only article devoted to Dickens and Beckett is "Dickens and Beckett: Two Uses of Materialism," by Victor Sage in 1977. Mary Bryden, in "Gender in Transition: *Waiting for Godot* and *Endgame,*" provides a valuable reading of the two Nells of *Endgame* and *The Old Curiosity Shop*, even if she regards the linkage as temporary and offers it only tentatively. James Acheson gestures towards, yet does not execute, a Dickensian reading of *Endgame* in his influential article "Chess with the Audience" in which he states that if Hamm is related to the Ham of *David Copperfield* then the play displays "displeasure with Victorian sentimentality" (36). Such moments are rare in the Beckett critical canon. In James Knowlson's encyclopaedic biography of Beckett, Dickens is mentioned only twice, compared, for example, to nine mentions for Samuel Johnson and ten for Sartre. But those two mentions are themselves important. The first is a comment directly attributed to Beckett in which he describes his father's library stocked with a set of Dickens and a host of encyclopaedias, neither of which Beckett's father ever read. The second, again direct from Beckett, speaks of the enthusiasm with which he read *Oliver Twist* as a boy (Knowlson 10 and 139). Given such hints from Beckett's biography and his oeuvre, it is surprising that Dickens has so long been all-but absent from critical reactions to Beckett's work.

In direct contrast, Shakespeare has been a constant presence in critical accounts of Beckett. As early as 1963, J. Russell Browne could write confidently of "Mr. Beckett's Shakespeare." Browne was quickly followed by Ruby Cohn in her seminal essay "*The Tempest* in an *Endgame*" of 1965. From then on, Shakespeare has never left the critical discourse surrounding Beckett in general, and *Endgame* in particular. There is no space to do justice to the sheer volume of work directly or indirectly addressing the relations between Beckett and Shakespeare, but the importance of that relation might be emphasized by the fact that such figures as Theodor Adorno, Jan Kott, and Harold Bloom have all felt the need to turn to Shakespeare when dealing with *Endgame,* albeit in different ways and with different intentions.

While major commentators have focused on Shakespeare and largely ignored Dickens in relation to Beckett, Beckett himself, on at least one occasion, could bring together the figures of Shakespeare and Dickens in the same mental breath. In "Dante... Bruno. Vico.. Joyce," Shakespeare and Dickens are used to illustrate and justify Joyce's experimentations with language:

> Nor is he [Joyce] by any means the first to recognize the importance of treating words as something more than mere polite symbols. Shakespeare uses fat greasy words to express corruption: "Duller shouldst thou be than the fat weed that rots itself in death [sic] on Lethe wharf." We hear the ooze squelching all through Dickens's description of the Thames in *Great Expectations*. (Beckett, 1983, 28)[1]

Here Shakespeare and Dickens are presented on the same plane. In order to justify what to many was the radical nature of the language of *Finnegans Wake*, Beckett places Joyce firmly in the tradition of the two writers most acceptable to those "Ladies and Gentlemen" who are too decadent to accept Joyce's "direct expression" and to whom the essay is ostensibly addressed. There may have been an element of strategy in placing Dickens in such close alliance with Shakespeare, but the fact remains that Beckett felt able to do so. One of the questions this essay hopes to entertain is why the critical community has not followed suit; why has the role of Dickens in *Endgame* remained so muted, and that of Shakespeare so trumpeted?

The immediate answer is, of course, that *Endgame* directly alludes to Shakespeare. "Our revels now are ended" (39) Hamm comments after his father has sunk back into his bin and closed the lid, never again to emerge, at least not for as long as the current staging of the play lasts. Immediately, the word-for-word quotation takes us to *The Tempest* and Prospero abandoning the masque arranged by his art for Miranda and Ferdinand. Less direct, but no less recognizable, is the mauled allusion to Richard III, defeated and desperate on the field of Bosworth as he cries "My kingdom for a horse." In Hamm's world, this becomes the bitter, but perhaps no less desperate, "My kingdom for a nightman!" (22), as he cries for his binned parents to be thrown out by the man whose job it is to dispose of human effluence.

These two allusions, one a direct and one an adapted quotation, both call for and then legitimize a reading of the play in Shakespearean terms. As easily recognizable as they are, they sanction the consideration of further possible allusions to Shakespeare's work. It is a short step from these direct allusions to see Hamm as a "Hamlet in the final ditch" (Bloom 505) or a version of Lear, or to see Clov as Caliban and/or Ariel. Once the practice of looking at *Endgame* through the prism of Shakespeare has been established through direct allusion, the possibilities multiply, grow more complex and, as a result, appear all the more compelling and credible.

2

Unfortunately there are no direct or mauled quotations from Dickens's works in *Endgame*. As such, Beckett's allusive use of the novelist differs in kind from his overt use of Shakespeare. Rather than using recognizable quotations which activate the presence of a Shakespearean text within the text of *Endgame*, the allusions to Dickens are more situational and relational and hence, literally, muted. Nevertheless, Dickens's presence can be felt in a variety of guises within the text, and the parallels which can be drawn are so numerous as to suggest an important and comprehensive pattern which, once noticed, might change our perception of *Endgame*.

Whilst James Acheson may be reminded of Dickens's Ham and therefore suggest that *Endgame* condemns Victorian sentimentality, other aspects of *David Copperfield* suggest that the intertextual relations conform to a paradigm of deterioration, whilst that deterioration reveals a profound relationship within *Endgame* between want and power.

This relationship between want and power can be most clearly discerned in Hamm and Clov's two predecessors in Dickens's world: Mr Omer and his granddaughter Minnie. Mr Omer is the undertaker in Yarmouth who coffins David's father and mother and with whom David slowly becomes acquainted during his trips into East Anglia. During their last meeting, Mr. Omer's buoyant spirits are in direct contrast to his physical state. Omer has lost the use of his legs and is dependent on his "little elephant," Minnie, to push him around in a makeshift wheelchair, or "his easy-chair [that] went on wheels" which "runs as light as a feather, and tracks as true as a mail-coach" (674). Minnie is a willing little helper who butts her grandfather's chair into motion with a childish energy, allowing Omer to look back at David "as if it were the triumphant issue of his life's exertions" (676). Hamm in *Endgame* is of course pushed around in his own makeshift wheelchair, "an armchair on castors" (11), although, judging by the difficulties they have in taking a turn around the room it would seem unlikely that Hamm's easy-chair on wheels runs as smoothly as Omer's. Clov's attitude of grudging obedience hardly reminds one of the cheerful, helpful energy of the little elephant's, but their function—pushing the invalid in his easy-chair—is identical, and the decline from Minnie to Clov conforms to a trajectory of deterioration.

In direct contrast to Hamm, Omer embraces his infirmity. Finding himself in his second childishness and dependent upon the good-will of others, Omer relishes the opportunity to both bestow and receive kindnesses, as he says of himself whilst speaking in the third person:

> being wheeled about for the second time, in a speeches of go-cart; he should be over-rejoiced to do a kindness if he can. He wants plenty [...] because, sir, the way I look at it is, that we are all drawing on to the bottom of the hill, whatever age we are, on account of time never standing still for a single moment. So let us always do a kindness, and be over-rejoiced." (675)

He looks forward to doing a kindness for the wastrel Martha, and sees his lack of abilities as the opportunity for others to show their kindness. He "wants" plenty, but this lack is happily filled by the kindnesses of others, be it Ham reading to him of an evening, or Minnie cheerily shunting him from parlor to bedroom.

Hamm's physical situation is admittedly worse than that of Omer. Indeed, Dickens's invalid is grateful that only his limbs have failed him: "If it had been my eyes, what should I have done? If it had been my ears, what should I have done? Being my limbs, what does it signify?" (675) The pattern for Hamm's further deterioration is here set by Omer. Just as Beckett worsened Hamm's physical state over the many drafts and typescripts which culminated in *Endgame,*[2] so Omer's reason to be thankful—he still has his eyes—becomes Hamm's further affliction. One almost has a sense of Beckett challenging the optimism of Omer by offering an answer to the question "what should I have done" if blind.

While the Dickens character's degree of decrepitude might not be as great as Hamm's, nevertheless Omer's physical lack is an occasion for another form of plenitude as the failure of his limbs calls forth a greater degree of human love and kindness. Hamm's only reason to delight in his own infirmities is the opportunity it grants him to further torture Clov. His own decrepitude gives Hamm the "prophetic relish" of claiming that Clov will be reduced to the same state, only worse so: "Yes, one day you'll know what it is, you'll be like me, except that you won't have anyone with you, because you won't have had pity on anyone and because there won't be anyone left to have pity on" (29). With characteristic self-delusion, Hamm's prophecy creates a situation in which human love, kindness and pity have finally died. The world he actually inhabits is, of course, one in which pity has already died, killed in part by his own vicious caprices. Clov flatly tells Hamm he does not love him, possibly due to the suffering he has endured at Hamm's hands, and Hamm's pleading for forgiveness is only greeted by Clov's deadened and deadly "I heard you" (14). It is little wonder that Clov cannot bring himself to touch Hamm, let alone to kiss him. Love is also absent from Hamm's relations with his parents. Nagg is the "accursed progenitor" and Nell a "damned busybody" for whom, according to Hamm, limbless life in dustbins is too good, and Nagg rises to his own viciousness when recalling Hamm as an infant:

> Whom did you call when you were a tiny boy, and were frightened, in the dark? Your mother? No. Me. We let you cry. Then we moved you out of earshot, so that we might sleep in peace [...] I hope the day will come when you'll need to have me listen to you, and need to hear my voice, any voice [...] Yes, I hope I'll live till then, to hear you calling me like when you were

a tiny boy, and were frightened, in the dark, and I was your only hope. (38-39)

Hamm's prophecy for Clov's fate is here revealed to be an accurate description of his own. No one, least of all his father, has had pity on him, and he has had pity on no one.

This motif of lovelessness that I have here briefly sketched gains sharper relief from two further allusive parallels to *David Copperfield*. The room which the characters of *Endgame* inhabit has been likened to the inside of a skull, a post-apocalyptic bunker, a rendering of Freud's diagrams relating to the ego, id and super-ego, and, of course, to a denuded Prospero's isle. However, a *Copperfield* possibility has not been noticed. The right window of the *Endgame* room looks out over a "corpsed" earth, a "zero" space where "nothing stirs." The left window is no more promising as it looks out over a leaden sea of uncompromising grey (or light black) with not so much as a gull, a sail, a fin or smoke to break the monotony. David Copperfield finds refuge on the edge of the coast in the home of Dan Peggotty. The boat in which Mr. Peggotty and his charges live is situated in "the wilderness" or "dull waste"(36) of the Yarmouth mud-flats looking out across the sea and is, of course, reminiscent of the Ark which the Biblical Ham inhabited (and here several allusive possibilities within *Endgame* intersect). The house is not only symbolically a refuge in its resemblance to the Ark, but literally one as it gives security and succor to the orphaned and widowed. Mrs. Gummidge, Ham, Emily, and David himself, temporarily, are all given refuge in Dan Peggoty's unconventional family in this unconventional home on the edge of a grey, flat sea. The situational parallels between Dan Peggotty's home and the last refuge of Hamm, Clov, Nagg and Nell emphasize that the former was created through the extension of human kindness; the latter is a bitter world bereft of such kindness.

A perhaps slighter allusion might be added. Mother Pegg in *Endgame* is felt only as an absence in the text. She is first mentioned as being naturally "extinguished" (31) along with her light, and later Clov blames Hamm for her demise: "When old Mother Pegg asked you for oil for her lamp and you told her to get out to hell, you knew what has happening then? [Pause] You know what she died of, Mother Pegg? Of darkness." (48) Again, as with Ham(m) or Ham(m)let, the parallel is activated by a similarity in name: Pegg; Peggotty. In *David*

Copperfield the one-time servant Peggotty offers David the unconditional love and support of a mother that his own mother was unable to supply. Throughout the novel, Peggotty is as much of a true mother as the text has to offer, and it is this attribute which her near namesake in *Endgame* accentuates: she is always and memorably *Mother* Pegg. The Mother Pegg figure went through a series of transformations as Beckett worked towards his final version of *Endgame*. Early typescripts had Clov poorly disguised as a woman, Sophie, upon whom the ur-Hamm has a momentary urge to beget (Gontarski 49). These sexual elements, somewhat Oedipal in nature, are removed from the final text of *Endgame* leaving the focus to fall on the maternal nature of the figure alone. Childless herself, Peggotty is surrogate mother to David and so, in the final chapter of the novel, "A Last Retrospect," it is the maternal nature of Peggotty which is stressed: "her rough forefinger, which I once associated with a pocket nutmeg-grater, is just the same, and when I see my least child catching at it as it totters from my aunt to her, I think of our little parlor at home, when I could scarcely walk" (803). Through his own child and the never-failing loving presence of Peggotty, David is taken back to his own childhood, one in which, under the loveless rule of the Murdstones, Peggotty was the only reliable source of maternal care and affection. The giving and receiving of affection in the David-Peggotty relation is again precisely what is missing from the Hamm-Mother Pegg relation. When she begs him for oil for her lamp, he refuses, even though he has oil to give. Mother Pegg's privation is an opportunity for kindness which Hamm absolutely shuns. Like the infant Hamm, Mother Pegg is left in the dark bereft of love, this time fatally.

The death of Mother Pegg, through a lack of love and human kindness, is given a counterpoint in the relationship between Nagg and Nell. Nagg may be solicitous towards his wife, offering her the greater part of his biscuit, for example, and weeping at her apparent death, but, due to their physical condition, Nagg and Nell's relationship is one of remnants and remembrance. Nell may ask whether is it "time for love?" but the answer is surely that the time for love, just as the time for teeth, legs and kisses, was "yesterday!" (18)

The issue of human love and kindness raised by the textual relations with *David Copperfield* in turn accentuates the role of the orphan in *Endgame*. Arguably, adoption has always been part of the discourse surrounding the play. Hamm's chronicle has often and fruitfully been read as the thinly veiled autobiographical tale of how Clov was separated from his father and came to be in the service of his present master. The putative child beyond the confines of the last refuge would seem to fit into this pattern of orphans coming into Hamm's service. Recently, Paul Lawley has written perceptively of the figure of adoption in the play, subtly arguing that the "aesthetic dimension of [Hamm's] chronicle and the experiential dimension of the chronicler move into identity through the figure of adoption" and that "adoption is the figure for the fictional process itself, the only acceptable means of self-perpetuation for characters who reject the processes of nature" (122). Referring to holograph material, S.E. Gontarski points out that the theme of adoption was at one stage of the play's development even more pervasive: "Another note suggests that [the Hamm figure's] father and son are adopted; that is Nagg too may have been someone taken into the shelter as a servant: 'A un père adoptif / un fils adoptif'" (52).

The motif of adoption in *Endgame* is reflected in Dickens's almost obsessive interest in the state of the orphan. George Newlin has calculated that in the major works there are 82 characters with no father, 87 with no mother, and 149 with neither father or mother; leaving just 15 characters with a full complement of parents (285). In *David Copperfield,* partial or full orphan status is the norm rather than the exception: David, Emily, Ham, Steerforth, Dora, Traddles, Agnes, Uriah Heep; all have lost one or both of their biological parents. If one widens the concept of adoption to include those taken into care when abandoned or destitute, then Dan Peggotty acts as protector not only to Emily, Ham, and temporarily David, but also Mrs. Gummidge, and of course Betsey Trotwood gives her formidable protection not only to David, but also to Mr. Dick. Finally, after his failed adoption of the child-wife Dora, it is David's turn to act as protector, giving refuge to his aunt, Mr. Dick and Peggotty, all under the auspices of the angelic Agnes.

Such a beneficent form of adoption as practiced by the two Peggottys, Dan and his sister, and by Aunt Betsy, is not to be found within Hamm's household. Rather than gladly giving succor to those in need, Hamm uses need to force the adopted Clov into servitude. If the chronicle can be taken as a version of how Clov came into his service, then Hamm turns an opportunity for charity into one for the wielding of power. The father comes begging for "bread for his brat," an appeal for alms which Hamm effectively turns into a means of ensuring the man enters his service and, what seems to have been the objective all along, that the child enters his service also. The moment Hamm has been waiting for is when the father asks "would I consent to take in the child as well" (37), allowing Hamm to not only get the child into his service but also to do so at the request of the father. Lawley is surely correct to assert that in a world where the natural processes, except those of decay, have been rejected or have ceased, it is to adoption that the characters turn in the hope of perpetuation. According to the chronicle, Hamm feels that he "wasn't much longer for the world" when he met with the begging father; the possibility of adopting the son into servitude therefore acts as a means of Hamm's perpetuation, and, arguably, the possibility of a new child in the wilderness means that Hamm can again seek to perpetuate himself through adoption and hence has no need of Clov: "It's the end, Clov, we've come to the end. I don't need you anymore" (50).

Whether Hamm adopts Clov for the mere exercising of power or for the subtler motives of perpetuation, it is clear, if the chronicle is to be taken as autobiographical, that the adopted child was always intended for service. Here, the Dickensian model of adoption suffers a reversal. As the figure of Dan Peggotty suggests, adoption of a child is such that one places one's self at the service of the child; he selflessly takes in Ham and Emily, and, as far as the latter is concerned, dedicates a large portion of his life, fortune and energies in her service. Peggotty is again a model of selfless service, first to David's mother and then to David. In the cases of both the Peggottys, the adopting adult sacrifices themselves for the good of the adopted child. There is sacrifice in *Endgame* too, but it is the sacrifice of the biological parent. Hamm so engineers the encounter with the father that it is the latter who asks, one might say begs, for the child to be taken into service. He seems to intuit Hamm's intentions even in the act of begging for his son to become a servant, for he gazes at Hamm with "mad eyes, in defiance of my wishes" (37). Nevertheless, one supposes for the greater good of the child inasmuch as he will at least survive, the biological bond is broken. Clov, as his father surely realized, is destined to become the abused servant son of Hamm.

On the other hand, adoption in *David Copperfield*, and much of David's life itself, can be seen as the formulation of successful family units not sanctioned by conventional blood ties. When David enters Dan Peggotty's home, he naturally assumes that the adults and children represent a family unit, and indeed they do, but it is unit sanctioned not by marriage and direct ties of blood but by an economy of love and affection. This economy is made all the more obvious by Mrs. Gummidge who acts as drain on the "family's" resources until the disappearance of Emily demands that she abandons her role of being "gormed" and morose in favor of being active and self-sacrificing. In this respect, Emily's downfall replaces Mrs Gummidge's habitual depression as a means of binding the family unit together through an expression of affection occasioned by misfortune. Even so serious a scandal as that of Emily serves to bring forth the kindness in which Mr. Omer "over-rejoiced." The *Copperfield* adoptive family unit is one where blood ties have been replaced by ties of affection prompted and secured by distress or unhappiness.

Conversely, in *Endgame,* unhappiness might only seem to activate bitter laughter, yet Hamm can also be seen to create and then prey upon unhappiness and want. He actively destroys biological relations and enforces adoption, both in the case of Clov, in which the father is forced to knowingly give up his son, and in his own case. The traces of the comment in the holograph that Hamm has "un père adoptif / un fils adoptif" may be discerned and perform an important role in the final text of the play. Naturally (but is it or is it not natural: a question which *King Lear,* as *Endgame,* dwells upon), Hamm treats his own parents with no affection whatsoever and happily bins and screws down the lids whenever he can. He shows fury at Nagg precisely for his blood relationship, berating him as an "accursed progenitor" and asking emphatically "Why did you engender me?" It is hardly surprising, then, that Hamm dreads all form of natural procreation, even amongst the fleas and rats which still remain, and no less surprising that he also seeks orphan status for himself.

Clov as adopted son of Hamm and Hamm as orphan himself (despite the evidence of his parent's presence to the contrary), come together in the rich ambiguities of a single line. Clov has admitted that he can neither remember his father nor his home and that Hamm has been a father to him and this last refuge a home, to which Hamm replies: "But for me [*gesture towards himself*] no father. But for Hamm [*gesture towards surroundings*] no home" (29-30). In the same breath, Hamm asserts Clov's bounden status and makes a bid to grant himself the status of an orphan. While the meaning of the words in context suggests the former proposition is primary, the phrasing is such that it allows a contrary interpretation: "Yet, I, Hamm, had no father; Yet, I, Hamm, had no home." Hamm, through the prism of Dickens, sounds uncannily like that other false orphan, Josiah Bounderby of Coketown:

> '*My* mother? Bolted, ma'am' [...] 'My mother left me to my grandmother [...] and according to the best of my remembrance, my grandmother was the wickedest and the worst old woman that ever lived [...] I pulled through it, though nobody threw me a rope. Vagabond, errand-boy, vagabond, porter, clerk, chief manager, small partner, Josiah Bounderby of Coketown. Those are the antecedents, and the culmination.' (22)

The denouement of the novel reveals that Bounderby's mother, Mrs. Pegler, had not abandoned him but been banished by her son. For years she had remained true to the promise she made to her son and kept in hiding, daring only to steal a chance glance of her beloved boy once a year. In order to appear self-made, the next best thing to being self-generated, Bounderby thrust his devoted parent from him and willfully adopted the role of the orphan.

The parallels with Hamm are striking. Whilst no one would argue that Nagg and Nell are or have ever been devoted parents—and it is Nagg's viciousness towards his son that helps to convince us of his paternity—they have certainly been thrust into abandonment by the will of a son who would see himself as self-made. As a result, Hamm can claim to be self-authored and gain still further credit by overcoming greater misfortunes on his way to his illusory greatness. "But for Hamm no father. But for Hamm no home."

It would then seem that the Dickensian world of orphans bound by ties of human affection is used with bitter and systematic irony in *Endgame*. For Dickens, the conventional family structured on paternity is replaced by the family more firmly structured on affection. The very want of a parent, again to echo Mr. Omer, calls forth the need for kindness. In the Bounderby mode, Hamm seeks to be self-made through the abandonment of his parents, and he insidiously breaks the bond between, one assumes, Clov and his father. Blood as a means of continuance is shunned by Hamm (and can he really be blamed, given the evidence for how Nagg treated him in infancy?), leaving only the option of adoption. The adoption motif of *Endgame*, however, is not based on the reciprocal economy of want and kindness, lack and love; it is only the occasion for the exercising of power as Hamm brings Clov under his yoke and strives to claim the ultimate power of auto-genesis.

It is this play of difference between Dickens and Beckett that alerts us to an economy of want and power in *Endgame.* The misery of *Endgame*'s characters, often attributed to a miserablism or extreme pessimism on Beckett's part or, in a more sympathetic reading, to the author seeing the world about him without sentimentality or illusion, is here revealed to serve a further purpose; it generates power. In a post-war drama, the historical resonances perhaps do not need to be underlined, but it is worth noting that the early drafts of *Endgame* show a specificity of time and place, namely, Picardy / Normandy in the wake of the First World War. According to S.E. Gontarski, "The devastation in the Picardy / Normandy area was familiar to Beckett, and the World War I setting was not a very subtle means of deflecting the play's autobiographical level away from his World War II experiences in the region" amongst which was the time as a volunteer in the Irish Red Cross hospital in Saint-Lô (33). Gontarski suggests that the title of his report of the hospital's activities for Irish Radio, "Humanity in Ruins," might serve "as a gloss on *Fin de Partie*" (34). The relationship between want and power in *Endgame* would also be an appropriate gloss on, or a laying bare of, the economy that prompted the rise to power of totalitarianism, both of fascist and Stalinist hues, in the pre-war era. If there is hope in *Endgame,* it is in the relative impotence of Hamm, for at least the power based on want itself wants.

3

For a drama so concerned with adoption and perpetuation as *Endgame* it is perhaps fitting that the play's literary genealogy should be at issue. As I hope to have shown, the dialogue between Dickens and Beckett is a pervasive one which leads to a re-examination of the possibilities of meaning and significance within *Endgame*. The possibilities raised by a similar dialogue with Shakespeare have for so long been part of the critical reaction to Beckett as to seem all but unassailable. There is no intention here to question the validity of the practice of relating *Endgame* to *The Tempest*, or *Lear* or *Hamlet;* only to question what is at stake in the choice of Shakespeare as a literary precursor over and above Dickens. Why is Shakespeare as adoptive father of *Endgame* more readily conceivable than Dickens?

When compared with Shakespeare, as when compared with Dickens, the world of *Endgame* is marked by loss and deterioration as the plenitude of the past becomes a diminished present. Alfred Schwarz captures this movement when he claims that in contrast to Prospero, Hamm's "is the anguish of a devalued being in a decayed world, without hope of reprieve" (351). Whether one figures this in accordance with the philosopher Theodor Adorno as the "liquidated dramatic subject" of Hamm in relation to Hamlet, of whom he is a "grim abbreviation" (107), or with Ruby Cohn, who asserts that *Endgame* mockingly reflects *The Tempest* (334), the motif of deterioration is ever-present. If loss and deterioration are the guiding motifs of thinking about Beckett intertextually, the question of from which high-point has the Beckett world charted its decline is of great importance. The journey from Hamlet to Hamm may be one of loss, but it is not the same journey of loss as that traveled from Mr. Omer to Hamm.

Among the many commentators who have placed Beckett within a Shakespearean context, Harold Bloom argues most strongly for the pervasiveness of Shakespeare in Beckett's play. *Endgame,* he writes, "moves out from a Shakespearean paradigm that grafts elements of *Lear, The Tempest, Richard III* and *Macbeth* onto *Hamlet*" (500). Given that Hamlet is, for Bloom, the "largest Western representation of consciousness" (507), it might not be surprising that he chooses to see *Endgame* though the prism of *Hamlet* rather than through, for example, *Richard II* or *Richard III,* to which he also relates Beckett's drama. But the very act of focusing on the *Hamlet* resonances of *Endgame* (which are not legitimized by direct allusion), Bloom reveals how much is at stake in the Shakespeare-Beckett dialogue. The motif of deterioration here comes strongly in to play. Bloom argues: "Hamlet is a charismatic. His strong parody, Hamm, is anything but that; all that he definitely preserves of Hamlet is the play doctor and director of the play within the play" (507). The parodic relationship between Hamm and Hamlet is one based on diminution as the fullness of Hamlet gives way to the lessness of Hamm. The diversity and sheer bewildering personality of the Dane, who is at once the director of the play within a play, and greater than *Hamlet,* has been reduced to the theatrically bound, and hence, deeply unstable figure of Hamm, as "Shakespearean mimesis allows Hamlet both to play himself and be himself; Hamm perhaps can only play himself" (509).

The importance of this diminution should not be underestimated, for Bloom claims that " Hamm [is] the central man of twentieth century drama" and continues: "This is disconcerting and should be: [...] a dethroned king (of sorts) down to one servant who cannot sit, while he himself is blind and cannot stand" (509). It is in this claim—that Hamm is of such importance to twentieth-century drama—coupled with the assertion that, with *Endgame*, "Beckett had shaped our century's stage equivalent of Shakespeare" (509), that one can begin to discern the significance to be gained from stressing the intertextual relations between Beckett and Shakespeare, rather than the relations with such a figure as Dickens.

Yet one must be careful: Bloom never claims simple equivalency between Beckett and Shakespeare; the latter always remains supreme. Nevertheless, by laying the stress on "our century," Bloom charts a trajectory of decline; the denuded Hamlet (or Lear, or Prospero) that is Hamm is the fitting Hamlet for our own denuded age when, in Schwarz's words, man is a devalued being in a decayed world. The force of Hamm as a parody of Hamlet is made clear by Adorno, when he writes that: "Parody, in the emphatic sense, is the employment of forms at times when they have become historically impossible" (99). Adorno claims that *Endgame* addresses a crisis in meaning and representation precipitated by the horrors of World War II and the failure of Existentialism. Metaphysical meaning is no longer possible, and so the dramatic form is itself undermined, and, crucially for the present argument, within Beckett all "that appears of history is its result: decline" (88), leaving the human actor as a "non[-]identity" which comprises of two elements: "the historical disintegration of the subject as a unity, and the emergence of that which is not subject" (92). The rupture of the unity of the subject is captured in Hamm's narratives where he switches between the roles of the narrator and the role of himself, thus revealing, according to Adorno, the "very Self to be something else, the aping of something non-existent" (107). One can hear Bloom's words echoing here: "Hamm perhaps can only *play* himself" (My emphasis). The twentieth-century seems to have made the charismatic Hamlet impossible, leaving us to console ourselves as best we can with a lesser, fractured Hamm.

The critical tendency when considering *Endgame* and Shakespeare is to focus, on the one hand, on *The Tempest*, and on the other, the great tragedies, particularly *Hamlet*. The choice of these works to mark the high-point from which the Beckettian decline can be charted is significant and informs the quality of the no longer possible. The dialogue between *Hamlet* and *Endgame*, conducted both within the play and perhaps more importantly within the attendant critical community, allows for a consideration of the status of tragic significance. For Adorno, the issue is clear; *Endgame* parodies the now obsolescent tragic mode: "The dramatic constituents appear after their death. Exposition, intrigue, action, peripeteia and catastrophe return as decomposed participants in a dramatical inquest: the catastrophe is replaced by the announcement that there is no more pain-killer" (100). Just as the tragic forms are regurgitated in *Endgame*, so the tragedy of personality, the tragic fall of the charismatic hero, to adopt Bloom's conception of Hamlet, is made impossible by Hamm who can never break beyond the bounds of "playing himself." Bloom ambiguously writes that *Endgame* is in the tragic mode (499), thus allowing for the possibility that the play, as Adorno believed, took on tragic modes whilst being unable or unwilling to create tragic significance. A similar vein of thought inspired Jan Kott's re-imagining of *Lear* in the terms of *Endgame* in which the tragic, sanctioned by the divine, has been replaced by the grotesque: "The downfall of the tragic hero is a confirmation of and recognition of the absolute; whereas the downfall of the grotesque actor means mockery of the absolute and its desecration" (132). This journey from the possibility to the impossibility of tragic significance, from Hamlet to Hamm, has one crucial staging post: World War II, through which, according to Adorno, "everything, including a resurrected culture, was destroyed, although without its knowledge" (85).

At this moment of a cultural destruction without any possibility of resurrection, the role of *The Tempest* in *Endgame* takes on a further significance. Although there is here insufficient space to do justice to the relations between *The Tempest* and *Endgame* (and so much depends on one's interpretation of *The Tempest* because it is far from being a stable text), the note of reconciliation which is struck by

Shakespeare's play is utterly unthinkable within Beckett's. "Our revels now are ended" in *Endgame* marks the possible death of Nell; in *The Tempest,* the end of the glorious pageantry of Prospero's masque. This is not a simple journey from "the gorgeous palaces, / The solemn temples, the great globe itself" (V.1.152-3) to the destitution of the last refuge. There is a Beckettian strain in Prospero's speech, whereby all illusions are shattered and not a rack is left behind; such a world would indeed be an *Endgame*. However, as Alfred Schwarz has pointed out, Prospero's dismantling of his illusory world and his subsequent renunciation of power as he throws away his staff and drowns his books, becomes an occasion for reconciliation. All illusions may have been rejected, but man in his denuded state now asks for mercy, as Prospero asks of the audience at the close of the play:

> Now I want
> Spirits to enforce, art to enchant;
> And my ending is despair
> Unless I be reliev'd by prayer,
> Which pierces so that it assaults
> Mercy itself, and frees all faults. (Epilogue, l. 13-18)

Tragedy has been averted on Prospero's isle and reconciliation taken its place. If *Endgame* parodies and undermines tragic significance, it will not allow the Shakespearean alternative of reconciliation and mercy:

> Hamm: Forgive me. […] I said, Forgive me.
> Clov: I heard you. (14)

In *The Tempest*, tragedy is replaced by comic resolution, and that too in the *Endgame* world is no longer possible. Adorno writes that the laughter which *Endgame* provokes ought to choke on itself, for this "is what has become of humor after it has grown obsolete as an aesthetic medium and revolting without a canon of the truly humorous, without a place of reconciliation from where one could laugh, without anything left between heaven and earth that is really harmless, that would permit itself to be laughed at" (98).

Clov: [...] Well? Don't We laugh?
Hamm: [*After reflection.*] I don't.
Clov: [*After reflection.*] Nor I. (25)

Not even unhappiness can raise the necessary comedy for long, as Nell points out: "it's like the funny story we have heard too often, we still find it funny, but we don't laugh anymore" (20).

The high-point from which Beckett then declines in a Shakespearean context is bound by tragic significance on one hand, and the resolution of tragedy through the comic on the other. Both these ways out of suffering are rejected by *Endgame*. We have traveled from the possible to the impossible, from the meaningful to the meaningless; and their may be a perverse pride in such an assertion.

The intertextual paradigm between Shakespeare and Beckett in which the tragic has declined to the parodic or the grotesque is unsustainable when Shakespeare is replaced by Dickens. Mr. Omer is no Hamlet. Beckett's dialogue with Dickens through *Endgame* calls into question just such a paradigm which charts a satisfying trajectory from the decline of the tragic hero to the decline of the tragic itself. Rather than a tragic figure as the high-point from which Beckett declines, we have in Mr. Omer a much more comic creation. Although Mr. Omer's afflictions are real enough, his reaction to them and Dickens's characterization of him are not only humorous but stress the benefits of humor, as physical frailty is met with apparently sincere pleasure and heartfelt "over-rejoicing." For one, such as myself, who has long been keen to stress the comedy within *Endgame* in particular and Beckett's work in general, this Dickens-Beckett axis offers a challenge. When the intertextual paradigm was one from tragedy to the tragicomic, or to the parodic or grotesque, then the humor of *Endgame* performed a crucial role and was to be given all due critical emphasis. If the trajectory of decline is one which begins in the comic, in what does it end? To say that tragedy is hereby reinstated would, I think, be to underestimate the complexity of the situation and would seriously mis-read the effect of the play. Humor, however, has been one of the saving graces of the play; the deeply dark comic moments have at least made *Endgame* bearable to watch and contemplate. Yet *Endgame* demonstrates in its intertextual relations that neither tragedy nor comedy are possible any more. Like the funny story told too many times, the comic has lost its comedy:

Hamm: The whole thing is comical, I grant you that. What about having a
good guffaw the two of us together?
Clov: [*After reflection*] I couldn't guffaw again today.
Hamm: [*After reflection*] Nor I. [Pause] I continue then. (41)

With Hamm as the destination, the journey from Mr. Omer may well
be bleaker than that from Hamlet. With *Endgame* as the terminus, the
deterioration from Dickens offers still less consolation than the
deterioration from Shakespeare.

Paul Stewart, Intercollege, Nicosia

Notes

[1] Christopher Ricks pointed out Beckett's misquotation from *Hamlet* (it should read:
"rots itself in *ease*") in *Beckett's Dying Words* (52). According to Ricks, the mistake,
if it is an unwitting error, reveals that "for Beckett the only ease is death."
[2] For a full description of the development of the play over a series of drafts,
typescripts and holographs (held at numerous locations) see S.E. Gontarski, 25-54.

Bibliography

Primary Texts

Beckett, Samuel. *Disjecta: Miscellaneous Writings and a Dramatic
        Fragment*, ed. Ruby Cohn. London: Calder, 1983.
—. *Dream of Fair to Middling Women.* Dublin: Black Cat Press,
        1992.
—. *Endgame.* London: Faber and Faber, 1987.
Dickens, Charles. *Hard Times.* (1854) London: Penguin, 1995.
—. *The Personal History of David Copperfield.* (1850) London:
        Penguin, 1996.
Shakespeare, William, *The Tempest* ed. Virginia Mason Vaughn and
        Alden T. Vaughn (The Arden Shakespeare). London:
        Thomson, 2003.

Secondary Texts

Adorno, Theodor W. 'Towards an Understanding of *Endgame*' in Bell Gale Chevigny, ed. *Twentieth Century Interpretations of* Endgame. Englewood Cliffs, NJ: Prentice-Hall, 1969. (82-114)

Acheson, James. 'Chess with the Audience: Samuel Beckett's *Endgame*' in *Critical Quarterly* 22.2 (1980): 33-45.

Bloom, Harold. *The Western Canon: The Books and Schools of the Ages.* London: Papermac, 1994.

Browne, J. Russell. 'Mr. Beckett's Shakespeare' *Critical Quarterly* 5 (1963): 24-39.

Bryden, Mary. 'Gender in Transition: *Waiting for Godot* and *Endgame*' in Steven Connor, ed. *New Casebooks: Waiting for Godot* and *Endgame.* Basingstoke: Macmillan, 1992. (150-164)

Cohn, Ruby. "*The Tempest* in an *Endgame*" in *Symposium XIX* 4 (Winter, 1965): 328-334.

Gontarski, S.E. *The Intent of Undoing in Samuel Beckett's Dramatic Texts.* Bloomington: Indiana University Press, 1985.

Knowlson, James. *Damned to Fame: The Life of Samuel Beckett.* London: Bloomsbury, 1996.

Kott, Jan. *Shakespeare Our Contemporary.* (1964) New York: Norton, 1974.

Lawley, Paul. 'Adoption in *Endgame*' in Connor (1992): 119-127.

Newlin, George. *Everyone in Dickens: A Taxonomy,* vol III, *Characteristics and Commentaries, Tables and Tabulations.* London: Greenwood, 1995.

Ricks, Christopher. *Beckett's Dying Words.* Oxford: Oxford UP, 1993.

Sage, Victor. "Dickens and Beckett: Two Uses of Materialism" in *The Journal of Beckett Studies* 2 (1977): 15-39

Schwarz, A. *From Büchner to Beckett: Dramatic Theory and the Modes of Tragic Drama.* Athens, OH: Ohio University Press, 1978.

Hamming it up in *Endgame*: A Theatrical Reading

Kate Dorney

> If all Beckett's characters are ruined philosophers of a kind, they continue to live their ruination philosophically, that it is to say, restlessly asking *why* things should be this way. And if Beckett's work enacts, as so many have supposed it does, the collapse of the metaphysical certainties that have sustained Western thought over the last two thousand years and before—the belief in God, in the unity of the world, in the knowability of experience, the communicability of reality through language, the idea of 'man,' and the corresponding notion of his historical purpose or destination—then it does so, as it were, from the inside rather than from the outside of these things. (Connor 3)

This quotation provides a neat summary of the prevailing themes in Beckett studies. It also indicates a degree of consensus among the critical community: there is no questioning those views of Beckett's work which read him as entirely preoccupied by philosophy, by the collapse of metaphysical certainties. One can just observe the location of the action. This essay seeks to challenge these predominant modes of engagement with Beckett in relation to *Endgame*, a play that is normally excavated for philosophical, scatological and eschatological meaning as outlined by Connor above. It proposes instead to focus on the *performative* nature of Beckett's engagement with theater and language.

This approach opens up space for a rereading of the play as a sly meta-linguistic and meta-theatrical commentary on both 'absurd theater' and other forms of theater contemporary with the play's first performances in the 1950s. Where others have described a meditation on the inevitability of a 'breakdown of communication' in the aftermath of war and increasing mechanization, I perceive a resolutely theatrical event: a pastiche of meta-theater, music-hall and set pieces satirizing intellectual and theatrical anxieties about the nature of performance. Rather than seeing Hamm as a post-war Fisher King presiding over the desolation of his own people, I want to present a study of a self-important actor-manager, who must be centre-stage at all times, rehearsing with his recalcitrant company.[1] Such a re-reading sees Hamm, "the great soliloquizer," continually undermined in rehearsals by his straight man (Clov) and upstaged by his stooges (Nagg and Nell)—themselves 'raconteurs' from another stage tradition. Extrapolated to breaking point, this reading sees Hamm on his own representing the actor or director-centered theatrical trends of the past—"me to play"—whilst Hamm in concert with his company reflects the move towards ensemble-based theater becoming increasingly popular in Britain (already popular in mainland Europe through the work of the Berliner Ensemble and the Comedie Francaise) in the late 1950s and early 1960s.[2]

By drawing on reviews of first performances, subsequent scholarly works on the play, and on Beckett's *oeuvre* as a whole, this essay seeks to contextualize the theatrical landscape into which *Endgame* was born and the critical environment in which it has been received. In doing so, my aim is to challenge monolithic readings of *Endgame* that see the play as an apocalyptic tragedy embodying Beckett's bleak vision of life in the twentieth century or those who interpret the play as an exercise in the breakdown of communication delineating the process of dehumanization undergone by the characters. As Michael Worton observes, the opaque nature of Beckett's work makes it more accessible rather than less so. Rather than encouraging monolithic or mono-focused readings, such opacity encourages a post-modern multiplicity of interpretations and endlessly alternative readings:

> Whether our favored field is the Bible, literature, philosophy or popular songs, we will each pick up some of the references and so accept that all is not even "nearly finished." Our strongest defense against the absurdity and the entropy of existence is the necessity—and the joy—of co-creating the text by continually changing its shape as we connect different ideas and images, as we perceived it to be unauthoritative because it is a *cento*, a patchwork of manipulated quotations. (85)

My own 'favored field' is the theater rather than solely Beckett's drama. Accordingly, in this essay I follow up the theatrical allusions within *Endgame*, and the implications of these allusions in performance. In the final section of the essay I also examine the meta-theatrical legacy of *Endgame* in post-war British drama, particularly the subsumption of this meta-theatrical knowingness into the theatrical mainstream via Harold Pinter and Tom Stoppard.

Endgame in Theater History

Until the cusp of the millennium, the received wisdom of the theatrical academy was that the sterile desert of post-1945 British theatre consisted of acres of Rattigan, Coward and Enid Bagnold; middle-class, middle-brow audiences mindlessly consumed drawing-room comedies and thrillers, interspersed with a healthy dose of saccharine musicals and domestic tragedies. So legend has it, these audiences fled when John Osborne's *Look Back In Anger* premiered at the Royal Court on 8 May 1956, appalled by the unacceptable face of urban squalor it presented (graduates living in rented rooms and women ironing in their husband's shirts). The publication of Dan Rebellato's *1956 and All That* in 1999, and Dominic Shellard's *British Theatre Since the War* in 1999 and *British Theatre in the 1950s* in 2000, issued a welcome challenge to this comfortable view of the post-war period, and attempted to make space for the impact of Beckett, Ionesco and absurd theater on this inert theater-going public. The new orthodoxy advanced that the 'shock of the new' had begun before the English Stage Company had even erected the ironing board.

Bull (1984), Lacey (1995), Rebellato and Shellard have all pointed out that *Look Back in Anger* was far from revolutionary in form: compared to the bafflement that greeted (and often still greets) *Waiting for Godot* and *The Lesson* in 1955, the mild grumblings that greeted *Look Back in Anger* were positively restrained. As the late Jack Reading, former vice-president of the Society for Theater Research, observed, Beckett's theatrical style was far more of a challenge to contemporary audiences than the essentially well-made *Look Back In Anger*. In a letter to Shellard, Reading wrote:

> *Waiting for Godot* left the members of its audience who sat it out to the end completely *stunned*. We knew we had seen things on the stage that could not be related to anything theatrical previously experienced. It was almost beyond discussion or rational appraisal. It had been an entirely new experience: a play (for want of a better word) that had taken its audience into a new extension of imagination.

> *Look Back in Anger*, on the other hand, was merely *stimulating*: the set had
> been accepted as not un-ordinary and not as ground-breaking as some later
> commentators now suggest; the characters, the story and the plotting were
> unremarkable; we knew of graduates who had declined to enter the rat-race
> of usual employment; the direction was pedestrian and the final curtain of
> animal talk had been squirmishly embarrassing. What had been different was
> the vehemence of the delivery of the off-the-top outbursts of Jimmy.
> (Shellard 28)

Reading's first-hand experience bears out the observations of Bull,
Bigsby, Lacey and a host of other theater historians. *Look Back in
Anger* may have grabbed the headlines, but theatrically speaking,
Waiting for Godot was the mould-breaker. And if Reading and his
contemporaries were startled by Jimmy's outbursts, then the histrionics
chez Hamm must have given a whole new meaning to the words
'family feud.'[3]

Endgame in Critical History

It signals NO HOPE to the human race – *Punch*, 10 April 1957

Endgame depicts the tensions between hesitation and severance, retention
and relinquishment of control by the self-consciously histrionic monarch of a
wasteland ambivalently approaching a ritual of renunciation. (Rabey 49)

These two opinions, divided by nearly half a century and an industrial
amount of scholarship, concur that *Endgame* is not for the faint-hearted
and certainly not for the light-hearted. When I first came to study the
play I was struck by the way in which critics seemed to have arrived at
a consensus about how depressing the themes of the play were. Was no
one else struck by the cruel joke which had Clov, with his "stiff
staggering walk" doing continual circuits of the stage and going up and
down ladders? Surely a funny walk is one of the staples of twentieth-
century comedy enshrined in Monty Python's "The Ministry of Silly
Walks" sketch and Morecambe and Wise's "Walk this Way" sketch, as
well as in every clown routine since the invention of big clown shoes?
Even if the play's original audience missed that point, the generations
of critics who grew up in the 1970s should surely be able to see the
funny side, having had the pleasure of watching this school of physical,
knockabout comedy develop on television? Evidently even those who

appreciated the odd gag preferred to think of Beckett's jokes solely as black comedy; as one last laugh on the way to apocalypse. The seeds of this dour, linguistically mistrustful and philosophically inclined Beckett seem to me to be attributable to two texts: Martin Esslin's *The Theater of the Absurd* (1962) and the "Three Dialogues" between Beckett and Georges Duthuit published in Esslin's *Critical Essays on Beckett* (1965). In the former, Esslin outlines the philosophical genealogy of the absurd movement, and extrapolates Beckett's choice of reading matter into a theory of communication breakdown. In the latter, Beckett, caught in a rare moment of volubility, utters the fateful phrase "Nothing to express, no power to express, no desire to express," and his reputation as a linguistic nihilist was sealed (17). Indeed, so secure is this critical stance that as recently as 2002, Jean Jacques Lecercle was yoking together Beckett and post-structuralist philosopher Gilles Deleuze, in order to explicate Deleuze's determination to right the wrong 'linguistic turn' that philosophy made all those years ago, and to reduce language to its proper place in the order of things (6).

The Linguistic Turn in Beckett Studies

'Loss of faith' in language and concomitant ideas of 'communication failure' are crucial markers of what Esslin's book christened the Theater of the Absurd. Ever since the book's publication, 'absurd' has become a convenient label to attach to any dramatic work whose characters are less than fluent or who express any reservations or dissatisfaction about the communicative efficacy of language. The stylistic research of Simpson (1989), Herman (1995), Culpeper, Short, Verdonk (1998) and Toolan (2000), has provided welcome new perspectives on 'communication failure' in drama by highlighting the fact that far from being uncommunicative, dramatic communication failure or dysfluency may be closer to unplanned, spoken discourse rather than planned, formal discourse. In doing so, stylisticians have been able to challenge the notion that "nothing happens," or that only "nonsense" is communicated in Absurd dialogue. However, an account of Absurd drama explicated entirely by means of Conversation Analysis or stylistics will always be geared towards explaining the mechanisms of language rather than of drama: to ignore the medium, is, especially in the case of Beckett, to ignore the message as well. By taking this research a step further however, it is possible to show that instances of so-called communication failure in the dialogue of Beckett and Ionesco can be reread as an ironic commentary on the idea of 'loss of faith' in language. The meta-linguistic discourses that proliferate in *Endgame* foreground acts of communication, or failures of communication, exposing them for what Judith Butler calls a series of "stylized repetition of acts" (136), which simultaneously draw attention to, and undermine, the idea that language is an ineffectual communicative tool.

As readers and audience members, our expectations of what constitutes meaningful dialogue in a theatrical performance, like our experience of what constitutes identity, are based on "a set of meanings already socially established." In the case of Absurd drama, these expectations were established before the Kitchen Sink, Epic and Absurd "movements" of British theater in the 1950s. Up to that point, theater in Britain had been dominated by "drawing-room comedies," domestic tragedies and other varieties of the "well-made play," in which characters exchanged fluent, articulate and witty repartee, or expressed the depth of their feelings in finely-turned prose. Demotic speech, vulgar jokes and comic routines were usually confined to music hall acts or "reviews." This was where the working classes went for their entertainment while the middle-brows enjoyed the well-made play.

Understandably then, when *Waiting for Godot* appeared on the London stage in 1955, it left the critics baffled and hostile: "a play," according to Vivian Mercier, "in which nothing happens twice" and conducted in conversation more usually heard in the playground, or in the music hall.[4] Accordingly, most critics latched on to the protagonists' idiosyncratic conversational style, describing it as "incomprehensible and pretentious" (Philip Hope-Wallace, qtd in Elsom 69-70), and, furthermore, hailing it as Beckett's metaphor for the meaninglessness of life, language and theater. Subsequent plays by Beckett, Ionesco, Pinter and Stoppard (among others) provided theatrical and academic criticism with an opportunity to trace common themes and turn a group of disparate plays into a movement reflecting the decay of language and communication: one of the perennially seductive myths of literary criticism.[5] From this movement came the birth of Esslin's *Theater of the Absurd*, a work credited with defining the movement in spite of his protests that the book was an attempt to explore common themes rather than pigeonhole a group of playwrights. Esslin explained the origins of Absurdism in the work of Sartre and Camus and traced the way in which this new philosophy surfaced in literary and dramatic works. In bringing together philosophy, literature and the pronouncements of the various playwrights, Esslin provided a compelling way of understanding the work of Beckett, Ionesco and others that has the tone for future public and academic reception of their works.

"Nothing to express, no power to express, no desire to express"

Beckett's famous epigram, taken from a discussion about modern artists, is perpetually cited as one of his few (and oblique) articulations of his own aesthetics. Famously closed-mouthed about his work, Beckett is, in many respects, the ideal 'absurd' writer, the absurdist's absurdist. His refusal to elucidate on the meaning of his plays, or to comment on interpretations of his work by others leaves the reader/critic/academic desperately looking for something that might contain a grain of his ideas on the subject. Chance remarks on other subjects, passages from the novels, plays, and academic writings have all been excavated for clues. One theory suggests that such is his loss of faith in language, that Beckett regards language as incapable of doing justice to his ideas (Kennedy). Another suggests that resounding silence is the ultimate demonstration of theory in action: no words, no reason, and no point (Kane, Steiner). I would like to suggest that there is a degree of humour in this enigmatic silence, a kind of self-reflexive joke. More significantly, lack of authorial elucidation leaves the field wide open for critics to explain, posit, and speculate without any fear of being gainsaid. Beckett's silence becomes the most eloquent testimony to the inadequacy of language ever *not* spoken. Instead of admitting a plurality of interpretations, meaning is anchored in authorial intention, voiced though the opinions and actions of that author's fictional characters.

A clear example of this tendency to allow the character's words to speak for the author can be found in Beckett's first play *Eleutheria*. Victor, the play's protagonist, refuses to speak, and the play is centered on discovering the reason for his silence. In true Beckettian style it is eventually discovered that Victor has made his most coherent speech off-stage and to the servants; another character loses his temper and parodies Victor's imagined speech and his audience's reaction:

> I see it from here. Life, death, freedom, the whole kit and caboodle, and the disillusioned little laughs to show that they are not taken in by the big words and the bottomless silences and the paralytic's gestures to signal that that's not it, it's a different matter, an altogether different matter, what can you do, language isn't meant to express those things. (134)

The accuracy with which Beckett parodies the Absurdist quandary about language suggests his attitude was perhaps more equivocal than is often supposed. It also offers an uncanny preview of the denouement of Ionesco's *The Chairs* (*Eleutheria* remained unpublished and unperformed until the 1990s). The play revolves around a husband and wife (the Old Man and the Old Woman) preparing for a party at which the Old Man intends to reveal his 'message' to the world. The couple greet and seat invisible guests, and await the Orator they have employed to disseminate the Old Man's message. They play the hosts' role to perfection, making polite small talk with the invisible guests, and in the process demonstrating the strength of the process of implicature, which here allows us to follow both sides of their conversations, despite the fact we can only hear one side of it. When the Orator arrives, the couple make their farewell speeches and jump out the window, at which point the Orator begins. Ionesco's stage direction reads:

> *The Orator, who has remained motionless and impassive during this scene of double-suicide, decides after a few moments to speak. Facing the rows of empty chairs, he gives the invisible crowd to understand that he is deaf and dumb. He makes signs in deaf and dumb language—desperate attempts to make himself understood. Then he produces the guttural groans and rasps of the mute.* (56)

The mute's gestures leave the imaginary audience wholly unimpressed and unenlightened, in the same way as Victor's imagined speech has left his family and the play's audience none the wiser as to the cause of his existential malaise. On both occasions, the audience is denied its expectations, both in terms of what they expect from a play, and what the plot has given them to expect.

Despite the fact that the idea of conveying a profound message is ridiculed in both of these plays, and, perhaps most famously of all in

Lucky's speech in *Waiting for Godot*, Esslin (1980) cannot resist the opportunity to match phrase to authorial intention. In a similar act of cross-referencing, Beckett's silence has led many academics to infer Beckett's attitudes from his reading habits. To paraphrase Beckett, we see it all from here, the youthful amanuensis Beckett reading Mauthner's *Critique of Language* to Joyce—the two of them using Mauthner to plot the communicational havoc they will wreak on European literature. Most treatises on Beckett and language routinely make some reference to the book, and attempt to map the book onto the writer, just as they try to match the character's ideas to the writer's. Esslin's mention leaves us in no doubt as to the conclusions he draws:

> Beckett read Joyce passages from the works of Fritz Mauthner, whose *Critique of Language* was one of the first works to point to the fallibility of language as a medium for the discovery and communication of metaphysical truths. (34)

Rather than assuming that both writers embraced Mauthner's thesis wholeheartedly, it seems equally plausible that this 'absurd' or 'suspicious' attitude to language evidenced in their work is a parody of such highbrow theorizing. It is not as if either of them were without a sense of humor, or incapable of such parody—one only has to turn again to Lucky's speech to verify that. Surely this tendency to make one-to-one correlations embodies everything Absurdism is supposed to challenge: the continual need to find and attribute meaning? As Pinter observed, reflecting on the variety of interpretations of his own work: "The desire for verification on the part of all of us, with regard to our own experience and the experience of others, is understandable but cannot always be satisfied" (ix).

Beckett, Linguistics, Philosophy and Critical Theory

In his essay on *Endgame* in *Must We Mean What We Say?* (1976), philosopher Stanley Cavell proposes a way to read through and around characteristically Beckettian obfuscations of language, meaning and motivation. According to Cavell, Beckett is trying to "uncover the literal." Thus a less nihilistic reading of the play can be achieved by taking every word literally, breaking open the clichés and curses and taking the meaning of the words at face value (120). Accordingly, Cavell reads Clov's "[*exasperated*] What in God's name could there be on the horizon?" (107) to show "Hamm [*sic*] really asking whether anything on the horizon is appearing in God's name, as his sign or at his bidding" (120).

According to this interpretation, *Endgame* shows Beckett not despairing of language as, for example, Esslin, Steiner and Gessner would have it—indeed, Cavell dismisses Esslin's interpretation as nothing more than "impositions from an impression of fashionable philosophy"—but rejoicing in the simplicity of language, "our inability *not* to mean what we say" (115, 117). Although this position offers a welcome change to the more traditional one outlined by Esslin *et al*, both Cavell's and Esslin's interpretations seem to ignore an additional branch of "fashionable philosophy" of the period in which Beckett wrote: J.L Austin's and John Searle's Speech Act Theory which led, via Derrida, to Judith Butler's notion of performativity.

Speech Act Theory provides an account of how language can function as action through the uttering of certain words. For example, an act is committed when the words "I now pronounce you man and wife" are spoken. When he outlined this theory in *How To Do Things With Words*, Austin (whose ideas were later developed by his student, John Searle) decreed that a speech act could only be performed if certain 'felicity conditions' were observed (rules setting out the circumstances in which words perform actions—for example, to pronounce someone man and wife meaningfully requires a specific authority). The speech act had to be performed 'genuinely,' a requirement that automatically outlawed speech acts performed in plays and in literature.

In the 1970s Derrida challenged the 'infelicitous' status of fictional and dramatic dialogue, arguing that a speech act could only be successfully performed if the formulation was recognised as a speech act. Without that recognition, the words would lose their performative force regardless of the felicity conditions. Derrida describes this process of recognition as 'iteration'; that for a 'mark' (word, expression, etc.) to have any valency as a referent, that is, to have any significance in an act of communication, it must be recognisable or authenticated as having been used before:

> Could a 'coded' or iterable utterance succeed if its formulation did not repeat a 'coded' or utterable utterance, or in other words, if the formula I pronounce in order to open a meeting, launch a ship or a marriage were not identifiable

> as *conforming* with an iterable model, if it were not then identifiable in some way as a 'citation'? (17-18)

Derrida offers the analogy of signing of a cheque to validate a purchase. In order for the cheque to be accepted, the signature must be authenticated by a similar signature on the corresponding cheque guarantee card. In order for the signature to have any significance in the transaction, one's signature must be authenticated by reference to the signature slip on the reverse of the card. Without the authentication, the purchase cannot be made; similarly, without the recognition of performative force, the speech act cannot perform its task.

Judith Butler expanded Derrida's idea into a theory of performativity that challenged dominant models of gender and sexual identity as fixed and stable categories. She suggested that the fixed appearance of an identity is the result of a "regulatory fiction," that gender is an act, a performance constituted in, by, and through its repetition in the same way that speech is:

> As in other ritual social dramas, the action of gender requires a performance that is *repeated*. This repetition is at once a re-enactment and re-experiencing of a set of meanings already socially established; and it is the mundane and ritualised form of their legitimation [....] Gender ought not to be construed as a stable identity or locus of agency from which various acts follow; rather gender is an identity constituted in time, instituted in an exterior space through a *stylised repetition of acts*. (136)

Butler's articulation offers a useful way of reading the meta-linguistic commentaries that pepper Absurd dialogue. Theater is, in and of itself, performance, and meta-linguistic commentary offers a double layer of performance—the speaker is at once inside and outside the text. Performativity thus offers a useful way of re-reading the 'problem of cliché' so often foregrounded in discussions of 'loss of faith in language.' It allows us to re-work constant anxiety about lack of 'originality' lessening the impact of our speech, into strengthening the impact of our speech by drawing on the power of its collective background. For example, cliché is simply a repeated stylization: when we say "I can't express how I feel" we are doing something with words, with the apparently useless language that doesn't allow us to express ourselves; we're expressing the magnitude of what we feel. Similarly, the anguished cry "I can't describe the horror" only retains performative force if the audience recognizes that the strongest

possible description of something is to label it "indescribable." In this
way then, Derrida and Butler effectively negate the validity of the
debate about the 'lacking word' and the corresponding anxieties about
originality of expression. There is no such thing as an entirely original
expression, because the expression must contain enough 'traces' of
former/similar expressions to be recognizable, otherwise it cannot
succeed in having its proposed effect. The manifestation of the
absurdist's quandary through halting speech can be read against the
grain of its content: absurd protagonists may feel unable to
communicate, but what they communicate to their audience is decoded
via the audience's recognition of these citations.

Absurd drama has provided a rich vein of scholarship for
linguists, theater critics, philosophers and literary critics for over 40
years. Some of the positions held by eminent practitioners from these
disciplines can be reconfigured to provide a new way of interpreting
this work. As Austin embraced the dramatic lexicon but rejected drama
as 'meaningful,' absurd drama can be seen to have literally acted out
the iterative process. Suffused with meta-linguistic and meta-theatrical
commentary, absurd dramatic dialogue has, through a series of
repetitive stylized acts, *cited* those features which seem to embrace
communication breakdown and given them meaning afresh.

"A stylized repetition of acts"—Beckett's debt to the music hall

Waiting for Godot, the play in which, famously, "nothing happens
twice," is the ultimate tribute to the idea of a stylized repetition of acts.
Vladimir and Estragon wait in vain for the mysterious Godot to appear
in both acts, and are visited instead by Pozzo and Lucky, and the Boy
and his brother. In addition to the physical gags they import from the
music hall, the duo (for that is what they are, a comedy double act)
perform the traditional music-hall turns of commenting on the
audience, but also of sabotaging the other's act by refusing to play the
role offered to them. Remarking on and insulting the audience is an
established part of comic routines from stand-up to music-hall.
Primarily based on the principle that if one is in a vulnerable position,
one should always attack first to demonstrate confidence and mastery
over one's opponent, audience-baiting can be a useful way of avoiding
heckling. It is, after all a brave audience member who will tackle a
performer as obviously on the offensive as Hamm. Yet, paradoxically,

dealing with hecklers can also be an integral part of a comic's routine, where the audience enjoys the gladiatorial aspect as much as the act itself.

Beckett's incorporation of these techniques can be seen as a way of simultaneously challenging critics and audiences and pre-empting their reactions. Examples of this in *Waiting for Godot* are frequently cited, but worth highlighting again here, as they link into a reinvigoration of music-hall techniques in British theatre in the 1950s and 1960s.

> [**Estragon** *moves to the centre, halts with his back to the auditorium.*]
> Charming spot. [*He turns, advances to the front, halts facing the auditorium.*] Inspiring prospects. (*Complete Dramatic Works* 15)

This initial taunt to the audience is fairly mild, and it also offers an ironic commentary on the bare stage that has replaced the usual sumptuous set of 1950s drama. The example below is much more barbed. Not only is there the inference that the actors are not enjoying themselves, they also parody the likely reactions of the audience:

> **Vladimir.** Charming evening we're having.
> **Estragon.** Unforgettable.
> **Vladimir.** And it's not over.
> **Estragon.** Apparently not.
> **Vladimir.** It's only beginning.
> **Estragon.** It's awful.
> **Vladimir.** Worse than the pantomime.
> **Estragon.** The circus.
> **Vladimir.** The music hall.
> **Estragon.** The circus. (34)

As Kennedy points out, "[t]he irony of this internal reference to 'what is going on here in the theatre' gives the audience a chance to reflect on its own 'charming evening,' and the attendant risks of 'it' not yet being over, as the digressions multiply" (1992, 26). *Endgame* elaborates on this joke: meta-theatrical reviews proliferate as characters judge each other's performance from the audience's perspective, as well as commenting on their own routines as the audience might see them.

> **Clov.** Why this farce day after day?
> **Hamm.** Routine, one never knows.

Of even more significance is the doubly ironic moment when Clov goes to the front of the auditorium and looks through his telescope, observing that, "I see ... a multitude ... in transports ... of joy" (106). Firstly, we know that there are no survivors besides Hamm and his family in the world of the play; and secondly, judging by the early critical reception, audiences were far from ecstatic, and so the actor playing Clov is unlikely to see anyone in transports as he surveys his audience.

Beckett's fondness for repetition is foregrounded in both delivery and reception. Before turning to *Endgame* however, I would like to look briefly at John Obsorne's *The Entertainer*, which opened at the Royal Court Theater just after *Fin de Partie* in 1957. The play follows the fortunes of Archie Rice (played by Laurence Olivier in the original production, and then in the film), a music-hall entertainer who struggles to keep his act alive against the competition from film and television. His father Billy was a legendary music hall performer, and Archie has never really escaped from his shadow. As a consequence his embittered and embattled position makes his stage persona a particularly offensive one. After one joke that falls particularly flat, he says to the audience:

> Thank you for that burst of heavy breathing. You should have heard what James Agate said about *me*! But I have a go, lady, don't I? I 'ave a go. I do. You think I am, don't you. Well, I'm not. But *he* is! Here, here! Did I tell you about my wife? Did I? My wife—not only is she stupid, not only is she stupid, but she's cold as well. Oh yes, cold. She may look sweet, but she's a very cold woman, my wife. Very cold. Cold and stupid. She's what they call a moron glacee. Don't clap too hard—it's a very old building. (59)

Rice's remarks also act as cues for the audience: "laugh here."

In *Endgame* this process is at work at a much subtler level. The characters are equally aware of themselves as performers, and, more specifically, as performers whose skills are failing, hence their reliance on each other to work up their acts. As in traditional music hall however, a double act always means the troubling of a smooth performance, usually in the form of (un)intentionally foiling the other's attempt to dominate the conversational (as well as the physical) stage:

Clov. What is there to keep me here?
Hamm. The dialogue. [*Pause*] I've got on well with my story. [*Pause.*] I've got on with it well. [*Pause. Irritably*] Ask me where I've got to.
Clov. Oh, by the way, your story?
Hamm. [*Surprised.*] What story?
Clov. The one you've been telling yourself all your ... days.
Hamm. Ah, you mean my chronicle?
Clov. That's the one.
[*Pause.*]
Hamm. [*Angrily.*] Keep going, can't you, keep going!
Clov. You've got on with it, I hope.
Hamm. [*Modestly.*] Oh not very far, not very far. [*He sighs.*] There are days like that, one isn't inspired. [*Pause.*] Nothing you can do about it, just wait for it to come. [*Pause.*] No forcing, no forcing, it's fatal. [*Pause.*] I've got on with it a little all the same. [*Pause.*] Technique, you know. [*Pause. Irritably.*] I say I've got on with it a little all the same.
Clov. [*Admiringly.*] Well I never! In spite of everything you were able to get on with it!
Hamm. [*Modestly.*] Oh not very far, you know, not very far, but nevertheless, better than nothing.
Clov. Better than nothing! Is it possible?
Hamm. I'll tell you how it goes. He comes crawling on his belly—
Clov. Who?
Hamm. What?
Clov. Who do you mean, he?
Hamm. Who do I mean! Yet another.
Clov. Ah him! I wasn't sure. (121)

Hamm's prompting during this exchange lays bare the cues normally implicit in conversational interaction to keep the process moving. Clov's reluctance to engage in this process is sharply counterpointed by Hamm, the great soliloquizer, literally 'hamming' it up, in an effort to engage his audience, sighing and repeating the phrase "no forcing." Then, once Clov decided to cooperate, he becomes deliberately over-interested and obstructive by continually asking questions. Not content with ruining this effort, Clov destroys any attempt at sentiment when Hamm has another stab at running through his soliloquy later on:

> Hamm. Then let it end! [**Clov** *goes towards ladder.*] With a bang! [**Clov** *gets up on ladder, gets down again, looks for telescope, sees it, picks it up, gets up ladder, raises telescope*] Of darkness! And me? Did anyone ever have pity on me?
> Clov. [*Lowering the telescope, turning towards* **Hamm.**] What? [*Pause.*] Is it me you're referring to?

Hamm. An aside, ape! Did you never hear an aside before? I'm warming up for my last soliloquy.
Clov. I warn you. I'm going to look on this filth since it's an order. But it's the last time. [*He turns the telescope on the without.*] Let's see. [*He moves the telescope.*] Nothing ... nothing ... good ... good ... nothing ... goo- [*He starts, lowers the telescope, examines it, turns it again on the without. Pause.*] Bad luck to it!
Hamm. More complications! [**Clov** *gets down.*] Not an underplot, I trust. (130)

As well as deliberately misconstruing Hamm's words, Clov also goes out of his way to distract the audience from Hamm's speech by his elaborate comic business up and down the ladder, ruining the atmosphere in the process and hogging all the attention for himself. We may infer that Hamm's final phrase in this excerpt is not just a comment on the 'plot' of the play, but also on Clov's attempts at upstaging him.

These meta-theatrical interludes are frequent, as are the failures of actions to ever raise a laugh. Hamm's attempt at levity in the face of failing bodies and a deserted world meets an indifferent reception:

Hamm. Sit on him!
Clov. I can't sit.
Hamm. True. And I can't stand.
Clov. So it is.
Hamm. Every man his speciality. [*Pause*] No phone calls? [*Pause*] Don't we laugh?
Clov. [*After reflection*] I don't feel like it. (97)

The reason for its failure is hinted at below. Repetition is funny for a while, and then it becomes deadly, or at least, painful:

Clov. [*Sadly.*] No one that ever lived thought so crooked as we.
Hamm. We do what we can.
Clov. We shouldn't.
[*Pause.*]
Hamm. You're a bit of all right, aren't you?
Clov. A smithereen.
Hamm. This is slow work. [*Pause*] Is it not time for my painkiller? (97)

This is one of the critical moments in the play when both Hamm and Clov realize that their act is old and stale, and not as fluid or as funny

as it once was. As Hamm observes: "This is not much fun. [*Pause*]
But that's always the way at the end of the day, isn't it Clov?" (98) The
performers get tired of doing the same routine.

Interestingly (perhaps reflecting the waning popularity of
music-hall) Hamm and Clov have reached this point a lot quicker than
the old-stagers Nagg and Nell, who have been telling each other the
same stories for a life-time and only very recently have grown tired of
them. Fittingly, the parents Nagg and Nell cling to the old tradition.
They are closer to unadulterated music hall and circus, the original
comedy double act, harking back to a tradition where you could come
on, tell a funny story then a few jokes to break the monotony, and then
bring the house down. Their routine is also getting tired, as Nell
observes as they try, and fail, to kiss. "Why this farce, day after day?"
(99) This question is echoed later by Clov and answered by Hamm:
"Routine. One never knows" (107). Continuing the theme of physical
deterioration, Beckett gives Nagg and Nell one of the oldest jokes in
the book:

> [*Pause. They turn away from each other*]
> **Nagg.** Can you hear me?
> **Nell.** Yes. And you?
> **Nagg.** Yes. [*Pause*] Our hearing hasn't failed.
> **Nell.** Our what?
> **Nagg.** Our hearing. (99)

Even deafness cannot save Nell from Nagg's constant desire to
perform. As with Hamm and Clov, she is willing to give up the
performance, but he refuses to quit his role. The difference in their
relationship allows Nell greater freedom to be rude, but Nagg is
indomitable:

> **Nagg.** Will I tell you the story of the tailor?
> **Nell.** No. [*Pause.*] What for?
> **Nagg.** To cheer you up.
> **Nell.** It's not funny.
> **Nagg.** It always made you laugh. [*Pause.*] The first time I thought you'd die.
> **Nell.** It was on Lake Como. [*Pause.*] One April afternoon. [*Pause*] Can you
> believe it?
> **Nagg.** What?
> **Nell.** That we once went out rowing on Lake Como. [*Pause.*] One April
> afternoon.
> **Nagg.** We had got engaged the day before.
> **Nell.** Engaged!

> **Nagg.** You were in such fits that we capsized. By rights we should have
> drowned.
> **Nell.** It was because I felt happy.
> **Nagg.** It was not, it was not, it was my story and nothing else. Happy? Don't
> you laugh at it still? Every time I tell it. Happy! (101-102)

Nagg's indignation speaks of wounded professional pride; laughing to
death is the comic's greatest wish for his audience, and the idea that his
story might not have been the only reason Nell was helpless with
laughter all those years ago maddens him. He immediately launches
into the story as if to demonstrate its comic greatness. "Let me tell it
again. [*Raconteur's voice.*] An Englishman, needing a pair of striped
trousers in a hurry [...]" (102). Hamm suffers similar problems with
Clov, when even their comic business fails to entertain him. Having
repeatedly sent Clov off to fetch the glass/telescope, then told him not
to bother, he comments, "This is deadly." Clov stumps back on with
the telescope and begins the laborious business with the ladder,
continuing the stooge's role of contradiction and confusion by
observing "Things are livening up":

> [*He gets up on ladder, raises the telescope, lets it fall.*] I did it on purpose.
> [*He gets down, picks up the telescope, turns it on auditorium*] I see ... a
> multitude ... in transports ... of joy. [*Pause*] That's what I call a magnifier.
> [*He lowers the telescope, turns towards* **Hamm.**] Well? Don't we laugh?
> (106)

The obvious allusion to a small and joyless audience could hardly be
clearer. And these performers know all about joyless audiences, having
weathered the critical storm of *Waiting for Godot* and *Fin de Partie*.

   Whatever the reason we assign to Beckett for incorporating
music-hall into his plays on so many levels, we should remember that
the music-hall existed alongside his plays and the plays of others
during the 1950s, particularly outside of London and the West End. In
its purest form the genre was waning, as film and television gradually
replaced live entertainment, but the legacy lives on in the plays of this
period: in *Look Back in Anger*, *The Entertainer*, *Oh What a Lovely
War!* and in the works of John Arden and Peter Nichols. As John
Osborne noted in *The Entertainer*:

> The music hall is dying, and, with it, a significant part of England. Some of
> the heart of England has gone; something that once belonged to everyone,
> for this was truly a folk art. In writing this play, I have not used some of the

techniques of the music hall in order to exploit an effective trick, but because
I believe that some of the eternal problems of time and space that face the
dramatist, and, also, it has been relevant to the story and setting. Not only has
this technique its own traditions, its own convention and symbol, its own
mystique, it cuts right across the restrictions of the so-called naturalistic
stage. Its contact is immediate, vital and direct. (7)

Reading Osborne's impassioned declaration, the audience might
perhaps draw its own conclusions as to why Beckett embraced aspects
of music hall in his plays.

The allusive possibilities of Beckett's work, however, have led
many critics to stress the literary rather than the theatrical. Morrison
concentrates on the "narratives" which might be alluded to in the
narratives of Beckett's characters, favouring the Biblical and the
classical as Beckett's sources for *Endgame* and *Waiting for Godot*. She
ingeniously explains how Didi and Gogo's little canters have their
roots in Chaucer and *The Decameron*:

the structure of *Godot* is much more like a music-hall review or, to use a
more literary analogy, a frame narrative such as *The Decameron* or *The
Canterbury Tales*. In *Waiting for Godot* the "frame" is the abiding static
situation of waiting, and the various episodes Vladimir and Estragon engage
in are the means by which they enhance the "beauty of the way." Their
various "canters" have as much variety in subject matter, style and pace as
does any collection of tales marshalled to hearten the pilgrims. "For trewley,
confort ne myrthe is noon/To ride by the weye doumbe as a stoon" is a
judgement Vladimir and Estragon would share; and if they seem less
genuinely merry than Chaucer's sundry folk, it may be simply that for them
martyrdom is both more immediate and certainly less meaningful.
Nonetheless, they set themselves "to talen and to pleye." (14)

If the structure resembles a music-hall review and the structure belongs
to a play, that is, to the *dramatic* genre that focuses on live
performance, why pick a *literary* analogy? As discussed above, the
influence of music-hall can be detected in more than just the structure
of *Godot*: Chaucer's *Canterbury Tales* and Boccaccio's *Decameron*
may have their fair share of trouser-dropping and farting gags, but they
tend not to have extended jokes at the expense of the audience, or to go
for the visual gags of hats and boots.

Given *Godot*'s legendary status as a play which sent its first
audiences fleeing into the night, Didi's expansive gesture to the
auditorium and his reassurance to his partner that there is nothing
there, "not a soul in sight" (14), suggests that the live aspect of their

performance is not a random choice of genre, but a calculated challenge to theater audiences and producers alike. Reading contemporary reviews of the play, the observation "nobody comes, nobody goes. It's terrible" sounds like a line from the play, and similarly, many of the lines in the play sound like a premonition of the play's critical reception every bit as much as it whispers of man's existential terror. Morrison's reading of *Endgame* is, I would suggest, hyperopic: rather than seeing what is directly in front of her, her vision picks out more clearly what is at a great distance. Analysing Hamm's chronicle, she observes:

> Hamm refers by name to his "chronicle" and is self-conscious in his narration of it, aware of himself assuming the role of historian, aware of himself adopting a special voice and the manner setting off these words from his other speech. (27)

In such a theatrical reading, the adoption of a special voice and manner suggest that Hamm is performing, that he acting, rather than embodying "the Moses of a garden desolate, the Polidore Virgile of a wrecked kingdom" (28).

Endgame—An Endless Rehearsal?

It is seductive to think of Hamm as a tyrannical actor-manager from the 1920s (for example, Anew McMaster, Charles Doran, or later, Donald Wolfit), insisting that his company continue to rehearse the same old play regardless of their total lack of audience. The conceit is intensified by fact that Hamm was played in the first production by George Devine, the Artistic Director of the Royal Court (just as actor/director Roger Blin, to whom the play is dedicated, had played Hamm in the premiere of *Fin de Partie*). The recalcitrance of Hamm's fellow performers, the competition over who is audience and who is actor, the fatigue they express at running through their routines again, suggest a company sick to death of its own acts. At one point, Clov "implores" Hamm: "I'm tired of our goings on, very tired," and then says, "[*Imploringly*] Let's stop playing!" (129-130). Yet as Hamm acknowledges at the beginning, like his father he finds it impossible to retire: "Yes, there it is, it's time it ended and yet I hesitate to [*he yawns*]—to end" (93). Even Clov's attempt to bring the curtain down by walking out on the production—"This is what we call making an exit" (132)—fails. Hamm will not be denied the last word, and those words sound ominously cyclical, as if the whole thing might be about to begin again:

> Since that's the way we're playing ... [*he unfolds handkerchief*] ... let's play it that way [*he unfolds*] and speak no more about it [*he finishes unfolding*] speak no more. [*He holds the handkerchief spread out before him*] Old stancher! [*Pause*] You ... remain. [*Pause. He covers his face with handkerchief, lowers his arms to armrests, remains motionless.*] (133-134)

Following Morrison's observation that stanch can refer to a staunch friend as well as a stauncher of blood (the handkerchief) it seems plausible that Hamm's last gesture might be to command his partner to stay, an imperative, rather than a declarative (40). The act goes on...

'Wham, bam, thank you Sam': the legacy of *Endgame*

> **Player King**: [The dumb-show is] a device, really—it makes the action that follows more or less comprehensible; you understand, we are tied down to a language which makes up in obscurity what it lacks in style. (Stoppard 56)

Given the readings I have offered here, and Beckett's assertion that "Hamm is a king in this chess game lost from the start," it seems fitting to end with the consideration of a Player King and Beckett's meta-theatrical meta-linguistic legacy (Cohn 152). The Player King in Stoppard's *Rosencrantz and Guildenstern are Dead* (1966) epitomizes the ways in which communication is fetishized in drama through meta-linguistic and meta-theatrical commentary. Both are, and always have been, standard theatrical fare. The reason for analysing them here is to draw a parallel between the way in which the meta-theatrical and the meta-linguistic interact, and how standard meta-linguistic expressions about being at a loss for words are taken literally, rather than performatively, in some contexts, but not in others. If we contrast the reception of Beckett and Stoppard, Beckett's professions of linguistic decay are usually taken literally, as in Cavell's article discussed above, while Stoppard's are interpreted performatively and praised for adding to the theatrical experience. Writing in the *Manchester Guardian*, Philip Hope-Wallace implied that the jokes in *Endgame* actually made the play more depressing:

> This wry comment on the hopelessness of our human situation with our
> failing faculties and futile fidgets, accumulates almost imperceptibly a leaden
> weight of despair which the occasional little jokes, some perhaps rather too
> puerile, only increase. (qtd in Elsom 69-70)

In contrast, despite the fact that the quandary articulated by the Player-King about language, expressivity and theater is a common theme in Stoppard's earliest plays—*Rosencrantz and Guildenstern Are Dead*, *The Real Inspector Hound* (1968), *Jumpers* (1972), and *Travesties* (1974)—and is the main means of deriving comedy, it is never taken quite as seriously by the critics.

There is an obvious debt to *Waiting for Godot* in the games of linguistic 'tennis' in *Rosencrantz and Guildenstern*, in the 'playing' at being Guildenstern and Hamlet: Vladimir and Estragon "play at [being] Pozzo and Lucky," but Stoppard's meta-playfulness is usually interpreted as virtuoso grandstanding rather than Absurdist anxiety (Stoppard 31-33, 35-36; Beckett 68). Reviews of these plays emphasize the *theatrical* nature of Stoppard's achievements in a way that completely eluded contemporary reviews of Beckett's work. Milton Shulman's review of *Rosencrantz and Guildenstern Are Dead* praises the play for avoiding the gloom of its philosophical and theatrical antecedents: "Easy as it is to find echoes of Sartre, Beckett and Kafka in the introspective exchanges of R. and G., it is an exceedingly funny play" (qtd in Elsom 89-90). Michael Billington's 1974 review of *Travesties* acclaims it as:

> a dazzling pyrotechnical feat that combines Wildean pastiche, political
> history, artistic debate, spoof-reminiscence, and song-and-dance in
> marvellously judicial proportions. The text is a dense web of Joycean
> allusions, yet it also radiates sheer intellectual joie de vivre, as if Stoppard
> were delightedly communicating the fruits of his own researches. (51)

This is in spite of the dangerous heresy of Dadaism that the play investigates, which, one would have thought, was every bit as degenerate as existentialism. Perhaps the difference in these critical responses can be attributed to the different contexts in which these meta-linguistic debates occur. In the case of *Waiting for Godot* and *Endgame* it seems to be the removal of any identifiable surroundings that contributes most significantly to the 'nihilism' of Beckett's plays, whereas Stoppard's usually take place in a recognizable context: for example, *Hamlet* for *Rosencrantz and Guildenstern* and *The*

Importance of Being Earnest for *Travesties*. His characters are always from the educated classes, so it is natural for them to be articulate, and to reinforce the expectation of Wildean and Cowardian levels of wit in everyday conversation. In addition, as Billington identifies, Stoppard delights in letting his audience know what Stoppard the playwright has learned about for his latest play. Thus the audience feels that they are learning from the play, rather than being asked questions by the play or being forced to confront their own *ennui*—something Beckett's plays tend to foreground quite strongly. Pinter's early plays suffered a similar fate to Beckett and Ionesco (with whom he was constantly compared). Again it seems the main reason for interpreting Pinter's work metaphysically rather than literally is because, in spite of the recognisable settings, his characters tend towards conversational inarticulacy and taciturnity rather than fluency. As with Beckett, Pinter's refusal to shed any light on his plays, other than the joking remark about "the weasel under the cocktail cabinet," contributes to the interpretative free-for-all that prefers elaborate extrapolation rather than an examination of the play as a play.

It seems fitting, under the circumstances, that the last words should belong to the showmen:

> **Hamm**. Do you not think this has gone on long enough?
> **Clov.** Yes! (114)

Or perhaps, given the cyclical nature of the play I have advanced:

> **Clov.** The end is terrific!
> **Hamm.** I prefer the middle. (115)

Kate Dorney, The Victoria and Albert Theater Museum, London

Notes

[1] The allusion here, of course, is to Hamm's obsessive questioning of Clov during and after their "little turn." "Hug the walls, then back to the centre again. [**Clov** *pushes the chair.*] I was right in the centre, wasn't I?," and then "Back to my place! [**Clov** *pushes chair back to centre.*] Is that my place?`[…] Am I right in the centre?" (104)

[2] Of relevance here is the establishment of the English Stage Company at the Royal Court in 1955, the Theater Workshop at Stratford East in 1953, and the formation of the Royal Shakespeare Company in 1961 and the National Theater in 1962.

[3] The ramifications of taking into account the view of audience members like Reading are currently being investigated by the author, Shellard and Jeffrey, both in an oral history project and the research development of the British Library's Theater Archive. The project is in its infancy at the time of writing, but what is certain is that theater history will be radically altered in the aftermath.

[4] *Waiting for Godot* was first performed in English in August 1955, five months after Ionesco's *The Lesson*. Ionesco's play was similarly criticized, but failed to attract sufficient attention to mark it out as the beginning of the Absurd debate.

[5] From Bacon to the Romantics, to the War Poets and the Holocaust, the idea that language cannot express original and authentic feeling recurs. See Roy Harris' *The Language Myth* and George Steiner's *Language and Silence* for further explorations of this topic.

Bibliography

Play Texts

Beckett, Samuel. *The Complete Dramatic Works*. London: Faber and Faber, 1986.

—. *Eleutheria*. New York: Foxrock, 1995.

Ionesco, Eugene. *The Chairs* trans. Martin Crimp. London: Faber and Faber, 1997.

Stoppard, Tom. *Rosencrantz and Guildenstern Are Dead*. London: Faber and Faber, 1968.

—. *Jumpers*. London: Faber and Faber, 1972.

—. *Travesties*. London: Faber and Faber, 1975.

—. *The Real Inspector Hound* in *The Real Inspector Hound and Other Entertainments*. London: Faber and Faber, 1993.

Secondary Texts

Beckett, Samuel and Duthuit, Georges. 'Three Dialogues' in Martin Esslin ed. *Samuel Beckett: A Collection of Critical Essays*. London and Englewood Cliffs, NJ: Prentice-Hall, 1965. (19-20)

Billington, Michael. *One Night Stands*. London: Nick Hern Books, 2001.

Bull, John. *New British Political Dramatists*. Basingstoke: Macmillan, 1984.

Butler, Judith. *Gender Trouble: Feminism and the Subversion of Identity*. London: Routledge, 1990.

Cavell, Stanley. 'Ending the Waiting Game. A Reading of Samuel Beckett's *Endgame'* in *Must We Mean What We Say?* Cambridge: Cambridge University Press, 1976. (115-162)

Cohn, Ruby. *Back to Beckett*. Princeton: Princeton University Press, 1973.

—. *Just Play: Beckett's Theatre*. Princeton: Princeton University Press, 1980.

Connor, Steven ed. Waiting for Godot *and* Endgame: *New Casebooks*. Basingstoke: Macmillan, 1992.

Culpeper, Jonathan, Mick Short and Peter Verdonk eds. *Exploring the Language of Drama: From Text to Context*. London: Routledge, 1998.

Derrida, Jacques. *Limited Inc*. Evanston: Northwestern University Press, 1998.

Elsom, John. *Post-war British Theater Criticism*. London: Routledge and Kegan Paul, 1981.

Esslin, Martin. *The Theater of The Absurd*. Harmondsworth: Penguin, 1962, 1980.

—, ed. *Samuel Beckett: A Collection of Critical Essays*. Englewood Cliffs, NJ: Prentice-Hall, 1965.

Herman, Vimala. *Dramatic Discourse: Dialogue as Interaction in Plays*. London: Routledge, 1995.

Hope-Wallace, Phillip. Review of *Waiting for Godot* in *The Manchester Guardian* (28 October 1958).

Kane, Leslie. *The Language of Silence*. London. Associated Press, 1984.

Kennedy, Andrew. *Six Dramatists in Search of a Language*. Cambridge: Cambridge University Press, 1975.

—. 'Action and Theatricality in *Waiting for Godot'* in Connor. (16-28)

Lacey, Stephen. *British Realist Theatre*. London: Routledge, 1995.

Lecercle, Jean-Jacques. *Deleuze and Language*. Basingstoke: Palgrave Macmillan, 2002.

Morrison, Kristin. *Canters and Chronicles. The Use of Narrative in the Plays of Samuel Beckett and Harold Pinter*. Chicago and London: University of Chicago Press, 1983.

Osborne, John. *The Entertainer*. London: Faber and Faber, 1957.

Pilling, John ed. *Cambridge Companion to Beckett*. Cambridge: Cambridge University Press, 1994.

Pinter, Harold. 'Writing for Theater' in *Plays One*. London: Faber and Faber, 1990.

Rabey, David Ian. *English Drama Since 1940*. London: Longman, 2004.

Rebellato, Dan. *1956 And All That*. London: Routledge, 1999.

Searle, John R. *Speech Acts*. Cambridge: Cambridge University Press, 1969.

Shellard, Dominic. *British Theatre Since the War*. London and New Haven: Yale University Press, 1999.

—, ed. *British Theatre in the 1950s*. Sheffield: Sheffield University Press, 2000.

Simpson, Paul. 'Politeness Phenomena in Ionesco's *The Lesson*' in Ronald Carter and Paul Simpson, ed. *Language, Discourse and Literature: An Introductory Reader in Discourse Stylistics*. London: Routledge, 1989.

Steiner, George. *Language and Silence*. Harmondsworth: Penguin, 1969.

Toolan, Michael. '"What makes you think you exist?" A speech move schematic and its appliance to Pinter's *The Birthday Party*' in *Journal of Pragmatics* 32 (2000): 177-301.

Worton, Michael. '*Waiting for Godot* and *Endgame*: theatre as text' in Pilling. (67-87)

Works Consulted

Brater, Enoch and Ruby Cohn eds. *Around the Absurd*. Ann Arbor: University of Michigan Press, 1990.

Dobrez, L. A. C. *The Existential and its Exits: Literary and Philosophical Perspectives on the work of Beckett, Ionesco, Genet and Pinter*. New York: St Martin's, 1986.

Hale, Jane A. '*Endgame*: How Are Your Eyes?' in Connor. (71-86)

Hinchcliffe, Arnold. *The Absurd*. London: Methuen, 1969.

Innes, Christopher. *Modern British Drama: The Twentieth Century*. Cambridge: Cambridge University Press, 2002.

Petrey, Sandy. *Speech Acts and Literary Theory*. London: Routledge, 1990.

Endgame and Performance

Julie Campbell

Endgame has attracted very diverse responses over the years. My aim is to explore the play in relation to performance, in an attempt to discover why reactions tend to be extreme and so widely varied. Samuel Beckett described it as "the favorite of my plays" (Gontarski xv), or alternatively as "the one I dislike least" (McMillan 163). Hugh Kenner calls it Beckett's "single most remarkable work" (165), while Harold Bloom states that "*Endgame* is Beckett's masterpiece" (8). Katharine Worth recognizes that it "draws out reactions of dislike" (9), and reports one theater critic who describes Katie Mitchell's production as "Chinese water torture" (56).[1] This is a fairly recent response, and it might be useful is to go back to much earlier responses to Beckett's first plays. Harold Hobson and Kenneth Tynan were two British critics who, rather against the tide of contemporary theater critics, reacted favorably to the British premiere of *Waiting for Godot*.[2] That English audiences did not immediately take to *Godot* was for Hobson "hardly surprising," as they "notoriously dislik[e] anything not understandable" (Hobson 1955, 93). *Godot* is now considered a classic. Nowadays many may well be surprised at its early reception, and may even question whether "understanding" Beckett's drama is really the issue.

Tynan begins his review of *Godot* by suggesting that "a special virtue attaches to plays which remind the drama of how much it can do without and still exist" (Tynan 1955, 95). This seems to me remarkably astute. He cares, he tells us, "for the way it pricked and stimulated my own nervous system," and the way "it forced me to re-examine the rules which have hitherto governed the drama; and, having done so, to pronounce that they are not elastic enough" (97). Again, very useful insights are being expressed here: he recognizes the profound effects upon the individual of this innovative drama, and also appreciates the way Beckett has stretched the rules of drama through a process of reduction—a remarkable achievement.

In his review of *Fin de Partie* (the original French version of *Endgame*)[3] Hobson describes it as "magnificent" (Hobson 1957, 164) and contends that the play "has outraged the Philistines, earned the contempt of half-wits and filled those who are capable of telling the difference between theater and a bawdy-house with a profound and somber and paradoxical joy" (161). Tynan is neither a Philistine nor a half-wit, and his review of *Godot* makes this perfectly clear. But for Tynan in *Godot* there was "a human affirmation" that is missing from *Fin de Partie*; in this play Beckett is described as "stamping on the face of mankind" (Tynan 1957, 165). Tynan's response has lost the appreciation of dramatic rule-breaking and is much more involved with the content, even 'the message' as he sees it: "For a short time I am prepared to listen in any theater to any message, however antipathetic. But when it is not only disagreeable but forced down my throat, I demur" (166). What has happened? Can this be the same production that filled Hobson with "a profound and somber and paradoxical joy"? Can this be the same critic who, in response to *Godot*, celebrated the re-examination of dramatic rules and their transgression? There is a movement here—and one that is not acknowledged—from the formal considerations in his response to *Godot* to a far more individual reaction to content, and to an interpretation of what the play 'means.' The idea of Beckett having a 'message' is a telltale signal. Beckett famously stated, in relation to Joyce, that "form is content, content is form" (Beckett 1983, 27).[4] Should his own work be viewed in the same way? Isn't Tynan making the mistake that in his review of *Godot* he so perceptively avoided, which is to judge Beckett's drama by rules that don't apply? Many forms of drama do contain a message, and this is especially true of realism. But Beckett is not a realist. It is a mistake to approach his work as if he is, as the result must be that he will be judged as failing to abide by realist conventions and the expectations they have set up. Tynan has interpreted the play. It speaks to him, and says: "man is a pygmy who connives at his own inevitable degradation" (Tynan 1957, 165). Interpretation when applied to Beckett's work cannot avoid being an individual and personal response, and in my discussion of the play I want to keep as far as possible from an interpretative approach as I can, for reasons that will become clear.

Beckett has described *Endgame* as a "one-set howl" (Knowlson 426), "a gloomy graceless act" (Knowlson 427), and as "rather difficult and elliptic, mostly depending on the power of the text to claw, more inhuman than *Godot*" (Harmon 11) and yet, James Knowlson tells us, "he rated [it] more highly than [...] *Godot*" (435). It *is* a difficult play. Vivian Mercier, a scholar and a well-respected commentator on Beckett's work, describes it as the "grimmest of his plays" (7). He declares: "Personally, I loathe the play and wonder whether the ability to make one's audience suffer is a valid artistic criterion" (174). His reaction is extreme—one of repulsion: "In fact," he tells us, "after seeing the first New York production of *Endgame*, I turned away in disgust from Beckett's work as a whole" (177).[5] Interestingly, Brooks Atkinson found the same production "quite impressive," which he qualifies as: "Impressive in the macabre intensity of mood, that is" (171). Mercier considers that the play has no "philosophical validity" (175), but Atkinson is prepared to consider it in terms of performance and dramatic effect:

> Whether or not [Beckett's] theme is acceptable or rational, his director, Alan Schneider, has had the grace to take him at his own evaluation and stage his play seriously. Although there is not much physical movement in it, it has continuous tension and constant pressure. (172)

He remarks on Beckett's ability to "create a mood by using words as incantations," and decides that the play is "a superb stroke of theater" (172). Again, can this be the same play? The responses seem heartfelt, and Mercier acknowledges the personal nature of his disgust. What interests me are the extremes of the opposing responses, between Hobson and Tynan, and between Mercier and Atkinson. Something is going on here, and something pretty divisive. I want to explore what this could be.

I recently saw Matthew Warchus's production of the play, which was impressive on just about every count.[6] The reviewer in *The Independent* described it as "a stunningly good production [....] that confirmed my growing conviction that Beckett is the greatest dramatist to use the English language since Shakespeare"[7]—high praise indeed. A colleague of mine, after seeing this production, came to my office to discuss it, and decided that the play was a "perfect play—the most perfect play of the twentieth century."[8] This set me to thinking. What is a "perfect play"? Would Beckett, who so valorizes failure, recognize such a term as appropriate? I suppose the term "perfect play" summons up, for me, terms like "well made play," which surely couldn't be applied to *Endgame*.

I want to set aside interpretation, and look at the play initially in terms of structure, whilst at the same time keeping in mind that form cannot necessarily be separated from content. I also want to keep in mind the fact that, with a play like *Endgame*, the interpretation and response to both form and content will differ widely, according to each member of the audience, in relation to the expectations and the life experiences they bring with them, which cannot fail to influence their reception of the play. Worth makes some interesting observations about the way responses to Beckett have changed over the years. She notes that: "[p]eople have got used by now to the idea of Beckett's being funny as well as formidable," and that audiences who are familiar with Beckett and his plays will have a "sense of anticipation as a set piece of drollery approaches" (66). Once familiar with *Endgame* an audience member will know what is going to happen, and will feel less lost: expectations concerning structure now fit the play, and even shape the play in the mind, rather than working against it. The original shock of the new cannot be re-experienced, although newcomers to plays like *Endgame* will often react in similar ways to the early reviewers—with delight or with confusion and bewilderment—and they may reject it and dismiss it out of hand.[9]

We can recall Tynan's words about Beckett's drama reminding him (or reminding "the drama") "how much it can do without and still exist" (Tynan 1955, 95). *Godot*, he tells us, has "no plot, no climax, no *denouement*; no beginning, no middle, no end" (95). I wonder if spectators still see it that way. Many spectators have become familiar with the play. I expect today that it is recognized as not exactly true to say that either *Godot* or *Endgame* lack such dramatic elements, although Beckett's drama certainly moves away from the expectations concerning what a dramatic plot 'should' be—expectations that have been produced by many kinds of traditional drama, especially realist drama. It is not surprising that his plays do not conform to realist conventions, as Beckett is not a realist. Beckett often plays with traditional dramatic elements: there is parody and there are shocks and surprises. Tynan recognizes that Beckett, with *Godot*, has gone beyond the traditional conventions, and succeeded. Why does he feel that he has not succeeded with the play that followed?

Perhaps many theater-goers and critics in the fifties had their dramatic expectations too directly formed by the drama of the time. *Godot* and *Endgame* shared the British stage in this period with plays by John Osborne, Arnold Wesker and Shelagh Delaney: playwrights who were changing the expectations of drama but in terms of content rather than form. The new content focused upon working-class characters and situations, but the form was not new, and maintained the stable beginning, middle and end audiences had come to consider were essential elements of drama, and of course their plays conveyed a message. In 1961 Beckett spoke to Tom Driver of a new form, not a renunciation of form, but a "form [that] will be of such a type that it admits the chaos [....] a form that accommodates the mess" (219). If we think of the structure of *Endgame* as a movement towards a form of art that "admits the chaos" and "raises questions that it does not attempt to answer" (220), we can begin to place clear water between what *Endgame* is doing and what many other kinds of drama are doing, especially the British realist drama of the fifties.

Perhaps in order to create something new, going backwards is the first step—back before the later nineteenth century and the kind of realist theater introduced by Ibsen, which has had such a strong influence on writers and directors in the theater, on film and on television. Beckett can also be seen to be stepping outside the domains of "legitimate" or "serious" drama, into popular forms such as the music hall and pantomime: forms that celebrate and feature theatricality in a way that realist drama will not, by definition. In relation to structure, critics have often gone back to earlier, traditional forms in discussions of *Endgame*. Mercier suggests that this play has an affiliation with tragedy (14), while Andrew Kennedy suggests that the "one-act structure [...] gradually closes in like the final scene of a traditional tragedy" (47). Theodor Adorno also cites tragedy in his discussion of *Endgame*, seeing it as a form of drama that has been "renounced [...] because its stylization and resulting pretentiousness seemed alien to secular society" (26). Such stylization has been renounced by realist drama, as a matter of course, in its aim to create an illusion of life as it seems to be, rather than as a poetic expression abstracted from "reality." For Adorno, in *Endgame*, "dramatic components reappear after their demise. Exposition, complication, plot, peripeteia, and catastrophe return as decomposed elements" (26). And intriguingly Kennedy suggests a traditional structure underlying the play. For him it not only resembles the fifth act of a tragedy, but, following Adorno, he considers that there is a condensation: a kind of distillation of the whole tragic process. Kennedy discusses the sixteen scenes Beckett formulated for the Berlin production of the play, which he directed, in 1967.[10]

> The opening and closing tableaux (scenes 1 and 16 [...]) constitute a kind of prologue and epilogue [....] Scenes 2-10 [...] form the first major movement of the play, reaching a climax in the lines borrowed from the *Tempest*: 'Our revels now are ended!' [...] The remaining scenes are dominated by the end. (64)

It is a fascinating idea: a Chinese box structure which has affinities with the closing act of a tragedy while also containing further levels that echo traditional dramatic structure the deeper we delve. We can discern the traditional pyramid structure in Kennedy's analysis: exposition, rising action, climax, falling action and *denouement*, but it is a structure that is well hidden beneath the oddness of the surface, and it is not surprising that it can go unnoticed on the conscious level. But it is no doubt attended to on a more subliminal level and could be one of the reasons for the sense of satisfaction that many spectators feel after watching the play.

When Beckett directed *Endgame* he placed great emphasis on formal elements: "There are no accidents in *Endgame*. It is all built on analogies and repetitions" (qtd in Gontarski xiii). He also stressed simplicity: "it's got to become simple, just a few small, precise motions" (xvi), and in his direction he worked "to clarify and develop the lines of conflict and sharpen the play's ambiguities" (xix). "'The play is full of echoes,' he told his German cast. 'They all answer each other'" (xxi). S. E. Gontarski summarizes the importance of repetition and balance in Beckett's approach to the play:

> Pattern is as crucial to Beckett's eye as to his ear, and that patterning dominates his theatrical notes: motion is repeated to echo other motion, posture to echo other posture, gestures to echo other gestures, sounds to echo other sounds. The principle of analogy is fundamental. (xx)

The final tableau should echo the opening one (Gontarski 48): "the much rehearsed and serene ending echoes the beginning—a deliberately theatrical tableau" (Kennedy 50), and the importance of this final stasis for Beckett, and the way he wished it to linger in the memory of the audience, is clear when he tells his actors that a curtain call is "repugnant" to him, as "it would have hurt me to break up the picture at the end" (qtd in Gontarski 71). Beckett told Jonathan Kalb "that it was essential 'to visualize a play on your own mental stage while you're writing,' and went on to explain that the reason he preferred *Endgame* to *Godot* was that it was better visualized in that way and is thus 'a more complete and coherent movement'" (72). Knowlson considers that, when Beckett directed *Endgame*, "What [he] did was to see the work in terms of clear visual patterns with movements so carefully charted that the word 'choreography' can quite properly be applied to a meticulously planned direction" (qtd in Gontarski, Introduction).

Pattern is present in what Kalb has called the "perfectly balanced ambiguities" (82) of the play. Paul Lawley considers that "few texts can be more explicitly structured upon binary oppositions than *Endgame*," and cites the "onstage/offstage, inside/outside opposition" alongside "past/present, land/sea. nature/non-nature, light/darkness" (1992, 124). Pierre Chabert speaks of polarities in terms of the dramatic tension they produce:

> Just as there is an intrinsic tension between silence and words, so there is an intrinsic tension between immobility and movement. Words emanate from silence and return to it, movement emanates from immobility and returns to it. (qtd in Kalb 39)

Drama is conflict, and there is a strong conflict in the play. Beckett stressed this when he decided that "there must be maximum aggression between [Hamm and Clov] from the first exchange of words onward. Their war is the nucleus of the play" (qtd in Gontarski 50). He also described the basic conflict: "Clov has only one wish, to get back into his kitchen—that must always be evident, just like Hamm's constant effort to stop him. This tension is an essential motif of the play" (48). This central tension was picked up by Hobson in his early review (162), but Tynan seems to have missed the kind of tensions the play is built upon, and writes of his sense of "little variation, either of pace or emphasis" in his response to the same production (166). Yet, surely, "the fluctuation of tension" in the play, which Kennedy notes as "a device that fills the stage with the illusion of dramatic action" (57), is an essential element of the play and is foregrounded throughout.

A significant reason for my own estimation of the play as dramatically effective concerns the very variety that Tynan considers to be lacking in the play. There is variety of pace, including consistent alternations between movement and stasis, speech and silence. There is a wide variety of tone: directions on speech shift continuously. Instructions as various as "tonelessly," "proudly," "gloomily" (12), "irritably," "gloomily" (13), "shocked," "relieved," "coldly," "louder," "violently" (14) are present within the first four pages of the text. The mood is not one of unrelieved gloom: there are many comic moments and styles of performance that recall music hall double acts, Laurel and Hardy, or Marx Brothers films, while the introductory mime sequence and other comic business bring to mind the silent comedy of Buster Keaton. The range is extensive: comic, tragic, bombastic, maudlin, elegiac, poetic, sad, ludicrous, desperate, stoic, exasperated. It is never monotone; it never stays still; it is always moving.

Kennedy points out the way "the whole play is conceived in thoroughly theatrical terms" and speaks of the "highly play-conscious nature of Beckett's art" (61). This area seems to be an essential one to explore when considering the play's success as a theatrical event. Beckett has said: "It is a playful piece" (qtd in McMillan 218). There is a very strong sense, right from the beginning of the play, of actors who are conscious of their roles as actors (as of course all actors really are). Beckett spoke of the play as being "full of echoes" (qtd in Gontarski xxi): the metatheatrical elements produce a play full of mirrors, as the self-reflexive play concerns drama mirroring drama, actors self-consciously acting, and the audience members made aware of their own roles as spectators. Kenner suggests that Hamm's name points to his status as "the generic Actor" (160). He is centre stage, always in need of an audience, and always tending to overact his part. His first words—"Me [...] to play"—are redolent of his consciousness of role-playing: "Can there be misery [he intones] loftier than mine?" (12) It is histrionic but robbed of any sense of authenticity by the way he repeatedly undercuts his lofty rhetoric, punctuating it with his own spoken doubts as well as with the repeated yawns that signify an actor who isn't entirely "in part" as yet. Clov's first words—"Finished, it's finished, nearly finished, it must be nearly finished" (12)—denote not only a surprising way to begin a play, and a kind of pocket-sized exposition of the "endgame" to follow, but can also be seen to signify an actor at the beginning of a play who wishes that it was already over. This metatheatrical device recurs throughout. *Endgame* is not like a realist play, where the actors are careful not to shatter the illusion that what the audience sees is "really" happening. There are explicit references to acting and the theatrical situation: Antony Easthope has listed "'farce,' 'audition,' 'aside,' 'soliloquy,' 'dialogue,' 'underplot,' 'exit'" (54). Such signals are clearly alerting the spectator to the fact that this is theater—it is *not* real. But of course there is a double play: it is really happening. It is a play, acted in front of the audience, on the stage. The play refers to itself rather than to an illusory situation beyond, unlike realist drama. Richard Gilman recalls Kenner's influential discussion of the play when he suggests that *Endgame* can be viewed as "a play about playing, a performance 'about' performance" (84).

Rather than considering this self-reflexive play in relation to Brecht—who was certainly encouraging the spectators to remember that they are watching a play and not slipping passively into the illusion that what is happening is "real"—it seems essential to recognize that Beckett is attempting something quite different from Brecht.[11] Ruby Cohn refers instead to Pirandello, who clearly has much stronger affinities with Beckett than Brecht has. But Cohn is able to bring in a subtle and telling difference between the playwrights' use of self-reflexivity when she speaks of how Pirandello was "distinguishing between art and life, between fictional characters and actual people" (76), whereas Beckett, she argues, "dramatizes authors." Hamm, "the first of this lineage," is an author within the play, the "play author" who mirrors his own creator by telling stories and ensuring a "stage audience" with the bribe of a sugar plum (77). Thus not only is the playwright-as-storyteller mirrored within the play through Hamm, so is the audience through Nagg. There are other kinds of self-reflexivity in quite other kinds of theater, of course, which help to highlight its pervasiveness. Clowns, pantomime dames and villains, and comedians generally will appeal to their audiences directly, breaking through the fourth wall and laying bare the performance as performance. Soliloquies are another form of theatrical device which break the illusion of the stage world as separate and "real," and they constitute an important feature in

Endgame.[12] They of course have a strong presence in pre-realist drama, both tragedy and comedy, and Hamm alludes specifically to Shakespearian soliloquies when he echoes Richard III and Prospero. Metatheatricality is present in Classical drama, in Medieval drama, in Early Modern drama, and is able to produce an intriguing double effect—a jolt—a reminder of the playwright's role as fictionalizer, the actor's role as actor, the spectator's role as spectator. It often involves a comic quality in that this device is simultaneously recognizing, and jolting the audience into recognizing, that this is a performance—it isn't real, and yet it is—a real performance, happening in front of our eyes. It is telling the truth, but a truth that realist drama is consistently concerned with not acknowledging in favor of creating an illusion of truth in terms of the content. For realism, the form needs to be as transparent as possible so that the illusion of the "real" (in terms of characters and events, etc.) is upheld.

Lawley comments on the "uncompromising stylization which is a characteristic of the play's every facet" (1988, 87). The stylization of the play is striking evidence of its theatricality and is an important feature that critics have returned to again and again. Gabriele Schwab, for instance, speaks of Hamm and Clov as "highly stylized" characters who are both "condensed and overdetermined" (93). Kennedy sees all "the four characters of *Endgame* [as] even more stylized—in terms of role, speech, physical appearance and movement—than are the characters of *Waiting for Godot*" (53), and there is certainly a strong move in *Endgame* towards a greater theatricality and abstraction than is discernable in *Godot*. Emmanuel Jacquart considers that, unlike a realist dramatist, "the author is not looking for a literal representation [...] but for a highly stylized *equivalent*" (79). Schwab's point that the characters are "not only acting but also playing with these roles" (89) is of interest here, and relates to the discussion above concerning the self-consciousness that pervades the play. For spectators unfamiliar with poetic drama the abstract, stylized quality of the characterization and acting must create certain problems and a feeling of alienation.

Tynan's fierce response to the production he reviewed seems to stem from a discomfort with the distancing effect: it was "portentously stylized" with the result that it "piled on the agony until I thought my skull would split" (166). Kenner's discussion of the characters as like chess pieces (156-60) is useful, as it helps to make the stylization very clear, along with the difficulty an audience will have if they try to get involved in the way they are encouraged to do with more psychologically rounded characters. This relates to the more "literal representation" of realist drama that Jacquart suggests the play is *not* attempting to provide, but also to those impressive and moving, yet far more poetic representations of humanity we meet with in Greek and Early Modern tragedy. Mercier pinpoints the abstraction of the characters in *Endgame* acutely when he suggests that with Hamm and Clov "we can laugh at them [...] we can fear them, but we cannot pity them nor identify with them" (14). "We can laugh at them," just as we can laugh at circus clowns, where the characterization deals with physical absurdity and discourages both identification and sympathy; "we can fear them," just as we can fear melodramatic or Gothic villains who are again one-dimensional, and who work against psychological wholeness and the shades of gray we recognize in dramatic characters drawn to appear as lifelike and credible representations of humanity. Kenner recognizes that Hamm has many of the properties of a "ludicrous stage villain" (164). Straightforward pity is not encouraged; we are distanced to an unusual degree, except in more popular forms of theater, not so concerned with portraying subtle levels of human complexity but rather with the black and white abstractions of clown or villain. This leads us back to the chess game and the black and white of the opposing pieces on the board. Beckett has spoken about *Endgame* as "pure play" (qtd in McMillan 14), and has commented on the chess analogy:

> One must make a world of one's own in order to satisfy one's need to know, to understand, one's need for order [....] There for me, lies the value of the theater. One turns out a small world with its own laws, conducts the action as if upon a chess board [...] even the game of chess is still too complex. (15)

Beckett is aiming for "the extreme simplicity of the dramatic situation and issue" (Harmon 24), and it is illuminating just how often phrases like "Keep it simple, everything simple" (qtd in McMillan 204) and other admonitions for simplicity recur in Beckett's direction.

There is a key and central issue here, and one that goes some way towards explaining the antipathy of critics such as Tynan and Mercier. Beckett described the play as "more inhuman than *Godot*" (Harmon 11), and this certainly is true. It is also—and this is allied with its "inhuman" quality—more abstract and more theatrical. If we think of it as "pure play"—like a chess game, but even simpler—we are approaching a source of its theatrical power. Tynan missed the "human affirmation" that he had gleaned from *Godot* (1957, 165). He was, I suggest, reading the play as a "literal representation" rather than as "pure play." *Endgame* is "a small world with its own laws," not what Tynan is reacting to, which is quite another kind play. Tynan is responding to something that isn't *Endgame*—he criticizes it for not being the kind of play that encourages us to respond to it as an apparently direct, realist representation of the world beyond the stage. Mercier, too, with his description of the characters as "grotesque[s]" and "monsters rather than men" (14) also judges the play according to dramatic conventions to which it, intentionally, does *not* adhere. The characters are not designed to be pitied or identified with in any straightforward or traditional way. Something else is happening: "something is taking its course" (*Endgame* 17).

Endgame* is poetic drama. It convinces me that the "rules that have hitherto governed drama," and especially realist drama, are "not elastic enough," as Tynan suggested in relation to *Godot*. Beckett has created "a small world with its own laws." I have so far kept away from interpretation, dwelling instead on formal and theatrical aspects of the play, such as dramatic structure, self-reflexive play and abstract characterization. I now want to clarify just how important avoiding interpretation can be, in order to get a genuine sense of why this play works, and also to suggest further reasons why it doesn't work for others. Beckett was very wary of providing interpretations, and this becomes more and more noticeable when reading the descriptions of his own direction of the play.[13] He has famously told Alan Schneider that when "it comes to these bastards of journalists I feel that the only line is to refuse to be involved in exegesis of any kind. That's for those bastards of critics" (qtd in Harmon 24). He also cautioned Schneider not to "seek deep motivation everywhere" (29). To actors he has given such enigmatic responses as: "I only know what's on the page [....] Do it your way" (qtd in McMillan 179); "Don't look for symbols in my plays" (181); and "I don't know what's in Hamm's head" (182). This might seem unhelpful, yet for me it seems essential. He retreats from exegesis—"I'd rather not talk about it" (230)—as talking about the play, apart from in theatrical and formal terms, would produce the kind of closure that the play itself is resisting in just about every way. It is an endgame, but without a traditional ending, without closure, in both dramatic and interpretative terms. The play needs to remain open.

Kenner has stated, with genuine insight, that "the play contains whatever ideas we discern inside it; no idea contains the play" (164). This openness to individual interpretation is necessary, as this is where a great deal of the play's effectiveness comes from. Hobson's review of *Fin de Partie* shows genuine insight. What is admirable is the way he has, even with such small acquaintance with the play, managed to state something which holds just as true today, after many years have passed and many productions have taken place, and something that certain directors surely should have taken more notice of: "Beckett is a poet; and the business of a poet is not to clarify, but to suggest, to imply, to employ words with auras of association, with a reaching out towards a vision, a probing down into an emotion, beyond the compass of explicit definition" (Hobson 1957, 162). His words are a useful way into the thorny debate concerning directorial interpretation. Although Beckett has directed the play on more than one occasion, he is insistent that his is not the definitive version: "I don't claim my interpretation is the only correct one. It's possible to do the play quite differently, different music, movements, different rhythm [...]" (qtd in Gontarski xviii). Kalb presents a very useful summary of the kind of "explicit definitions" directors have imposed upon the play (77-87). He analyzes this propensity by suggesting that "even theater practitioners who consider themselves open-minded enough to accept frameworks of indecision sometimes end up pinning them down to particular meanings out of fear that audiences will not understand" (77). But "understanding" isn't the point here. Even with the best intentions:

> [d]irectors frequently express their love of and respect for Beckett's work by overlaying their ingenious illustrative ideas on it. What begins as an attempt at creative collaboration ends up as a private explanation of what was originally created to resist explanation. (77)

Easthope returns to Hobson's idea of Beckett as a poet: "Beckett's work is 'poetic.' What the adjective really points to in Beckett's plays [...] is the extraordinary ability of the language and the stagecraft to imply, suggest, connote, evoke, and set off expressive nuances" (57). "Clever" conceptual direction closes down the ability for this poetic indeterminacy to work. Hobson describes Beckett's drama as "beyond the compass of explicit definition" (1957, 162), and yet, as Kalb points out, many directors lack the courage to trust Beckett, and end up "filling in the 'missing' specifics in an effort to explain the unexplainable" (94).

The debate about directorial freedom has been an ongoing one in Beckett circles. It has surfaced again and again at the Beckett seminars held at Reading University[14] and keeps recurring in the discussions of the Samuel Beckett Working Group.[15] Angela Moorjani made a very persuasive case against the heavy-handed impositions of certain directors in her paper for the Working Group in 2004, suggesting that directors should do "less, rather than more, in bringing the unspoken light to the audiences, leaving them [...] to grapple with glimmerings in the dark" (13). She argues in favor of the spectator and against "directorial closure" (14), which may mask Beckett's poetry. Beckett's drama is able "to imply, suggest, connote, evoke, and set off expressive nuances" (Easthope 57). Directors need to take care not to get in the way of all of this, because this is where the crucial drama happens: in the spectator's response to the poetry of the play. The reason, for me, that *Endgame* works as performance is *because* it is "beyond the compass of explicit definition" (Hobson 1957, 162). This has to do with its carefully balanced structure, its self-reflexive play with dramatic elements, as well as the way in which the characters themselves are theatrical components (rather than simply representations of "real" people). For me this is poetry—dramatic poetry—the poetry of light and shade, movement and stasis, sound and silence, comedy and pathos. This is what we start from; interpretation follows, but on the terms Kenner has stated: "the play contains whatever ideas we discern inside it" (164). Like Moorjani, I want to place the spectator in the foreground when it comes to interpretation.

Kennedy suggests that, despite all critical efforts, the play "cannot be interpreted [...] definitively"; rather interpretation is an "endless process" (48). Such an idea will evoke a genuine feeling of pleasure (in me) or perhaps quite other feelings, such as exasperation, irritation, frustration (in others). Schwab discusses how the play "has occasioned numerous speculative interpretations" (93). She summarizes some of these and then makes a crucial point: that interpretations will tend towards reduction and closure, whereas the play itself resists both. Directorial decisions based on interpretations can close down the play at the site of the performance. Critical interpretations may not have a definitive influence over spectators, but the movement is again towards an imposition of meaning that the play itself resists and challenges. The play encourages the audience to feel "drawn into the game" of trying to make sense of it, but Schwab contends that the play also encourages us to begin to reflect upon our "own interpretative acts" (95). It is a fascinating discussion, and a convincing one. Schwab considers that

> [t]he effect is to make the audience conscious of how it projects meaning. This allows it to experience its projections as an attempt to close and center something inherently open and decentered. We might also call this effort a defense against the experience of otherness. At the same time the dis-illusioning strategies aim at altering our need for centering and closing open structures. (96)

This is thought-provoking and surely explains something important about this play, and what is happening in the minds of the spectators. According to this line of thought a great deal of the drama is prompted by what is happening on stage, and yet is located in the spectator's attempts at interpretation, and the "projection and closure" (95) this involves: the attempt and its frustration. This process is dramatic, and will for some (for me) provoke pleasure and exhilaration, and for others provoke "extremely defensive responses" (97).[16]

Wolfgang Iser follows Schwab in focusing on the "spectator's interpretative faculties" and how they are brought into play (168). He writes of the way in which there is a constant movement involved: an "alternation of building and dismantling" (168) in a spectator's response to Beckett's drama. Like Schwab, he recognizes the way in which we are encouraged into an awareness of our own interpretative acts, but we are also made aware of way that our projections are being challenged. We are "continually building and dismantling concepts, and ultimately—through this very same inescapable process—we are forced to realize (in both senses of the word) the deficiencies of our interpretations" (170). Iser recognizes that "[t]his experience is conditioned by various factors connected with our own disposition and, above all, with the expectations that we bring to art and that are deliberately exploited by Beckett's plays" (170). This is useful in my attempt to discover why *Endgame* works for some and not for others. Iser suggests that Beckett's plays can fail to satisfy "because they make us block our own paths to possible solutions" (175). He also contends, following Schwab, that the strategy of *Endgame* is "to bring the spectator into play" (178):

> Through this process, the dramatic focus of the play is shifted away from the plot [...] and onto the spectator [...]. The dramatic action, therefore, comes about through the projections of the spectator and occurs in the mind of the spectator, thus setting off a response pattern in which the spectator's projections are cast as an integral part of the dramatic performance. (187)

Spectators who are new to this kind of drama will experience many more problems in relating to the play than those with some experience of experimental drama, whether as audience members or practitioners.[17] People who are accustomed to the kind of clarity realist drama provides are almost certain to feel confusion. They have become habituated into looking for the kind of "literal representation" Jacquart refers to, and as a result there is an almost impenetrable barrier between them and the play. Realist drama encourages passivity in the spectator, with the dramatic elements clarifying and encouraging a large degree of consensus as to what is being portrayed and how it should be interpreted. Without this clarity many spectators feel lost and frustrated, and those new to Beckett's play may find it depressing. The characters are of the kind generally ignored by mainstream drama, which rarely deals with aging and disability. Interestingly, those who have experience of working with the physically impaired, such as care givers, hospital workers or health visitors, or who have relations or friends who are disabled, often find a way into the play through the knowledge they bring with them. The tendency is generally to make sense of the play by interpreting it as representational. This cannot distort it into realist drama, but the familiarity of responding to realism, which resembles the way we respond to the world, is hard to relinquish. It is familiar, it feels safer. This of course is where the ideas of Schwab and Iser come into play: their discussions of how familiar forms of sense-making are thwarted and resisted, and thus challenged. *Endgame* encourages the spectator to make sense of what is happening on stage, but then challenges this very procedure. I find that this play tends to be more revealing about the spectator than it could ever be said to be about itself. We are forced to bring more of ourselves into play than ever can be the case with realist drama, where so much of the explication is clear and unfolds before our eyes. It is also essential to note that not all theater-goers will have the kind of analytical skills that Schwab and Iser presuppose. Without such sophistication, the challenging nature of the play can fall flat and seem ineffective and pointless, and for some the response is one of boredom.

I have discovered that Beckett is not for everyone. This may seem obvious, but it is illuminating, and helps me tone down my proselytizing tendencies when teaching the play. Some will be intrigued from the first and welcome the challenge that the work poses; others will be dismissive, even repelled. I think that this is because his drama aims at far more hidden, unconscious levels of the self than other kinds of drama, which deal much more overtly with the surface, the seeable, the sayable, and, of course, the understandable. I also think that it is difficult for audience members who do not have a practical and/or academic experience of theater to appreciate just what is being done. There is a spell-binding quality in the way in which this play creates what for me is a thrilling theatrical experience out of what seems so little. It is simple, pared down to the bones, but manages to suggest so much: in dramatic terms as well as in relation to interpretation, it seems that, for some of us, the less we are given the more we make of it.

Mercier suggests that interpretations of Beckett's work "reveal more about the psyches of the people who offer them than about the work itself or the psyche of the author," and sees himself as no exception (vii). I agree, and this is one of the reasons that Beckett's work continues to fascinate me. But this can backfire. As quoted above, Mercier stated that "after seeing the first New York production of *Endgame*, I turned away in disgust from Beckett's work as a whole" (177). In his Prologue to *Beckett/Beckett*, however, Mercier qualifies this: "it was events in my personal life rather than any distaste for a particular work of his that impelled me to shun Beckett" (xiii). His wife became ill, and was diagnosed with multiple sclerosis. "It may seem paradoxical [Mercier writes] that this confirmation of Beckett's gloomy estimate of the human condition should have turned me against his work, but I wrote virtually nothing more on him until after [my wife's] death" (xiii). This decision doesn't seem paradoxical, but perfectly understandable. The paralysis and blindness his wife suffered would have seemed to be mirrored in *Endgame*, and of far too personal a nature not to have provoked a strong reaction.

Mercier's reference to the Rorschach test in relation to Beckett's plays is important (vii): it does have a greater ability to reach areas of the individual psyche than most forms of drama, and this can be a harrowing experience. We bring ourselves to the play. To a great extent we create it, and certainly we create what it means to us: this is one of the great strengths of the play. Beckett is not writing realist drama, but spectators can hardly fail to make connections with their own philosophical views, their own personal lives, and all this entails. Much as I will continue to contend that the play is doing more than giving us a "gloomy estimate of the human condition," I do recognize and respect Mercier's position, along with the numerous responses this play has encouraged—and will continue to encourage.

There is much I have not said about performance, in part because so much has been said elsewhere,[18] but also because the idea of total comprehensiveness was not my aim—I would also question its possibility in relation to this particular play. My aim is to show that the play is dramatic, although it may *seem* essentially undramatic. The structure that underlies it is simple, abstract and, for me, theatrically effective. Part of its power is its simplicity. The complexity is found in what the audience chooses to bring to it. It is poetry—poetic drama—and as such is not dealing in direct representation or the illusion of the real. Directors need to allow this poetry to happen; the play should never be closed down; the questions never answered; interpretation should be the province of the audience, and needs to echo the endlessness of the dramatic situation. It is a bleak play. It can be seen to be challenging the very processes we use to make sense of the world, and ultimately finding such processes lacking. Some will resist this and seek instead some safer ground where things are shown to make sense, and choose to see the kind of plays that end when they end, rather than continue to grow and question and disturb. There is no message in *Endgame*, there is no consoling panacea, but there is something indefinable and also magical going on. What *Endgame* does offer is, in Hobson's words, "a magnificent theatrical experience" (1957, 164), impossible to pin down, but endlessly fascinating, which fills me, as it did Hobson, "with a profound and somber and paradoxical joy" (161).

Julie Campbell, University of Southampton

Notes

[1] "The relentless drip, drip, drip of misery is like Chinese water torture" (*The Times*, 19 April 1996), on *Endgame*, dir. Katie Mitchell, first performed at the Donmar Warehouse, London, 11 April 1996 (quoted in Worth 56).

[2] London premiere of *Waiting for Godot*, dir. Peter Hall, first performed at the Arts Theater Club, London, 3 August 1955.

[3] Premiere of *Fin de partie*, dir. Roger Blin, first performed at the Royal Court Theater, London, 3 April 1957.

[4] Samuel Beckett, 'Dante...Bruno.Vico..Joyce' in Beckett 1983.

[5] American premiere of *Endgame*, dir. Alan Schneider, first performed at the Cherry Lane Theater, New York, 28 January 1958.

[6] *Endgame*, dir. Michael Warchus, first performed at the Albery Theater, London, 10 March 2004.

[7] Review of *Endgame* in *The Independent*, 11 March 2004.

[8] My colleague, Chris Slater, who has many years of experience teaching both drama and film at Southampton University.

[9] I have been teaching *Endgame* to first-year students at Southampton University for many years, and their initial responses to the play tend to be very varied, and also enlightening, and my references to first time spectators are largely in relation to their observations and comments.

[10] 'Beckett's instructions for the Berlin production of *Endgame* in 1967, identifying sixteen scenes as the units of the play's structure (cited in Kennedy 64-65):
1. Clov's mime and first monologue.
2. Hamm's awakening and his first monologue, and the first dialogue.
3. Nagg and Nell's dialogue.
4. Hamm-Cov dialogue, with Hamm's first turn around the room.
5. Clov's comic business with the ladder and the telescope.
6. Hamm's questioning of Clov with the burlesque flea scene.
7. Hamm-Clov dialogue with the toy dog scene.
8. Clov's rebellion, Hamm's story of the madman, and the alarm-clock scene.
9. Hamm's story.
10. The prayer ending with Nagg's curse.
11. Hamm's story continued.
12. Hamm's second turn around the room.
13. Hamm-Clov dialogue (farewell).
14. Hamm's role.
15. Clov's closing monologue and exit.
16. Hamm's final monologue.

[11] See Kalb for some useful discussions relating to the distance between Brecht's theater and Beckett's (44-7, 73-4, 146-7, 215-16, 218-19).

[12] See Chapter 4, 'All Mankind Is Us: Soliloquizers,' Cohn 1980, 58-75, for an illuminating discussion of soliloquies in *Endgame* and other plays.

[13] See Gontaski and Dougald McMillan, passim.

[14] The Beckett Seminars take place annually at Reading University, organized by the Beckett International Foundation and convened by Julian A. Garforth and Mark Nixon.

[15] The Samuel Beckett Working Group meets every two years at the International Federation for Theater Research Annual Conference and is convened by Linda Ben Zvi.

[16] This relates to the kind of defensive responses I often encounter in first-year students.

[17] I will be referring to some of the responses of my first-year students in the following section.

[18] See Cohn 1980, Gontarski, Kalb, Kennedy and McMillan, to name just a few.

Bibliography

Adorno, Theodor. 'Trying to Understand *Endgame*' in Harold Bloom, ed. *Samuel Beckett's Endgame*. New York: Chelsea House Publishers, 1988. (9-40)

Atkinson, Brooks. Review of *Endgame* in *The New York Times* (29 January 1958): 32. Reprinted in Raymond Federman and Lawrence Graver eds. *Samuel Beckett: The Critical Heritage*. London: Routledge & Kegan Paul, 1979. (171-172)

Beckett, Samuel. *Disjecta: Miscellaneous Writings and a Dramatic Fragment* ed. Ruby Cohn. London: John Calder, 1983.

—. *Endgame*. London: Faber and Faber, 1985.

Bloom, Harold ed. *Samuel Beckett's* Endgame. New York: Chelsea Publishers, 1988.

—. 'Introduction' in Bloom (1988): 1-8.

Cohn, Ruby. *Just Play: Beckett's Theater*. New Jersey: Princeton University Press, 1980.

Connor, Steven ed. Waiting for Godot *and* Endgame*: New Casebooks.* Basingstoke: Macmillan, 1992.

Driver, Tom. 'Beckett by the Madeleine' in Federman and Graver (1979): 112-113.

Easthope, Antony. 'Hamm, Clov, and Dramatic Method in *Endgame*' in Bloom (1988): 49-58.

Federman, Raymond, and Lawrence Graver eds. *Samuel Beckett: The Critical Heritage*. London: Routledge & Kegan Paul, 1979.

Gilman, Richard. 'Beckett' in Bloom (1988): 79-86.

Gontarski, S. E. ed. *The Theater Notebooks of Samuel Beckett: Endgame*. London: Faber and Faber, 1992.

Harmon, Maurice ed. *No Author Better Served: The Correspondence of Samuel Beckett and Alan Schneider*. London: Harvard University Press, 1998.

Hobson, Harold. Review of *Waiting for Godot* in *The Sunday Times* (7 August 1955): 11. Reprinted in Federman and Graver (1979): 93-95.

—. Review of *Fin de Partie* in *The Sunday Times* (7 April. 1957): 15. Reprinted in Federman and Graver (1979): 161-164.

Iser, Wolfgang. 'The Art of Failure: The Stifled Laugh in Beckett's Theater' in Wolfgang Iser, *Prospecting: From Reader Response to Literary Anthropology*. Baltimore: The Johns Hopkins University Press, 1993.

Jacquart, Emmanuel. "*Endgame*, Master Game" in *Journal of Beckett Studies* 4.1 (1994): 77-92.

Kalb, Jonathan. *Beckett in Performance*. Cambridge: Cambridge University Press, 1991.

Kennedy, Andrew. *Samuel Beckett*. Cambridge: Cambridge University Press, 1991.

Kenner, Hugh. *Samuel Beckett*. London: John Calder, 1961.

Knowlson, James. *Damned to Fame: The Life of Samuel Beckett*. London: Bloomsbury, 1996.

Lawley, Paul. 'Adoption in *Endgame*' in Connor (1992): 119-127.

—. 'Symbolic Structure and Creative Obligation in *Endgame*' in Bloom (1988): 87-110.

McMillan, Dougald and Martha Fehsenfeld. *Beckett in the Theater: The Author as Practical Playwright and Director*, Vol. 1. London: John Calder, 1988.

Mercier, Vivian. *Beckett/Beckett*. London: Souvenir Press, 1990.

Moorjani, Angela. 'Directing or In-directing Beckett: In Search of a Pragmatics of Indirection.' Paper presented to the Samuel Beckett Working Group at *The Director in the Theater World, International Federation of Theater Research* (St. Petersburg, 23-27 May, 2004).

Schwab, Gabrielle. 'On the Dialectic of Opening and Closing in *Endgame*' in Connor (1992): 87-89.

Tynan, Kenneth. Review of *Waiting for Godot* in *The Observer* (7 August 1955): 11. Reprinted in Federman and Graver (1979): 95-97.

—. Review of *Fin de partie* in *The Observer* (7 April 1957): 15. Reprinted in Federman and Graver (1979): 164-166.

Worth, Katharine. *Samuel Beckett's Theater: Life Journeys*. Oxford: Oxford University Press, 1999.

Essay Abstracts

Natka Bianchini, "Bare interiors, chicken wire cages and subway stations—re-thinking Beckett's response to the ART *Endgame* in light of earlier productions"

In December 1984, Beckett sought, through legal injunction, to halt performances of the American Repertory Theater's (Cambridge, MA) production of *Endgame* directed by JoAnne Akalaits, which had made changes to the text and setting. Although the dispute was ultimately settled out of court and the performances permitted, shortly afterward Beckett amended the contract that licenses his plays in production to prohibit any changes to the text, setting or stage direction. For twenty years, the public perception of Beckett as a rigid and recalcitrant playwright has persisted, formed largely on the basis on this sole event. This paper seeks to reexamine the controversy surrounding Beckett's response to the 1984 production in light of new evidence and interviews, and in light of Beckett's response to two earlier productions of *Endgame* in the United States: Andre Gregory's 1973 Manhattan Project *Endgame*, and Alan Schneider's 1958 American première. By examining Beckett's reaction to Gregory's production, which also radically deviated from his text, but drew a surprisingly different response from Beckett, and by understanding his relationship with his American director Alan Schneider, one will see clearly that Beckett was often flexible and permissive in regards to his work in performance, and that it was only later in his life, after mounting distress in response to several years of directorial meddling, that Beckett became more inflexible.

Julie Campbell, "*Endgame* and Performance"

Endgame has attracted very diverse responses over the years. Kenneth Tynan's review of Roger Blin's production of *Fin de Partie* expresses his distaste for the play, whereas Harold Hobson considers it "magnificent." Alan Schnieder's production of *Endgame* (1958) also drew quite different reponses from Brooks Atkinson and Vivian Mercier. The extremity of the responses, for and against the play, are fascinating, and I discuss some of the possible reasons that lie behind them. In place of considering interpretations of the play, I focus on the dramatic structure and effects, and responses from critics and reviewers, alongside reactions from less experienced spectators.

I consider the structure of the play, and the views of critics such as Mercier, Andrew Kennedy, and Theodor Adorno, who contend that there are elements of tragic form underlying the play. Jonathan Kalb, Paul Lawley and Pierre Chabert refer to the polarities and tensions in the play, which create dramatic rhythm and pattern. Hugh Kenner, Antony Easthope and Ruby Cohn are brought into the discussion, as they have many useful ideas concerning metatheatricality. Gabrielle Schwab and Wolfgang Iser both make a convincing and interesting case concerning how the play encourages the spectator's consciousness of how they project meaning.

Many will continue to be discomforted by a play that refuses to provide answers, and turn away from a play that seems to them bleak and alienating, whilst others will continue to consider that *Endgame* is a remarkably successful piece of theatre, with an enduring fascination.

Mary F. Catanzaro, "Masking and the Social Construct of the Body in Beckett's *Endgame*"

A central feature of *Endgame* is the pairing of two men in an unconventional duo, within a tradition stemming from *The Birds* of Aristophanes to modern film and television. Although Hamm and Clov's partnership might suggest a coded homoerotic variation of the buddy conceit, theirs involves psychological and physical codependency. Beckett concentrates on two conflicting issues: a master/slave dialectic and a parent/shame dialectic. The play is a ruthless devolution of power, where the source of Hamm's paralysis appears rooted in dysfunctional family dynamics and the inner demons that torment him. Inclined to lord it over family and valet, Hamm just barely suppresses his paranoia in order to maintain a state of needful companionship. The traces of sexual cruelty, seductive appeal, and his inflated ego are seen in the metaphor of his speech, flashy dress, and eccentric accouterments. These constitute his masks and are emblematic of the social construct of the body. The power inequities between the two men suggest that Beckett views enduring relationships as highly suspect.

Kate Dorney, "Hamming it up in *Endgame*: A Theatrical Reading"

My essay seeks to challenge predominant modes of engagement with *Endgame* in which the play is excavated for philosophical, eschatological and allegorical meaning, and proposes instead to focus on the *performative* nature of Beckett's engagement with theater and language to reread the play as a sly metalinguistic and metatheatrical commentary on both 'absurd theater' and other forms of theatre contemporary to the play's first performances in the 1950s. Above all things, this essay seeks to celebrate and emphasise the *humor* of *Endgame* and to move studies of it away from the philosophical and linguistic turns that have dogged the reception of Beckett's work ever since the publication of *Theater of the Absurd*. Drawing on reviews of the first performances and subsequent scholarly literature and research in post-war British theater history and literary linguistics, the essay contextualizes the theatrical landscape into which *Endgame* was born and received and follows those meta-theatrical cues in the text which mark it out as a trenchant swipe at theatrical conventions and expectations in the mid-1950s. From this perspective, Hamm is revealed as a self-important actor-manager rehearsing his shabby company, and determined on maintaining his place centre-stage (in the manner of many managers of British repertory companies in the 1940s and 50s). Hamm, 'the great soliloquizer,' is continually undermined in rehearsals by his straight man (Clov) and upstaged by his stooges (Nagg and Nell)—themselves 'raconteurs' from another stage tradition. Extrapolated to breaking point, this reading sees Hamm on his own representing the actor or director-centered theatrical trends of the past, 'me to play'; whilst Hamm in concert with his company reflects the move towards ensemble-based theater becoming increasingly popular in Britain (already popular in mainland Europe through the work of the Berliner Ensemble and the Comedie Francaise) in the late 1950s and early 1960s. The essay ends by looking at the effect of this meta-theatrical legacy on the work of Pinter and Stoppard.

Colin Duckworth, "Re-Evaluating *Endgame*"

This essay is a form of creative and dynamic interrogatory criticism. In the process of seeking to re-evaluate *Endgame* my investigation into the reasons for my longstanding resistance to the play brings several disparate factors into focus: *Endgame* and Ionesco's *Le Roi se Meurt*; problems raised by musical analogy (words—versus—music); Beckett's univeralisation of personal tragedy and of personal world-view; the function of framework reference, evocation of off-stage space and anterior lives, in comparison with other Beckett plays; further considerations of a musical—and biblical-linguistic—nature (Schubert, Messiaen, time/temps, delay/délai) relevant to the problem of interpretation; the end of what game?

The basic discrepancy between my appreciation of several other Beckett plays and *Endgame*, namely, that I have never directed *Endgame*, is explained and justified. In the second section, it is partially rectified by means of real-time re-creation of the on-stage conditions and resultant interpersonal relationships of actors/characters.

Jane E. Gatewood, "Memory and Its Devices in *Endgame*"

This essay analyzes the formal style and thematics of memory in *Endgame* by contextualizing it with Beckett's earlier and later plays, *Waiting for Godot* and *Krapp's Last Tape*. In *Endgame,* both Hamm's and Clov's narrations of memory echo and extend those of Didi and Gogo in *Waiting for Godot*, for while both Hamm and Clov attempt to remember and cannot, they also knowingly play with memory's equivocations. Such "playing," with its attempts to rework and control memory, anticipates moves to catalog, store, and order memory made in *Krapp's Last Tape*. In all three plays, the concern with memory exhibits a Beckettian anxiety concerning history and memory, while revealing more fully the existential crisis begun in *Waiting for Godot*: that the self can never know the past, that history is always conditional, contingent upon one unknowable—the inability of the self to be sure of its own existence.

This essay demonstrates that an abiding concern of Beckett's works is the impossibility of remembering one's own birth, and if one cannot remember this event, one cannot be certain of one's existence. Plays such as *Endgame* suggest, if one takes this conditional as the truth, the only surety this leap-of-faith provides is the surety of one's own death. Such an existential shift and bleak turn on the function and import of history and memory anticipates the loss of the subject and the culmination of history evident in later works of postmodernism. Yet while the essay situates *Endgame* as anticipating aspects of postmodernity in its reveling in the culmination of history and presentation of the loss subjectivity, it demonstrates that the play is not easily characterized as "postmodernist" or "modernist," for the play also exhibits Beckett's modernist anxiety concerning history and memory. *Endgame*, the essay suggests, is better situated in the space between the two movements.

Michael Guest, "Paul Ricoeur and Watching *Endgame*"

This essay applies Paul Ricoeur's post-phenomenological theory of narrative to *Endgame*. In particular, I explore the ideas Ricoeur presents in his three volume work *Time and Narrative*, concerning (i) an integral, reciprocal relationship that exists between time and narrative, and (ii) mimesis as an action consisting of threefold cyclical stages that culminate in a realization of the work in the experience of a real reader/spectator (which I subsume under the term *watching*). Noting Ricoeur's endorsement of reader response and reception theorists such as Wolfgang Iser and Hans Robert Jauss, I offer a reading of *Endgame* from a perspective that incorporates the watcher's role. The conceptual relationship between Aristotle and St Augustine that Ricoeur elucidates, which is such that narrative temporality offers a particular kind of response to the aporias that attend the phenomenological speculation upon time, is particularly pertinent to understanding *Endgame*. In configuring the aesthetic world of his play as a state of temporal paradox, Beckett himself draws aesthetically upon Aristotle and St Augustine in a way that is remarkably consistent with Ricoeur's philosophical approach to them. My reading emphasizes the metatheatricality of *Endgame* in particular respect to how the play stimulates an awareness of itself as an aesthetic work that "moves" in time toward the watcher, at once linearly and instantaneously. I explore subtle aspects of the dynamics of Beckett's theater illusion with respect to these ideas and demonstrate the value that Ricoeur's theory holds for appreciating Beckett's aesthetic strategies in *Endgame*.

Thomas Mansell, "Hard-to-hear Music in *Endgame*"

Endgame has been criticised for being both excessively abstract and exaggeratedly emotional—an ambivalence reflected in Beckett's own words on the play, which range from the purely musical to "groans and howls." Hence, while *Endgame* has understandably figured little in discussions of Beckett and music, the very severity of music's excision from *Endgame* suggests that it might be a key to the play.

Using Michel Serres's idea of "*dur*" ("hard" sensory data) and "*doux*" ("soft" intelligible information), this paper considers how three sounds in *Endgame* (the sea, the alarm, and the "headheart") undermine traditional distinctions between music, sound, and noise.

The established interpretation of "Hamm" as "hammer" is also capable of far greater subtlety, particularly if one attends to the German context of this clue. As well as blunt, heavy implements, "hammers" invoke thoughts of tuning-forks, ears, and pianos. Furthermore, by deriving "Clov" not from *clavus* ("nail") but from *clavis* ("key"), one arrives at a more complex image for the relationship between Hamm and Clov: "*Hammerklavier*." Indeed, from Pythagoras to Beethoven, hammers may be seen as not external to music, but integral to it.

Given this background, even the suspicion that Hamm is not only blind but also "hard of hearing" only bolsters the case for music's relevance to *Endgame*.

Antonia Rodríguez-Gago, "Transcultural *Endgame/s*"

This essay deals with three Spanish productions of *Endgame (Final de partida)* focusing on the cultural and theatrical appropriations introduced by three Spanish directors: Julio Castronuovo (1980), Miguel Narros (1982) and Rodolfo Cortizo (2001). My pivotal question is: allowing that cultural differences always affect theater productions—theater being a living thing which changes in time and place, always related to the given country's cultural and theatrical politics—to what extent can cultural difference influence a production without seriously damaging the original conception of the play in question? This question is difficult to answer in the light of Sirkku Aaltonen's statement that "throughout history translators and other theater practitioners have occupied foreign texts as tenants," and also given that since the 1960s and 1970s stage directors have acted more as co-authors than as interpreters of the plays they direct. A related argument explores how the necessity for freedom of interpretation affects Beckett's original conception of *Endgame,* whose *mise-en-scène* was carefully created by its author in the text itself, and was meticulously detailed by Beckett as director in his *Theatrical Notebooks.*

The Spanish political and cultural moment is reflected in the staging of the three productions of *Final de partida* discussed here, giving thus way to three "transcultural *Endgames"* which still retained the power and the dramatic impact of the original. Intercultural theater productions are always hybrid as these three productions illustrate. They don't belonging entirely to either the original or the received theatrical culture, yet they participate in both. Castronuovo created his 1980 *Final de partida* around the ideas of enforced living together after perhaps a "nuclear attack." Narros's 1982 production was more politicised and built around the idea of "the death of a dictator." Cortizo's 2001 production stressed the idea of "lost opportunities," where three generations waste their lives waiting for an impossible end. Thus, as Beckett suggested, each one of these directors contributed "his own music" in the staging of *Endgame.*

Paul Shields, "Hamm Stammered: Beckett, Deleuze, and the Atmospheric Stuttering of *Endgame*"

In his essay on *Endgame,* Nels C. Pearson envisions Hamm as a metonym for a defunct British imperialism and Clov as a remnant of the voiceless colonized. Clov struggles for a language that will speak without reference to the assumptions or logic of colonialism, yet, according to Pearson, the slave's attempts to find such a way of speaking paradoxically re-imprison him in the fetters of the colonizer. Another way to read Clov's hesitating speech, however, is to understand it as one faltering voice among many. Gilles Deleuze's essay "He Stuttered" helps to reveal an alternative postcolonial reading of the play, demonstrating how the atmospheric stuttering of *Endgame* emancipates, rather than impedes, the vanquished.

Russell Smith, "*Endgame*'s Remainders"

This essay argues that *Endgame* addresses itself to the historical situation of Europe after World War II, and in particular to the problem of loss and mourning and of what to do with what remains. Drawing on Freud's essay "Mourning and Melancholia" and recent essays by Dominick LaCapra and Slavoj Zizek, the greater part of *Endgame* can be seen as dramatising the "melancholic stratagem" whereby attachment to the lost object is preserved through fidelity to the remainder, in a comic parody of the tragic process of mourning. In particular, the relationship between Hamm and Clov can be read in terms of Giorgio Agamben's definition of melancholia: "the paradox of an intention to mourn that precedes and anticipates the loss of the object." However, the ending of the play, in which Hamm dismisses Clov and discards his remaining possessions, tragically completes the work of mourning, in a betrayal of the lost object that is inseparable from the callous task of going on living. *Endgame* can be read as a profoundly ethical critique of melancholy, and an affirmation of the tragic necessity of the work of mourning.

Paul Stewart, "But Why Shakespeare? The Muted Role of Dickens in *Endgame*"

Shakespearean dimensions of *Endgame* have been a mainstay of criticism of the play. Despite such broad hints as that from James Acheson's influential article, "Chess with the Audience: Samuel Beckett's *Endgame*," the role of Dickens in *Endgame* has been curiously undervalued. In fact, the intertextual resonance between Dickens and Beckett's play has been all but ignored. This essay asks one question: why has Dickens been ignored and Shakespeare so favored?

It is fitting perhaps that in connection with a play concerned with orphans, the literary genealogy of Beckett's play should be at issue. Close examination of *Endgame* and its characters show that allusions to both Shakespeare and Dickens conform to an aesthetic of lessening; the plenitude of the past becomes a diminished present, filled with the absences of that plenitude which was once possible. If this is the case, the privileging of Shakespeare over Dickens in critical discourse surrounding the play is in need of explanation. If one compares Beckett to Shakespeare, then the dynamic of influence moves from the tragic to the tragicomic, or from the tragic to the grotesque; from Hamlet to Hamm. If one compares Beckett to Dickens then the dynamic moves from the primarily comic to the primarily tragic; the optimistic Mr. Omer becomes the tragic Hamm. This chapter makes the case for Dickens in *Endgame* and reassesses the intertextual paradigms involved in Beckett's use of his Victorian precursor. It is argued that the satisfying trajectory of decline, which has so often been traced from Shakespeare to Beckett, is challenged by the question: If the trajectory of deterioration is one which begins in the comic works of Dickens, in what does it end?

About the Authors

NATKA BIANCHINI recently completed her Ph.D. in drama at Tufts University. Her dissertation is a study of the American premières and reception of Beckett's plays, titled: "Exactly as you Envisioned: Alan Schneider's Direction of Samuel Beckett." She has been a part-time faculty member at both Boston College and Tufts University, where she has taught Introduction to Theatre and Theatre History.

MARK S. BYRON is an Australian Research Council Postdoctoral Fellow in the Department of English at the University of Sydney, Australia. Since completing his PhD in 2001 at the University of Cambridge, he has taught at the University of Washington, Seattle, and at the University of Sydney. He principal publications include essays on Samuel Beckett, Ezra Pound and Gertrude Stein. He is currently co-editor of the Electronic Variorum Edition of Ezra Pound's *Cantos*, with Professor Richard Taylor, and is also working on an electronic edition of Samuel Beckett's novel *Watt*.

JULIE CAMPBELL is Lecturer in Literature and Drama at the University of Southampton. She has published widely on Beckett's prose fiction and drama. Forthcoming publications include "Samuel Beckett and Paul Auster: Fathers and Sons and the Creativity of Misreading," Linda Ben Zvi and Angela Moorjani, eds., *Beckett at 100: Looking Back, Looking Forward* (Oxford: Oxford University Press, 2007) and "Playing with Death in *Malone Dies*," *Borderless Beckett / Beckett sans frontièrs, Samuel Beckett Today / Aujourd'hui 19* (Amsterdam: Rodopi, 2008).

MARY F. CATANZARO (Ph.D., University of Wisconsin, Milwaukee, 1986) is an Independent Scholar living in Milwaukee. She has published articles on Beckett in series collections for Rodopi such as *Literature and the Grotesque* (1992), *Literature and Music* (2002), and *Literature and the Writer* (2004), ed. Michael J. Meyer; and in peer-reviewed journals as well. She is currently pursuing Beckett's exploration of the formation of personal identity in the context of male relationships.

KATE DORNEY is a theater historian who has worked with archives and other source material to re-evaluate various aspects of post-war British theatre history. She has worked with the AHRC British Library Theater Archive Project at the University of Sheffield reclaiming scripts missing from the British Library's Modern Plays Archive, researching and sorting the archive of Sir Ralph Richardson (Beckett's first choice for Estragon), and collecting oral history testimony from theater-goers and workers between 1945 and 1968. She has also worked with the Liverpool Everyman Theater Archive collecting oral history testimony from those who created and worked in the theater. She has published articles on Beckett, Joe Orton, post-war British theater and the aftermath of theater censorship in Britain and is presently working on an edited collection about regional theater in Britain and a monograph on the language of post-war British theater. Chapters tracing the development of queer theater in the 1960s and 70s, and a study of Ralph Richardson's life and work are also in press. Kate is currently Curator of Modern and Contemporary Theater at the Victoria and Albert Theater Museum in London.

COLIN DUCKWORTH is Emeritus Professor and Professorial Fellow (French), University of Melbourne. M.A. (Birmingham), Ph.D. (Cambridge), D.Litt. (Melbourne), Commandeur dans l'Ordre des Palmes Académiques. Writing: books, articles and conference papers on Beckett since doing critical edition of *En attendant Godot* (1965); member, Beckett manuscript edition team; critical editions of Voltaire (3), Flaubert and Renan. Translations and stage adaptations of Jarry, Rostand, Voltaire-Vanbrugh, Camus, Ionesco, Tardieu, Proust and Duras; biography (D'Antraigues); three novels (*Summer Symphony*, 2005); three opera libretti. Theatre credits: as director, many productions in English and French, including Beckett, Ionesco and Tardieu; as actor, major rôles from Shakespeare to Albee and Noel Coward; several film and T.V. credits (including three characters in *Neighbours*!).

JANE E. GATEWOOD is a Ph.D. candidate at the University of Georgia and is Associate Director of the University's Office of International Education, coordinating research and exchange agreements with foreign universities. She has a B.A. from Emory University (1998) and an M.A. from Montana State University-

Bozeman (2001). A former Mellon Fellow, she has conducted research at the Institute of Historical Research, London, and has presented conference papers on hypertext and the future of the book (Central New York Conference on Language and Literature, October 2000), the function of memory in Samuel Beckett's plays (CUNY Memory and Narrative Conference, March 2002), and on cinematic techniques in James Joyce's *Ulysses* (SAMLA, November 2003). Her dissertation, *The Language of the Silent Cinema in the Modern Novel*, analyzes the influences of early cinema on the narrative style of the modern novel, focusing upon works by Henry James and Joseph Conrad.

MICHAEL GUEST recently retired as a professor of Media and Cultural Studies at Shizuoka University Faculty of Informatics, Japan, where he lived since 1992. An active member of the Samuel Beckett Research Circle of Japan, he has published articles on Beckett's prose and drama and presented research in various fields of the humanities at prominent international conferences.

THOMAS MANSELL is a Ph.D. student at the London Consortium. His thesis on Samuel Beckett and music addresses the gap between Beckett's idealistic musical pronouncements and his actual experience of music, in particular at the piano. Thomas is a member of the London Beckett Seminar, and helped to organize the Beckett and Company event in London in October 2006. His work has been published in *Samuel Beckett Today / Aujourd'hui* and in *Performance Research*; he has also published reviews in the *Yearbook of English Studies* and the *Beckett Circle*.

ANTONIA RODRÍGUEZ-GAGO is "Profesora Titular" of English Literature at the Universidad Autónoma de Madrid where she teaches English Renaissance and Jacobean Drama and Contemporary Anglo-American theater. She has written many articles on contemporary theater in general, and on Beckett in particular. *Rockaby*, *Ohio Impromptu* and *Catastrophe* were premièred in Spain in 1985 using her authorized translations. The fifth edition of her revised, annotated bilingual edition of *Happy Days / Los dias felices* appeared in 2006. Her latest essay on Beckett, "Refiguring the Body Through the Mechanical Reproduction of Memory" is forthcoming in *Beckett at*

100: Revolving It All, ed. Linda Ben Zvi and Angela Moorjani (New York: Oxford University Press, 2007).

PAUL SHIELDS is Assistant Professor of English at Assumption College in Worcester, MA, where he teaches courses in theater and writing. He received his Ph.D. in English from Florida State University. He is a former associate editor for the *Journal of Beckett Studies* and is currently working on a manuscript that explores the relationship between Beckett and Gilles Deleuze's theories of the "man without qualities."

RUSSELL SMITH lectures in the School of Humanities at Australian National University, in literature, film and cultural studies. His work on Beckett has appeared in the *Journal of Beckett Studies* and *Samuel Beckett Today/Aujourd'hui* and he is currently editing a volume on Beckett and Ethics for Continuum. He has also published widely on contemporary Australian visual arts, and writes regularly for *Art Monthly Australia*, *Broadsheet*, *RealTime* and other journals.

PAUL STEWART is Associate Professor and Head of the Languages and Literature Department of Intercollege, Cyprus. He is the author of *Zone of Evaporation: Samuel Beckett's Disjunctions* (Rodopi, 2006), "The Need for Beckett," in *The Journal of Beckett Studies* (Vol 10 Nos. 1&2), "'All men talk, when talk they must, the same tripe': Beckett, Derrida, and Needle Wylie," in *After Beckett / D'après Beckett: Samuel Beckett Today / Aujourd'hui* 14 and numerous other articles on Beckett's work. He is currently working on a volume devoted to Beckett and sexuality.

Index

Names

Subjects